By the Same Author

nonfiction

As Good as I Could Be

Note Found in a Bottle: My Life as a Drinker

Home Before Dark

Treetops

A Woman's Life

fiction

Elizabeth Cole

Doctors and Women

The Cage

A Handsome Man

Looking for Work

My Name Is Bill

Bill Wilson: His Life and the Creation of Alcoholics Anonymous

Susan Cheever

Simon & Schuster

New York London Toronto Sydney

SIMON & SCHUSTER
Rockefeller Center
1230 Avenue of the Americas
New York, NY 10020

For information about special discounts for bulk purchases,
please contact Simon & Schuster Special Sales:
1-800-456-6798 or business@simonandschuster.com

Designed by Jeanette Olender
Manufactured in the United States of America

10   9   8   7   6   5

Library of Congress Cataloging-in-Publication Data
Cheever, Susan.
My name is Bill: Bill Wilson: his life and the creation of
Alcoholics Anonymous/Susan Cheever.
p.   cm.
1. W., Bill. 2. Alcoholics Anonymous. 3. Alcoholics—Biography. I. Title.
HV5032.W19C44 2004
362.292'092—dc22   [B]   2003059196
ISBN 0-7432-0154-X

Photographs 1–3 courtesy of the author; 4–19, 21–23 courtesy of the Stepping
Stones Foundation, Katonah, New York; 17 courtesy of Mel B. of Toledo, Ohio.

FOR MY FATHER: 1912–1982

Contents

My Name Is Bill

PART ONE

A Rural Childhood

Chapter One:

The Wilson House

The evening before Thanksgiving on November 25, 1895, Mrs. Emily Griffith Wilson, twenty-five years old, very confused and very pregnant, might have been found in the Wilson House hotel kitchen as the afternoon cold settled in outside and the steam formed on the windowpanes. She was preparing to bake an apple pie, cutting the apples and then rolling out the crust, and keeping an eye on the popcorn just warming up in a cast-iron pan over the woodstove. The big north-facing room where she worked smelled of cooking: of flour and the sweetness of apples, of a batch of sugar cookies and the sausage frying for the stuffing. Usually, she found these smells delicious, but this afternoon they were nauseating. Pregnancy ruined everything, she thought.

Emily could hear the others thumping around upstairs, Grandma Wilson and Gilly, and the rhythmic thunk, thunk of someone splitting wood in the big shed where the sheep and goats were penned in for the winter. Up the hill a dog barked. Out the back windows the kitchen garden, where a few pumpkins still lazed against the cold earth, was framed by the white columns of the porch, the big pine tree, and the road that followed Mad Tom Brook down to the peaked roof of the railroad station. She could hear the trains going through three times each day—the Green Mountain Flyer and the midnight sleeper when she was up late. The track came down from Montreal, past Dorset Pond just a few miles north, then right past the general store and the cheese factory, and then down the valley toward Manchester Depot and Manchester Village on the way to Albany, where you could change for Boston or New York City. Grover Cleveland was president, New York City police had just cracked down on an illicit distillery, and Oscar Hammerstein was packing them in at his Olympia Theater.

Across the green, as night fell and the pains made it harder for her to stay and work at the kitchen table, Emily could just see the parsonage where she and Gilly were planning to live once the baby was born. Then the lights went on in her parents' little white house with the cheerful red door and the green shutters. They would be over for dinner tomorrow, but the thought of them at prayer in the cozy little parlor where she had grown up made the pains subside for a moment. Not that their life had been perfect—life was always hard —but right now, alone for a moment, she remembered the innocent girl she had once been. Things had seemed so simple then. Slow-moving oxen pulled the great blocks of marble out of the mountains and loaded them onto railroad cars. There was maple sugaring in the spring and apple picking and cider in the fall. There was the General Store, where Mr. Barrows always smiled at her; the town meetings over in Dorset Village; the Grange Hall, where men argued about politics; the blacksmith shop where the family horses got new shoes; and the cobbler where she went for her own new shoes.

On the other side of the tracks were the marble mills where the blocks were cut into the slabs that were as common as grass all over town. East Dorset marble was the best marble in the world. There was her family's church and another church for the Irish who had come when the Freedleyville Quarry opened. There was school and playing and wonderful books. Emily had always imagined herself as Becky Thatcher in Mark Twain's book *Tom Sawyer*—adventurous, daring, and a little too smart for her own good. Her family, the Griffiths, were local nobility. They were the wealthiest family in

town although they would never say so. Her father, Gardner Fayette
Griffith, had fought for the Union Army during the Civil War. He
had been at Gettysburg with the Vermont 14th Regiment and
helped repel Pickett's charge and win the war for the righteous. He
owned the town's waterworks. He and his cousin Silas had the idea
of selling wood cut from the forests that blanketed the surrounding
mountains, and it had been a very good idea.

For what seemed like a long time the Griffiths had lived happily
in their house on the green with their children, their beloved son
Clarence and their daughters Millie and Emily. Everyone knew how
smart Emily was. After grade school she had gone off to train at the
Normal School over in Castleton, and she had become a teacher in
the local one-room schoolhouse. Emily had her heart set on more
than teaching, though. "Success, success, success, let that be your
watchword!" she exhorted her son years later. Now she exhorted
herself. Even then, as she carried that first child through the summer and fall of 1895, she imagined being something greater, something a man might be, perhaps a doctor or a lawyer.

Emily loved her parents—her father often seemed to be the only
person who really understood her. He understood that she was too
big for life in their little village. She was aiming for larger things.
Her mother was always reminding her that she was a woman and
that she should act like a woman, but her father didn't seem to feel
that way. She was like him, she told herself. She had high ambitions
for everyone around her, ambitions that transcended gender. What
her mother called stubbornness she saw as determination; determination like her father's. Even though her father was her best friend,
the events of the last few years just seemed to have overwhelmed
their friendship.

First Emily's little brother, Clarence, was sick. There was something wrong with his lungs. He couldn't breathe. Dr. Liddle came
over from Dorset and said Clarence had to be sent to Colorado. Of

course her parents followed instructions, but it was awful to see the little boy off on the train. Then they got word that the Colorado air hadn't worked. Clarence was dead. Ever since that boy died so far away, and no one knew who was there to comfort him in his last hours, Fayette had been different. Losing his ten-year-old son broke his heart. Even now, she knew her father didn't like complaining. Pregnancy wasn't something she would talk about with him; she had to concentrate on putting her fears aside.

Fayette Griffith expected that even children would adjust their feelings to life's little practicalities. She remembered the way he had reacted the one time she allowed herself to get sentimental about a farm animal. "Thanksgiving dinner with rousing fires in all the stoves to keep out the zero cold, and plenty of good cheer all around," she remembered forty years later. "The dinners were mostly always turkey. Occasionally we had chicken," she continued, "and once a little young barbecued pig—and that little pig was my pet—and the unusual sight of him made me feel kind of sick and faint." She wasn't allowed to leave the table.

A handsome Yankee woman with long chestnut hair, Emily couldn't believe how quickly she lay her ambitions aside and did what seemed to be expected of her, embracing marriage and motherhood. She was feeling angry at her husband Gilman, who was already not quite shaping up to be the man she had imagined he could be when they married a year before.

It was almost an arranged marriage. She and Gilly had known each other all their lives. Her family was no-nonsense and well off and lived on the north side of the green; his family was social and gregarious and owned the Wilson House on the south side of the green. Maybe that was the problem. She had grown up in a house; Gilly had grown up running an inn with his widowed mother, drinking with the guests and entertaining them even when he was a boy. Gilly was a charming man, a personable bachelor who had gone to Albany College in New York State. He had already been made manager of the North Quarry, and Emily had hoped that marriage would turn him into a responsible man.

Their family history seemed to affect Gilly in a different way than it affected her. At twilight on the night of November 25, as preparations for Thanksgiving dinner animated the big kitchen, she began to double over with the contractions—a kind of pain which dwarfed everything in her previous twenty-five years of life, even the bouts of anxiety that sometimes made her see blackness and feel that nothing was worthwhile.

The village of East Dorset is still a storybook sort of place. Picturesque but workaday, it's a town that has always been about industry—even if the product was as lovely as marble or as sweet as maple sugar. Its red and white frame houses huddle around a central green in front of a white clapboard Congregational church with a square, eight-pointed spire, in the narrow valley where Mad Tom Brook meets the Batten Kill. Called the Valley of Vermont, this verdant, limestone path in the land lies between the Green Mountains to the east and the Taconic Mountains to the west. A few miles north of East Dorset, at Dorset Pond in North Dorset, the valley narrows until only a few hundred yards separate the two mountain ranges. Mount Aeolus in the Taconic Range, named for its windy summit by a party of nineteenth-century climbers from Haverford College, slopes above East Dorset on the west side, while Bromley Mountain in the Green Mountain Range rises above the town to the east.

Sugar maples and oaks, pine and spruce trees, line the two village streets. The woods are still filled with birdsong and wildlife, owls hoot at night, and at the end of summer, flocks of geese honk their way across the sky. The sidewalks are paved with the snowy white marble veined in pale gray that comes from the local quarries. These underground shafts crisscross the surrounding mountains hundreds of feet under the rocky soil but occasionally erupt in a white burst against the green surface of the hills.

At the corner of Village Street and Mad Tom Road stands the Wilson House, still a rambling old dark red three-story building with white trim. Its rooms have been redone with flowered wallpaper and filled with sturdy oak furniture. Facing the rounded shape of Mount Aeolus, the long porch is the baseline for a jumble of clapboard dormers, shutters, and gables above it. Except for the church, it's the largest building in the small town, and it has been an inn since settlers first moved to this narrow valley back before Vermont was even a state, in the eighteenth century.

By the end of November the brilliant red and yellow of the New England fall is almost over and the trees throw skeleton shadows in the thin winter light. "No pen can describe the turning of the leaves," wrote Rudyard Kipling, who was living nearby in Brattleboro, Vermont, in his beloved house Naulahka and working on *The Jungle Book*. "The hillsides as far as the eye could range were afire, and the roads paved with crimson and gold. . . . Then a wet wind blew . . . till nothing remained but pencil-shading of bare boughs, and one could see into the private heart of the woods." In those days between the brilliance of fall and the great snows of the Vermont winter, the air is sharp and cold. The sun disappears behind the mountain and the dark comes filtering down early. Nights are long. By the end of November, the huge piles of stacked firewood are already beginning to shrink, and the smell of snow and woodsmoke and the occasional baking apple pie swirls around the churchyard, past the old schoolhouse and across the brook toward Mount Aeolus and the world beyond.

CHAPTER TWO:

EAST DORSET

The Green Mountains of Vermont, just after the Civil War, were the cradle of the taciturn New England virtues—thrift, honesty, industry—and also the cradle of New England vices. These vices included tobacco, which Bill Wilson started smoking as a teenager, homemade hard cider, cellar-brewed beer, illegal whiskey from across the Canadian border, and a hotheadedness that historians now call independence of spirit. Ethan Allen, from a Dorset family, was the leader of the Green Mountain Boys during the Revolution. A young man who might in another state and another time be classified as a juvenile delinquent, Allen used his hatred of authority and his willingness to take insane risks to become a great American hero and the epitome of Vermont values.

Allen had boldly forced the British to surrender at Fort Ticonderoga on Lake Champlain by infiltrating the fort with his small band of young men and waking the sleeping British captain at dawn on the morning of May 10, 1775. "The captain came immediately to the door with his breeches in his hand," Allen said later, "when I ordered him to deliver me the fort instantly." Allen's endurance matched his bravado. Later that year he managed to transport the cannons from Fort Ticonderoga, over the icy Taconic Mountains and huge snowdrifts to Boston, where they were the deciding factor in the retaking of Bunker Hill and the recapture of the city.

There was another side to Allen's courage: his bravado about drinking. One Yankee tall tale describes a friend of Allen's, napping next to Allen one afternoon, who noticed a rattlesnake nestled on the hero's chest. The snake was repeatedly biting Allen. Allen did not wake up from his own nap. But as he raised his gun to shoot the snake and save this homespun hero, the friend saw the rattler's tail droop and his head loll to the side. The snake was drunk. When Allen finally woke up, he complained about the mosquitoes.

New England, when Bill Wilson was born a hundred years later, still held the righteousness of the Revolution as a sacred memory. The independence that had been so hard to win and which had been won against all odds, was independence of spirit as well as freedom from the domination of George III. If an army of a few ragged and passionate men could defeat the greatest army in the world; if a country with no navy but some fishing boats and a borrowed fleet could withstand the Royal Navy; then anything could happen. The new colonies had experienced the force of human will. The existence of the United States itself was proof that belief could conquer numbers and experience. It was a country created by great hearts over the protests of wiser heads.

At the end of the nineteenth century, with the Civil War behind it, New England became a laboratory for all kinds of optimistic spiritual and technical experiments. Down at Harvard, Oliver Wendell Holmes held forth in the shadow of a history that included two Adams presidents and the intellectual center of the new colonies. Nearby, a young teacher of deaf students, Alexander Graham Bell worked on the telephone in a rented room on Essex Street in Boston. The country was young and it belonged to the young. Bell and his assistant, Thomas Watson, were both adventurous kids in their twenties, working on a device that even their backers didn't think could ever make money. They could only afford one bed between them; Bell designed during the night while Watson slept, then Bell slept while Watson translated his designs into wire and wood and electricity. Inventors—like Bell and Watson, and Samuel Morse—were celebrities who won instant wealth and fame. Edison, the wizard of Menlo Park, had invented the lightbulb, which had led to a society no longer at the mercy of nature's old-fashioned day and night. Philosophers such as William James speculated brilliantly on the meaning of life. Critic Van Wyck Brooks described the flowering of New England, and transcendentalism—the belief that true knowledge comes from intuition rather than experience—was in the crisp mountain air of the towns north of Boston.

Down in Concord, Massachusetts, men like Ralph Waldo Emerson, Bronson Alcott, and Henry David Thoreau—who built a cabin on a piece of land Emerson lent him on Walden Pond and wrote a book about it—had recently reinvented the relationship of man to God and nature. No longer did they imagine that God was a punishing, inhuman Calvinist who doled out an eternity of salvation or damnation on the basis of piety; they imagined a human-loving God who appeared in the guise of other people's goodness and the astonishing beauty of the natural world. This was a God who would appeal to those who needed him, a God who made redemption a real possibility.

In many ways, these two different visions of authority—the old punishing way with its acceptance of life, devotion to prayer, and an unreasoning God, and the newer humanistic way—split Bill Wilson's life into two parts. Still, there was hope in the air of New England in the second half of the 1800s. Lincoln had changed things; the great men and women who wrote about transcendentalism had changed things. Change was a new way of looking at the old world.

The flowering of the age of temperance began in the late 1850s and revived with renewed force after the Civil War, when a group of temperance movements swept the country. Some were religious, like the Women's Christian Temperance Union, which fought the "demon" of alcohol and called for an end to the sale of liquor and for the introduction of antialcohol education in the schools. Others were political, like the Prohibition Party, founded in 1869, which urged all states to adopt the "dry" laws that quickly spread throughout New England. The WCTU established "reform clubs" where ex-drunks gathered to talk about their stories and their desires not to drink again. Other groups, like the Washingtonians, and the Anti-Saloon League, established themselves and began to grow.

The Washingtonians were very successful and numbered in the hundreds of thousands at the beginning of the nineteenth century. They seemed to be able to get men sober. Their success, however, drew them into involvement with the political issues of their time, specifically the issue of the legality of slavery. The Washingtonians were abolitionists, and this righteous conviction destroyed them, splitting the organization down the middle and distracting it from its purpose of helping alcoholics.

Everywhere, alcoholics who had somehow reformed themselves established groups to abolish drinking. The evangelist Carry Nation won wide popularity with her urging of national prohibition. The Hearst newspapers supported prohibition, and even celebrities like Jack London, who had given up drinking and written about it in his sobriety memoir—*John Barleycorn*—called for an end to liquor sales.

Before the war a doctor in Maine had begun preaching that alcoholism was not a failure of will power but that it was a disease. Other medical practitioners agreed, and although medicine at the time was a primitive art, the idea that alcoholism is a disease became popular. A group of physicians formed an American Association for the Cure of Inebriates and sponsored a series of asylums where alcoholics could be sent to have their disease treated by doctors. Unfortunately, medical cures for alcoholism were still in the dark ages. The famous Keeley cure involved ingestion of a secret substance that was actually a simple form of chlorine, and many imitators offered chemical substances which were said to cure alcoholism. In New York City in the 1920s, Towns Hospital became famous for its belladonna-and-laxatives cure, dubbed by its celebrity patients "purge and puke."

Temperance swept the nation and was hailed as a cure for everything. It would alleviate poverty and end political corruption, its proponents preached. By the 1890s, according to Mark Edward Lender and James Kirby Martin in *Drinking in America,* the promise of temperance had "captivated millions of Americans. While there would never be a full national consensus, a majority ultimately agreed that the temperance ideal was desirable as a national policy goal." Temperance crusaders believed that temperance was a cause like the cause of independence which had started the Revolutionary War and the cause of abolitionism for which they had fought the Civil War.

Vermont was a dry state when Bill Wilson was growing up, a state where self-righteousness about not drinking lived side by side with self-righteousness about drinking anyway. Many people joined temperance movements, and many people drank nevertheless. In the arguments he heard on the subject, arguments that seemed to further split his mother's family from his father's family, Bill Wilson got an education in the evils of drink, the methods for treating alcoholism, and also in the pleasures of drink. In East Dorset, "I have business in Cambridge" was what people said when they needed a drink—Cambridge, New York, just across the border from Arlington, was the location of the nearest liquor store.

Antitemperance sentiment won a victory in 1902 when the citizens of Vermont voted in a "local option" provision by which every town could vote whether or not they wanted to sell liquor. Although some towns went wet, the general tide was against them. Prohibition was only eighteen years away.

In nineteenth-century East Dorset, life was local. Most of the people the Griffiths saw, they saw every day. Other towns had their identities and communities, but East Dorset was a rough quarry town, its character molded by the quarriers who populated Mount Aeolus and the dozens of quarry shafts. There was electricity in town, but no indoor plumbing. Most people ate with spoons and knives. Quarry work was dangerous, and the railroad was even more dangerous. There was a *carpe diem* attitude among the quarriers as there is among quarriers everywhere. The basic human appetites, for food, sex, and shelter, were met as often as possible with as little fuss as possible. Gilman Wilson seemed to define his masculinity with an eager sexuality. When Emily was away, he was unrepentantly involved with other women.

Vermont villages were also worried by the emigration of their children to the big cities where they could drink, and by gangs of Canadian laborers who swarmed across the border at harvest time and then swarmed back with big profits from picking and from occasional larceny. Vermont had a thriving dairy business and a burgeoning fruit-harvesting business. Vermont horses were the finest in the thirty-eight states, Vermont breeders had developed the Spanish Merino sheep famous for the quality of its wool, and Vermont maple sugar was the sweetest thing in New England. Another Vermont crop—tourism—was just beginning to show a profit. "They are willing to pay, they don't care for fishing grounds, they don't care for hunting . . . they want a little good food, they want a little milk to drink that has not been skimmed; they want a little good butter that they can swear by," wrote Victor I. Spear in his Farm Management Report for the Vermont State Board of Agriculture in 1893. "No crop [will be] more profitable than this crop from the city."

In the summer, up and down the Batten Kill Valley, people were coming from New York and Boston, building rustic A-frame shingle camps on Dorset Pond, and putting up airy great frame houses with velvety lawns and porches for sipping lemonade over in Manchester Village. The influx of people who had so much money that they could transport an entire household with horses, bedding, and even boats up from the hot city for the long, green Vermont summers made the provincial Vermont valleys pockets of urban learning and sophistication.

The Yankee tradition with its pride and discomfort embraced these doctors and lawyers who built second homes and restored the old saltboxes along the river. There was money there, there was class, and there was real knowledge to be had. These summer people with their civilized ways and their strange urban customs would have a dramatic effect on the towns in the Batten Kill Valley and an even more dramatic effect on the life of the Wilson and Griffith families.

Chapter Three:

The Wilson Family and the Griffith Family

Bill Wilson was always his mother's boy. He was always asking for her permission or trying to find a way to get her attention. He abandoned projects she didn't approve of and responded to her cheerleading with redoubled efforts. He remembered her round face contorted in anger as she beat him with a hairbrush, and her determined voice raining down on the contrite husband who was always just a little bit late, always just a little bit too happy. Even when things were good, she was off on a trip for her health or taking his sister, Dorothy, to visit Florida.

When he was world-famous and a trusted leader of hundreds of people, Bill would still complain to his mother that he was sick and be comforted by her as if he were a little boy again. He often mentioned the strength of his maternal connection and the way he kept on looking for a mother even though he had one. He married a woman who was older than he was and who, in many ways, acted like his mother. Never afraid of self-examination, Bill late in his life wrote candidly that he had an unhealthy maternal connection to his wife.

Jolly Gilly, they called his father. He had grown up in the inn, helping to welcome and amuse the guests. An innkeeper had to know how to make people laugh, how to join them in a meal and a drink. Gilly was happiest in the social settings he loved. "My father's people were very amiable and were noted on all sides for their humanity," Bill wrote in his autobiography. "They were popular folk. They were easygoing folk. They were tolerant folk. . . . Incidentally alcoholism ran pretty rife on the Wilson side." Gilly was a typical Wilson. He talked to people by telling them stories. As long as circumstances were just right and he had a drink nearby, he knew how to make his audience laugh and cry. If there was a pretty woman listening, he was even more inspired. He told stories about Vermont history, and he told stories about the mountains. He liked to say that the Vermont seasons were ten months of winter and two months of "damned poor sledding."

The men were always at work when you needed them, Emily thought, or off in the woods, or down by the tracks drinking together, off to Manchester or down to Arlington. She had thought Gilly might take after his father. William Wilson's drinking had led him to take a series of temperance pledges. One Sunday morning in despair he climbed to the top of Mount Aeolus and beseeched God to help him. He saw a blinding light and felt a great wind, and rushed down into town to interrupt the service at the Congregational Church. Demanding that the minister leave the pulpit, Wilson described his experience to the congregation of his friends, neighbors, and family. Emily loved this story about her husband's father, and she told it to her son and husband as often as they would listen. In the eight years William Wilson lived after that experience, he never had another drink.

Emily's father was a strong, silent type, the stalwart Gardner Fayette Griffith. No dramatic spiritual experiences for him. No drunken garrulousness for him. "On my grandfather's side there was quite a different strain," Bill Wilson wrote, remembering village life. " . . . The Griffiths, though hard driving and people of immense will, immense valor, and great fortitude, had extreme difficulty in forming close relations with other people." Fayette Griffith was from a proud New England line of lawyers, teachers, and judges who had been among the original pioneers in the Batten Kill Valley. She inherited his contempt for anything that looked like laziness, even if it was disguised as high spirits and great storytelling. The men would always let you down, she thought. You always had to take care of them.

As it got dark on that night before Thanksgiving, Emily's pains drove her out of the kitchen and into the north parlor. She lay on a couch there, trying to breathe, doubling over as the contractions wracked her body. There was no anesthetic in those days, but her mother kept handing her a glass of something that tasted awful and burned all the way down. In and out of consciousness, she screamed and cried out as midnight passed. Inside the house, the midwife and her mother tried to comfort her. Outside, Bill's friend-to-be, Mark Whalon, remembered a crowd of local boys gathered on the porch listening to Emily Wilson's screams as evidence of the strangeness of the adult world. Later, Emily was fond of saying that Bill's birth had almost killed her.

"When they brought you to me you were cold and discolored and nearly dead," she wrote him years later. "And so also was I but I held you to me, close in my arms and so we were both warmed and comforted, and so we both lived." It was three in the morning, dark with a quarter moon and a carpet of stars in the northern sky up above the mountain. Bill Wilson weighed 6¾ pounds. Later, when he reached his full height, he was so tall that the Army had to provide specially tailored uniform and shoes to fit him. "The memory of it all could not be clearer in my consciousness even now if it had not been seared into my brain that night with a red hot branding iron, for I was given no anesthetic," Emily wrote. Often her letters to her son began in a loving way, but anger gradually bubbled up through the prose, and they ended on a sour and self-pitying note. By the end of the letter she had forgotten all about the love she felt for the tiny helpless baby her son had been so long ago on Thanksgiving. Soon enough she was berating him for ingratitude, ending her birthday letter with the complaint that raising Bill and his sister alone was a hard cross to bear. "I still stagger under it," she wrote.

Pioneer women were destined to cook and take care of the animals and children and endure childbirth without anesthesia, and that tradition persisted into the nineteenth century. Most of them died young. In 1895 the average life span for women was thirty years shorter than it is today. At the turn of the century and for years later, most women didn't work or have the opportunity to educate themselves or even have the right to vote. Survival was a full-time job. Some women did not even want the right to vote. "A Suffragette is a being who has ceased to be a lady and is no gentleman," wrote Emily Wilson's neighbor, Annette Parmalee, to one H. W. Abbott in Landgrove in 1910. "A woman who will lower herself enough to want to vote does not deserve to be called a woman," Mrs. Abbott said. It wasn't until 1920 that the Nineteenth Amendment to the United States Constitution was passed, granting women the right to vote. (The Eighteenth Amendment, passed a year earlier, prohibited the sale, manufacture, export, or import of liquor in the United States.)

By 1904, the charming Gilman Wilson received a promotion to head the Florence Mine in Rutland, twenty-five miles north up the valley. Gilman Wilson was a gifted quarryman who headed a number of successful quarries during his lifetime. In the third grade the nine-year-old Bill was transferred from the poky, familiar one-room schoolhouse in East Dorset to the huge, sophisticated world of Rutland, one of the largest cities in Vermont. Bill was enrolled at the Longfellow School on Church Street, just a few blocks from his family's first real home, a wood frame house on Chestnut Street. Now at last, Emily and Gilman thought, they could begin married life in earnest with their own house and their own lives out from under the shadow of their prominent parents and their small-town past.

Everything would be fine; Gilman celebrated by taking his children to the circus to see the great Buffalo Bill shoot the aces out of playing cards.

Bill's sister, Dorothy, wasn't old enough to go to school yet, so Bill was left to fend for himself in a new school with hundreds of students. The results were mixed. Bill began to find tremendous interest in science and chemistry. He was already big for his age, and this got him teased in the schoolyard. For his parents the results of the move to Rutland were not mixed; they were disastrous. The pressures of real life seemed to make things worse instead of better. Emily was felled by an attack of appendicitis that resulted in an operation. Back at home, she took a long time to recover. She spent hours by the window breathing through a paper tube to get fresh air. Gilman was not a good nurse. Slowly, painfully, the marriage on which Bill's short life was built really began to unravel. Gilman apparently got involved with a local minister's daughter. Emily took Dorothy on long visits to friends in Florida that were ostensibly for her health. She had a series of what her son heard called nervous breakdowns. For a while she was sent to a sanitarium. Then she decided that her breakdowns were caused by her marriage. When Bill was still nine, his mother called on her father to come up to Rutland and bring them home.

By the time Bill was ten, he, his sister, Dorothy, and his mother had moved back to East Dorset and the Wilson House, and his father was heading for Canada and marble quarries unknown. This separation was painful for both father and son, who had grown close. "I loved Father," Wilson wrote later, "but I admired and respected Mother." In fact, Gilman's departure, as well as the reasons for his departure and the marital separation, were literally not spoken about.

Certainly, no one said anything about sex or drinking, both of which were contributing factors to Emily's fury at her husband. Bill and his sister, Dorothy, were told that their father was on a business trip. In Rutland, Gilman Wilson had taken his son on a silent ride up the mountain one night and left him waiting in the carriage while he disappeared inside the quarry office. It was only much later that the boy realized that that strange, frightening ride had been his father's clumsy way of saying goodbye.

CHAPTER FOUR:

DORSET POND

In the spring of 1906, Emily Wilson took her children on a picnic to Dorset Pond, a few miles north up the valley. The pond, dyed a mysterious green by runoff from the marble quarries, is tucked in the narrow north end of the Otter Creek Valley, fringed by pines and with a wooded island across the shimmering water. It was a famously beautiful place; the Bennington & Rutland Railroad had a station there, and people came from as far away as Brooklyn, Boston, and even the Midwest to spend the summers in the healthy mountain air. Once the summer people outnumbered the Vermont natives, the pond's name was officially changed to Emerald Lake.

Emily packed sandwiches and cheese, and loaded the children into the buckboard for the three-mile trip up the valley. Even by the way she laced up the boots under the long skirts everyone wore and put on her hat, her son, Bill, could tell that something was wrong. The air seemed to thicken around them as they traveled. His younger sister, Dorothy, was on edge, and his mother rode silently with her jaw set in a way that he had come to fear. Instead of thinking about what might be happening, Bill thought about the world around them as they went. He was already an accomplished naturalist, and as the family settled down by the grassy shore at the southwest end of the lake, his anxiety seemed to stop time. He noticed the limestone bedrock that cradled the lake and the way the narrow valley that opened out as it traveled south between two distinct mountain ranges—on one side, the gentle slopes like Bromley and Peru mountains, and on the other the more dramatic peaks like Mount Aeolus and Equinox Mountain down in Manchester.

Bill seemed to see every detail. He noticed the grasshoppers in the field nearby, the joe-pye weed and the blue bachelor's-buttons scattered in the grass and the way the purple coneflower seemed to find the edges of the meadows. A red hawk soared effortlessly from side to side above them. For a moment the boy wished he were a hawk with nothing in life but flying and hunting. There were robins and cowbirds in the surrounding pastures, and he even heard the call of an ovenbird. Butterflies—monarchs and yellow lunas—flitted near the trees—paper birch and beech, white ash and hemlock—and he remembered the night before the way he had noticed the fireflies lighting up the pasture between the Wilson House and the church. His senses were so alert that he could smell the water of the lake, the fragrance of the hemlock groves and pines around it. Over by the island a fish jumped at a fly on the glassy surface.

This was no ordinary picnic. It was Emily's attempt to soften the blow. As the clear water lapped the shore at their feet, she explained to her children that their father wasn't ever coming back from his business trip. Then she told them that she had also decided to leave, to go to school in Boston. Dorothy would go with her for at least part of the time. Bill would live in the Griffiths' house with her mother and father. "To this day I recall the scene on the grass by the lake front," Bill wrote in his autobiography years later. "It was an agonizing experience for one who apparently had the emotional sensitivity that I did. However I hid the wound and never talked about it with anybody."

Soon enough, Emily Griffith Wilson had made her plans. Not for her the role of a left-behind single mother. First she needed a divorce from that no-good Gilman. She found a divorce lawyer—a rare thing in those days—down in Bennington, and with her father's help drew up and signed the papers. It was 1906. "Somehow I learned that the divorce was complete," her son wrote later. "This certainly did something to me which left a very deep mark indeed." But Emily wasn't going to stay around and nurse her wounds, or anyone else's. She would go to Boston more than a hundred miles away—a full day's journey—and study at the Boston College of Osteopathy and become a doctor. Her father approved of her ambition. No one seems to have wondered what would happen to the boy, abandoned by his mother in response to being abandoned by his father. In a world where divorce was unheard of, the effect of the divorce was compounded by the behavior of these two people—the feckless Gilman and the driven Emily.

Bill and Dorothy were transferred back across the green, past the churchyard to the Griffith house where Fayette and his wife, Ella, were charged with raising the two children while their mother went off to improve herself. Bill went from being the adored son of a popular family and from the social, happy, boozy precincts of the Wilson House, to the narrow staircase and cramped upper rooms and Yankee rectitude of the Griffith house. He was ten years old, but he was already so tall that, if he wasn't careful, he bumped his head on the lintel of the staircase every time he went up to his bedroom or came down to go outdoors. The room at the top of the stairs and around to the right at the end of the short hall was so narrow that to read he had to drape himself across his bed and the floor, or lie with his feet out the window. That was the least of it. "You and I were always extremists," Bill Wilson wrote his mother years later. "We have never known the average, the mediocre. All or nothing, that's us."

When Bill Wilson moved across the green, it was as if he was moving to another world, a world of taunts and gossip behind his back, where the kids who already called Bill "Beanpole" now had the power to really hurt. Instead of letting his feelings out, Bill began obsessively working on skills that might make him feel better. He would be Thomas Edison; he would be Ty Cobb.

With tools he found in the deserted blacksmith shed next to the Griffith house, Bill used his spare time to build anything he could think of. He perfected an ice boat and constructed bows and arrows, slingshots, and sleds. He built the first radio in town and learned the Morse code so that he could communicate with other radio operators. He was fascinated by engines, all engines, engines of any kind. When the first cars began pulling up to the Wilson House, Bill was there, asking questions and looking under the hood. During the day, his grandfather, who believed that manual labor built character, had him out in the fields, picking strawberries in the spring and corn in the summer, milking the cows that lived in the shed at the back of the house. Bill spent hours winging stones at targets, especially the old disused marble mill across the tracks from the Griffith house. As the years passed, the mill grew smaller and smaller as Bill Wilson knocked it down stone by stone. His arms grew stronger, his voice deepened, he got even taller, and in the process he found that he could see and feel things that he hadn't even dreamed about before. He entered puberty and no one noticed. Where had his parents gone?

Sometimes it seemed as if every family had at least one man who worked in the quarries. By the turn of the century many of the quarries had closed—quarrying was hard and dangerous work and the veins were getting deeper and deeper. Gilman Wilson was one of a dying breed. The building of the New York Public Library, which began in 1900, created a boom in East Dorset that carried the Wilson family through the first few years of its life, through the birth of Bill and his sister, Dorothy. Ten- and twenty-ton blocks of marble were carved out of the mountain and hauled by horse and wagon to the Manchester Depot finishing mill. The balancing of huge blocks of marble and the columns cored out of the mountainside on flatbed trucks that could barely be held still on the steep slopes of Mount Aeolus was a tricky business. When Bill was eleven, two flatbed cars slipped away from their locomotive and went barreling down the tracks right through Danby and East Dorset and crashed into an empty passenger coach down at the Manchester Depot station.

CHAPTER FIVE:

THE GRIFFITH HOUSE

The Griffith house and the Wilson House still stand within shouting distance of each other, on either side of the East Dorset village green. The Griffith house is plain and solid. The expansive, red Wilson House is still a country inn, still welcoming travelers on the Bennington–Manchester Road. Instead of coming on horseback or in buggies like the one with the fringe that Gilman rented to cheer his family with Sunday drives, they drive up in cars. A new, wide Route 7 has been built, and although it ends where the railroad tracks cross it in East Dorset, most cars are still going too fast to notice the peaked roofs and church steeples off to their right among the maple trees.

Because of everything that happened there and in spite of everything that happened there, Bill Wilson's heart always stayed in East Dorset. Describing himself at the beginning of his autobiography as an infant looking out through the bars of his crib through the north windows at the back of the Wilson House, Bill Wilson remembers a sunset gathering over the towering peak of Mount Aeolus. "[That is] the spot where I first saw that mountain, the spot in which I recall so many of the associations of my childhood; that spot whose native ancestry and ruggedness endowed me, I fancy, with both strength and weakness," he told his friend Ed Bierstadt in a New York hotel room in 1954 when it was decided that he should sit down and record his own memories. As an adult, he spent almost every Thanksgiving at the nearby Londonderry Inn at the other end of the old Mad Tom Road and often spent months there writing.

This childhood, a childhood of picture-postcard New England in which the lovely images of nature kept being exploded by adult insanity, left Bill awkward and confused. It was a world of contrasts, often extreme and more often heartbreaking. On the one hand, there were the mountains turning red and gold in the autumn, the blizzard of 1888 closing the roads and covering the village with a soft, miraculous blanket of snow and the roads being closed for days, the heavy fragrances of spring, the abundance of game in the woods and fish in the Batten Kill and Otter Creek on the other side of town. On the other hand, there were the angry, raised voices of his parents.

Later he remembered the night he had accidentally made nitroglycerin in the woodshed with a chemistry set. His father—who was still around at the time—picked up the beaker as if it were about to explode, dug a big ditch, and buried it in the woods. As a quarry foreman, he knew all about dynamite and all about explosions. His father didn't punish him that night; instead he gave his son the feeling that they had shared in a narrow escape. That tolerance was precious to the boy, especially since his mother seemed to have a judgment and a punishment for everything.

To the end of his life Bill Wilson remembered a blessed early moment in which everything was calm. "It is eventime at the parsonage," he wrote his mother, his difficult mother. "The parlor is softly illuminated by that wondrous old kerosene lamp with the large and imposing globe. You are sitting at the piano and as you play father sings. The song is concerned with Jerusalem and is ended in a climax marked by the word 'Hosanna.' Though I first heard this evensong well over fifty years ago, I am still moved by it. It made me feel secure and mysteriously happy because you two were father and mother and because your music told me of the Great Father whose arms are outstretched toward us all." When this happy family was shattered, Bill's security went right along with it.

The Griffith household was a different world from the old one with mother playing the piano while father sang "Hosanna." Fayette and Ella never fought as Emily and Gilman had fought. They didn't seem to care about each other enough to fight. Everything was under control at the Griffith house. Grandpa Griffith (the children called him Brampa) was intimately connected with the town. Cousin Silas Griffith's sawmill, which had made Silas Vermont's first millionaire, sat next to the cheese factory, and Mailey Griffith ran the general store.

Fayette Griffith had come home to Vermont after Gettysburg, married Ella, and built a family. The Civil War had been profoundly destructive to Vermont in general. The state had been fiercely abolitionist, and half of Vermont's able-bodied men had joined to serve in the war against the southern states. Vermont had lost relatively more troops than any other state. During the Battle of the Wilderness she lost a thousand men in a single day. One Vermont battalion lost 40 percent of its soldiers.

Fayette had moved his family to the little town of East Dorset and began buying land lots at tax sales. He prospered in lumber and real estate. Clarence took up the violin and the girls went to school and all seemed well. The war was behind them. Then Clarence got sick. That was the year Emily took up with Gilman Wilson, and their wedding was shadowed by Clarence's death.

By the time he agreed to take in his grandson and granddaughter, Fayette Griffith was an embittered old man, a sixty-four-year-old who wondered why all his honesty and all his belief in the principles of liberty had yielded so much grief and pain. He had found a kind of cold salvation in success and competitiveness, and he passed this instinct on to his poor lost grandson, a tall drink of a boy already prone to depression and lonely walks in the winter woods, a boy at the edge of puberty who had already lost everything a child can lose before he was twelve years old. Grandpa Griffith bought Bill the things he thought a boy should have—a rifle, a chemistry set, the materials to make one of the first radios in Vermont—but he was just going through the motions.

Fayette wanted to be a good grandfather to the boy, but the boy seemed eaten up with self-doubt. He stubbornly battered away at the things he couldn't do. One day in the summer of 1914, Fayette mentioned to Bill that no one outside of Australia had ever been able to build a functioning boomerang. It was with some chagrin that the old man watched his grandson's misery take the form of determination to build a boomerang. With some growing feelings of irritation, he observed the boy carve, build, and throw failure after failure. When the boy threw his homemade boomerang, he was so entranced by the possibility of success that he left his arm stretched out as if he could will the thing to turn around and come back. He spent hours in the attic carving and hours in his room reading. By the time Bill actually built a boomerang that worked—using a three-foot plank from the headboard of his bed—Fayette had been moved by Bill's irrational persistence, although the boomerang almost took his head off as it swirled home in Bill's first successful demonstration.

The creation of the boomerang was a turning point for the connection between Bill and his grandfather. The old man took his grandson under his wing, talking to him for hours about the principles on which their country was founded, and allowing himself to remember the Civil War. He explained the way democracy worked in general and the beauty of Vermont democracy—with its town charters and town meetings—in particular. He gave Bill his law books—Blackstone and Sumner Welles—and even turned over to him Clarence's old violin. Bill threw himself at the instrument as he threw himself at everything else in his life and slowly became a good fiddler.

At local dances Bill played "Turkey in the Straw" and "She'll Be Comin' 'Round the Mountain"; he played jigs and he played waltzes, and sometimes his sadness lifted while he played, and he forgot all the things that had happened to him, and he just let himself be carried away by the music and the stamping feet and the sparkling eyes of the girls who listened, and by the warmth of the hay in the barns where they danced, and the summer nights with their birdsong and the smell of cut grass. For a while, for years even, it seemed as if his father's departure and his parents' divorce would be the low point of his life, a point from which he could mark his ascension to happiness and success.

Chapter Six:

The State of Vermont

Vermont—named after the French words for "green mountain"—was originally explored and claimed for the French by Samuel de Champlain and was lost to the British in 1763 during the French and Indian War. The first building in any village was the tavern, and as the state grew, town meetings were often held in taverns, and taverns also served as local courthouses.

Dorset was created in 1761 by Governor Benning Wentworth of New Hampshire, a man who hoped to expand his own territory and curry favor with George III by naming the town after his crony Lionel Crawford Sackville, the first Earl of Dorset. The town's earliest settlers, led by Zachariah Curtis in 1769, had to endure the dangers and discomforts of the pioneers, including Indian raids—their children were kidnapped and their houses ransacked—by the native Iroquois, packs of wolves raiding their herds of sheep, and the difficulties of clearing and farming the rocky soil. They persevered, and Dorset held its first town meeting in 1774.

Dorset people considered themselves Vermont royalty, and Dorset became Vermont's true center in 1775 and '76, when the state was chartered during the four so-called Dorset conventions. At the heart of Vermont, with its traditions of autonomy, democracy, and Unionism, was the town of Dorset, split into hamlets—East, North, and South—by the looming mass of Mount Aeolus.

Soon after that, Isaac Underhill started hammering blocks out of a ridge of marble at the foot of the Morse Hill Road on the Boomer farm, and the country's first commercial marble quarry was open for business. By 1920, when the marble quarries ceased most of their operations, East Dorset marble had found its way not only to the New York Public Library, but also to the United States Supreme Court Building, and the lintels at Harvard Medical School. East Dorset marble was particularly white but also particularly soft. Harder Italian marble was preferable, and when it became available at the same price, the demand for East Dorset marble dried up. In its heyday, however, marble was not East Dorset's only valuable product. The town was also the perfect forge for the Yankee character, as exemplified by its history of successful rebellion, and its tradition of government by the people in the annual March town meetings.

The Wilson family were among the first residents of East Dorset, having emigrated from Scotland and Ireland. In 1865, William Wilson married Helen Barrows, who lived in the largest house in East Dorset, across from the churchyard. The Barrows were direct descendants of Elder William Brewster, one of the leaders of the band of Pilgrims who came to the New World on the *Mayflower* in 1620. Although they were a kind of white Anglo-Saxon royalty, the Barrows lived in a world where everyone was white and Anglo-Saxon, and they were innkeepers, not people who cared about genealogy. Bill Wilson never mentioned the fact that he was a *Mayflower* descendant. For years the house—called the Old Barrows House— had been a tavern and an inn, but young William Wilson—Gilman's father—liked innkeeping and tavern keeping so much that the couple changed the name to the Wilson House.

Because of Vermont's geography, it was, and remains, a stubbornly rural state with journeys between towns made difficult in the summer by mountains, and impossible in the winter. Even the town of Dorset is divided by a mountain. Its politics have been marked from the beginning by an odd mixture of conservatism and a refusal to bow to authority. When John Adams put Vermont's congressional representative in jail for sedition, Vermont reelected him as he served his sentence. As Frank Bryan explains in his *Yankee Politics in Rural Vermont:* "To be a Vermonter still means to possess certain traits of character . . . which create bonds of communal spirit."

The village charter of East Dorset is astonishingly similar to the charter that hangs at the front of every meeting room of Alcoholics Anonymous—the bylaws of a society that has no laws—and is called the Twelve Traditions. Here is the idea of the power of community and the magic of service. Here is the idea that in a democracy, as Bill Wilson later said, "the leaders should be on tap, not on top." Here, in the New England transcendentalism that was as much a topic of conversation as the end of the wool business (Vermont's sheep population went from a million to a few thousand in the last years of the nineteenth century), is the idea of redemption through a spiritual experience. The traditions that animate the Batten Kill Valley between Manchester and Danby are traditions of great courage and great fear. The original settlers' horses and wagons creaking along the river path must have sounded like thunder in the silent wilderness at the foot of the nameless Mount Aeolus. The woods were filled with food, with timber for building and stones for making walls, and also with grave danger.

This combination of courage and fear was passed down to the boy who was born on Thanksgiving night there in 1895—not much more than a hundred years after the first settlers began farming the lush little valley. He would ramble for days in the woods. He could rise to any challenge. He could drive a team of horses, bring back a brace of squirrels or rabbits for dinner, or land the biggest trout from the Batten Kill. But he was always terribly afraid—of death, of loss, of sickness. His older friend Mark Whalon tried to take care of him. Later, Whalon remembered a summer when Bill

Wilson went around with his hand under his shirt to check that his heart had not stopped beating.

* * *

People in Alcoholics Anonymous sometimes say that Bill Wilson was chosen by God to carry a message. In hindsight, it seems as if Bill Wilson's experience and education were a systematic preparation for his role as cofounder of Alcoholics Anonymous and its principal writer. Because of his background, his Vermont childhood during a time when temperance was taught in school, and even his practical turn of mind, Bill Wilson was able to discover, implement, and disseminate the program that became Alcoholics Anonymous with what seems, in retrospect, miraculous effectiveness and dispatch. Looking backward, the story of Wilson's life almost seems like a blueprint.

A.A. survives partly because of its bylaws, first called guidelines and now called traditions, which prescribe an antihierarchical democracy in which each person has an equal voice, and no money or power is allowed to accumulate. All A.A. officials are elected, the groups are ruled by a majority vote called the "group conscience," and no one can give A.A. more than $1,000 a year. In New England, Wilson saw a fierce democracy in action, and he grew up in a community of farms and quarries where practical experience and strong community connections were more valuable than wealth or education.

The spiritual awakening Bill experienced at age thirty-nine, which was a spur to the creation of Alcoholics Anonymous, was an awakening in the context of a thorough knowledge of spirituality and alcoholism. Many of the ideas put forth in the twelve steps and the twelve traditions of Alcoholics Anonymous can be traced back to the rolling hills and shady pastures of the valley where the Mad Tom Brook meets the Batten Kill. Lois Burnham and her family, who were intimately involved with Bill Wilson, were devout Swedenborgians, and educated him in the enlightened humanism of their religion. Edwin T., or "Ebby," Thacher and his large Manchester Village family became a linchpin of Bill Wilson's success and of his failures. Most of all, though, it was Bill Wilson's faith in the goodness and perfectibility of human nature, and his canny understanding of the forces which corrupt that goodness—beliefs that he breathed in with the air of Vermont as he grew. Although he never had children, Bill Wilson was always a family man. Vermont, with its breathtaking landscapes, glorious history, and flinty good will, was his home, and the Vermonters who nurtured him as a boy really were his family.

Chapter Seven:

Mark Whalon

After the cataclysm of the Civil War saw their able-bodied brothers and sons head south to fight in the Union Army, many small New England towns just gave up the ghost. Those who stayed home to tend the land and the livestock had a hard time making a go of it. A walk today in the woods of Vermont or New Hampshire is punctuated by the crumbling stone walls built by farmers who gambled on making a living in this rocky soil and lost, and ruined foundations of houses and barns are all that is left of what were once thriving pioneer homesteads.

Although agriculture suffered, there were other more positive results. The men who did come back from the war were stronger and more sophisticated than many rural farmers, and the towns that survived for their homecoming became islands of education and storytelling. Fayette Griffith was one of those veterans, and another, more talkative vet, Bill Landon, lived next door. Landon's wife, Rose, ran the East Dorset lending library, and Bill spent many evenings listening to Bill Landon's stories about Gettysburg and Antietam. Then he would walk home across the green, a book in his hand.

Mark Whalon became Bill's guide through the complications of life, literature, and education. Mark was ten years older than Bill, and he often seemed a great deal wiser. It was Mark's friendship and his grandfather's support that allowed Bill to recover from the blows of his childhood and grow into a strapping, accomplished young man. Mark Whalon was East Dorset's Big Man on Campus. He knew everyone and he showed his young protégé the ropes. He had worked in the quarries, and he'd been a lumberjack; he had worked for the phone company; he had also taken some university classes.

When they met, he was working for the General Store in a capacity that allowed him free access to the store's delivery wagon. Later he became the East Dorset mailman. There were newspapers and even a few telephones in town, and between fishing and apple picking and the marble quarries and the cheese factories, everyone was busy all the time. Mark wrote that he became the mailman because he had unsuccessfully tried "cheesemaking, cow doctoring, mush-rat trapping and water witching." He became a rural poet, published a few books, and wrote an evocative poem called "Rural Peace" about coming into a cow barn during a snowstorm.

"Among all my childhood friends there is only one person with whom I ever had a close tie," Bill Wilson wrote. "He was a sort of uncle or father to me and I think in those years I had a certain dependence upon his superior knowledge of the ways of the world, and upon his wonderful charm." Mark Whalon went with Bill sometimes when he played the fiddle, and later when they were out in the woods after grouse or woodcock or fishing further up the creek or down in Dorset Hollow, they talked about what they would do when they were older. They talked about the books they read; Mark Twain and Charles Dickens were a nice complement to the more serious readings in philosophy and law that Fayette Griffith liked to discuss. The two young men stopped at a restaurant and tavern late one summer afternoon on their way home from a successful squirrel-hunting trip. Without saying anything, Mark tied the buckboard up to the rail and the boys swung down and walked through the doors.

Almost before he knew what was happening, Bill found himself with a tall glass of cider in front of him on the worn wooden table. Mark was drinking something that definitely looked illegal. No one in the Griffith household drank; they were a temperance family. Bill was a boy who was never going to drink—for him, drinking was what had caused all those losses. He still missed his father. He would never get over missing his father, even seven years later when he actually traveled to Vancouver to visit him for the first time. But he never forgot the warmth of the tavern and the way the men there seemed to melt together into one person—a person immune to loneliness.

Long after Bill had left East Dorset behind, long after he had started drinking and then stopped drinking again, he remained friends with Mark Whalon. Mark's own drinking problem waxed and waned throughout his life. Later he became a kind of everyman's Robert Frost. He had delivered mail by bobsled and horseback, snowshoes and ox teams, in the Batten Kill Valley and on the slopes of Mount Aeolus. Alfred Eisenstadt traveled to East Dorset in 1943 to take a spread of photographs of Mark Whalon, mail carrier, with his trusty 1935 Plymouth, for *Life* magazine, and Mark became locally famous for saying that the only good thing about a Vermont winter is its end.

Mark Whalon loved to talk. He talked about the theory of evolution—which he explained to his young friend—and about the widow Rose Landon's lending library and about class and money. Bill had never heard anyone talk about the things Mark Whalon talked about. So Bill talked back. In the old delivery wagon they rattled north to Danby or south down through Manchester Village, where great summer houses lined Main Street and where, at the huge resort hotel, rich people sat on the porch and just did nothing all day.

Bill loved Manchester Village, which seemed as far from East Dorset as Mars with its wide-open greens and two golf courses. The

Wilson House was a hotel for travelers, Bill thought, whereas the Equinox in Manchester Village was a hotel people traveled to get to. President Taft had stayed there, as had Theodore Roosevelt, and Abraham Lincoln had made summer reservations at the Equinox when he was assassinated. Down the street from the Equinox, Lincoln's son Robert had built his ornate estate Hildene, one of the great nineteenth-century American houses.

As the East Dorset draft horses clopped past the road up to the elegant gray stone building that Bill knew was a school called the Burr and Burton Seminary for rich kids from all over New England, and past the imposing gates of the Ekwanok Country Club with its greens that spread right out to the horizon, and the majestic memorial to the Manchester men who had died in the Revolutionary War, the Civil War, and the French and Indian War, Mark would hold forth on the place of class and wealth in their world, the differences between the "summer people" who used these grand houses for only a few months a year and the "natives" like themselves. Bill would argue that education counted more than money. Mark would argue that there was even a difference between "new" money, the money made by businessmen in Manchester, for instance, and "old" inherited money. Manchester Village was "old" money, Mark said.

Bill realized that he had never really thought about money at all. Was his grandfather's money old or new? Perhaps it wasn't enough to even qualify as money. Grandpa Griffith had the authority of a wealthy man, but he had never played golf, and he couldn't imagine him lounging on the wide porches of the Equinox, laughing with young women in the new short dresses. Instead of having a tan, Grandpa Griffith's skin was weathered from what he would call honest work. Was the difference between old money and new money really just the difference between physical labor and professional work? These were the ideas that Bill and Mark batted back and forth for hours, and it was conversations such as these that made Bill dream of being a lawyer like Clarence Darrow, a man who got paid to argue.

If New England at the turn of the century was a breeding ground for original ideas, Mark was a propagator of those ideas. The two boys talked about ghosts and the spirits that some of their neighbors could summon with a Ouija board. Mark Whalon was also Bill's connection with local and world politics, which came to East Dorset through radio programs and occasional newspapers. In 1901, when Bill was only six and his parents were still together, President William McKinley had been assassinated in Buffalo by an anarchist, and his vice president, Theodore Roosevelt, succeeded him. The assassination of a president shook the nation, but Theodore Roosevelt became a great hero of Bill's, as he was of Mark's. Here was a man who understood the power of action as well as the power of thinking, a man who was a soldier as well as a statesman.

Always an independent state, Vermont rallied behind Roosevelt with its characteristic feisty self-definition. "In Vermont too we are fortunate that the powers of the legislature itself, the law making department of every representative government, are only called into exercise in the mildest degree," said new Governor John McCullough in his 1902 inaugural address. "The people govern themselves."

When they passed down the hill out of Manchester toward Bennington, Mark pointed out Dr. Clark Burnham's house with its surrounding lawns and shade trees. The family had lived in it for generations, he said. The Burnhams and the Thachers, who owned another of Manchester's fine houses, had helped lure Walter Travis to design the golf course for the Ekwanok Club on the other side of Main Street. An elegant house behind one of Manchester Village's broad marble sidewalks, the Burnham house seemed more lively than some of the grand houses on Main Street. Bill knew that the Burnhams had children and that they were one of the families who had bought a camp up at Emerald Lake. In the winter their house was empty because they lived in New York. In the summer they had horses and everything else they brought with them in a boat up the Hudson to Albany and then by buckboard to Manchester. Bill had been to New York on the train, but he couldn't imagine living there. Burnham was a doctor whose rich clients followed him everywhere, Mark explained wisely. Bill thought that Mark's observation proved his point about education.

* * *

It was to Mark Whalon that Bill Wilson felt he could confide details of his life that might have been misunderstood by those who didn't come from the Yankee tradition. Years later, it was to Whalon that this university dropout wrote his real feelings about being offered an honorary degree from Yale University in 1954. "The secretary of Yale University showed up and began to talk to me as if I was George Washington or someone of that kind," Wilson wrote Whalon from New York. "I've just written a letter declining. The reason of course is that if I don't take this it will act as a terrific restraint on big shots and power seekers in Alcoholics Anonymous in the years to come. I'm declining for that reason only, not because I'm so damn noble or anything." He wrote his mother a different kind of letter. "I did rather want this degree," he confided. "It symbolized the long and happily fruitful span between the parsonage parlor and the peerage of the so-called great."

Bill's friendship with Mark Whalon became a kind of emotional lodestone. Mark was the man who interpreted the world for him. The ideas he first heard from Mark and from his grandfather, ideas about the nature of democracy and the necessity of curbing human nature, ideas about spirituality and instincts and the awakening of the human soul, were planted as he rode around the countryside in the General Store delivery wagon or leaned against the barn fence with his grandfather after the cows were in. It was in those years— when everything was as vivid as emotional pain can make them— that the seeds of the ideas were planted which would grow and blossom and bear the fruit that became the program called Alcoholics Anonymous.

Later, in the confusion of becoming so famous that he often traveled under an assumed name and hesitated to go to the meetings in the program he had founded only a decade earlier, Bill Wilson turned often to his boyhood friend for advice and counsel. "I do believe that life is just a day in school," he wrote to Whalon in 1951, when his friend was already sick with Parkinson's disease. "All our experiences are but lessons in some form or other which condition us for our larger destiny. Of that I am very sure. Any way you look at it, it's a problem world. What matters, and what matters only is what we do with the problems."

When Mark Whalon died in September of 1956, Bill Wilson collapsed first into hysteria and then into one of the depressions that had become dreadfully familiar to him and to his wife and mother. "I simply couldn't face it—even to talk to you," he wrote Emily before he rushed north to go to Whalon's funeral and burial in the East Dorset churchyard. The East Dorset Cemetery is an oval on the western slope of a hill between East Dorset and Manchester. Cars rush past on their way down the valley to the south. Bill Wilson's own gravestone is there now, next to his wife's in the Griffith plot. Made of sugary East Dorset marble, they are marked only by the small pile of mementos, coins, notes—all the paraphernalia of sobriety that visitors have left in his honor. Instead of the Yale degree, he has this.

Chapter Eight:

Mount Aeolus

Bill Wilson knew he would never drink. As he got older and looked back at his first ten years, he saw how his father's drinking often came before the fights; he remembered the way his father would take off for a few days, even at the beginning. As he grew in strength and confidence, he became even more certain of another thing—he would never, ever allow anyone to tell him what to do. This brought him into direct conflict with many small-town traditions and ideas, and caused him to feel even more of an outcast. He wasn't the only Vermonter who had noticed the deleterious effect of drinking on the family.

One weekend the County Temperance Institute held a two-day conference at the East Dorset Congregational Church in collaboration with the Dorset Board of Hope. Still reeling from his parents' divorce, the explosion of his beloved family, and the dislocation of his life, the eleven-year-old Bill Wilson went unquestioningly to the Congregational Sunday School across the green. All the Griffiths went to church. The day came during the visit from the Temperance Institute when all the children in the East Dorset Sunday School were asked to sign a temperance pledge. His peers agreed without thinking about it. What did they know about drinking? Although Wilson knew a great deal about drinking and what drinking could do to a family, he wasn't about to let some Sunday School temperance preacher tell him what he had to do. He could feel a stubbornness taking control of his feelings. Who did they think they were to tell him how to live for the rest of his life? Whose rules were these, anyway? He wasn't going to drink, but he wasn't going to sign their pledge either. He refused in the stubbornness of the moment, but this refusal had an enormous effect on his future.

He walked away from Sunday School and away from church. He decided that he was an atheist. If there was a God, how could he have allowed all this to happen? If he was to have a decent life, he knew he would have to build it for himself, in spite of God, with his own intelligence and determination. He would learn everything he could. He would follow his best instincts. He remembered all the months he had spent whittling the boomerang when no one else thought he could make it work. He thought of the way he had taught himself to play Clarence's beat-up old fiddle. If he could make music from a few pieces of wood and some gut strings, if writers could make whole worlds come alive on the page just by putting down what was in their heads, then human beings had the power to shape their own destinies, he thought.

Instead of going to church that morning, he hiked up Morse Hill through the hayricks to Quarry Road, past the old North Quarry where his father worked; he could feel the tug of darkness at his heart. The tin maple-sugaring buckets were hanging from some of the trees on the road that ran across the side of the mountain. He passed a team of horses pulling a tank for the sweet syrup. The bearded men hailed him because everyone knew everyone in East Dorset. Soon he would collect the sap from the Griffith sugar maples and boil it down in a huge iron kettle at the back of the house.

Last year getting the watery sap to become maple syrup had taken much longer than he had expected. He lay wood on the fire and boiled it and boiled it. Night fell and Dorothy had come out to plead with him to stop and go to bed. But he didn't stop until it was transformed into thick, amber-colored syrup. That syrup was the sweetest thing he had ever tasted. Now, taking a steep path, he walked fast until he reached the top, the summit of Mount Aeolus. Up there the air seemed thinner, clearer. His heart was beating dangerously fast, and he wondered if he was going to die. He could see the whole valley spread out before him, and the fields and pastures, a herd of sheep over there on Bromley Mountain, a few teams of oxen on the road to Manchester. It was March and the woods were uncannily silent, he could almost hear the snow melting around him and water dripping and beginning to stream down the mountainside, over the tracks, over the old Quarry Road.

All around him the rivulets poured down toward the creek and then the river, past the ridges on the Boomer farm and the old cheese factory and through the McBrides' cow pasture. Off to the north, up the valley still green with pines and hemlock but patchy with brown now as mud season approached, he could see the smoke rising from the chimneys of the iron mills in North Dorset and the glimmer of Emerald Lake. To the south there was the city of Manchester laid out below him like a town made from wooden toys, with its buildings and houses already clinging to the hills which had once been pasture. He could see the spire of the church in Manchester Village and the gold dome of the Bennington County Courthouse. And directly below him, looking like a town in a picture book, was East Dorset, with the spire of its church and the bulk of the Wilson House next to the railroad running by the old Dorset Turnpike and the Batten Kill just before it met Mad Tom Brook in its journey to the sea.

Bill had hiked every path and road on this mountain, passing by the mouths of the seventy-five quarries, each surrounded with the sea of marble chips that looked as if someone had lobbed a snowball at the brown earth, each with its blocks of marble piled up like a northern Stonehenge. He knew the hole that was really the mouth of Devil's Cave and the other caves that reminded him of Tom Sawyer, and the terrifying Injun Joe. Sometimes on a warm day he

would tell Fayette, whom he still called Brampa, that he was going
hunting and take his best eleventh-birthday present—the Reming-
ton .25-20—and walk up here and just lie down on the cool moss
and read a book. Mark gave him books, and he borrowed some
from Rose Landon's lending library, but he would read anything,
even the big Griffith Dictionary, from cover to cover. He would
bring his energy and intelligence to bear on all the problems that
faced him. If he could build a boomerang, surely he could build a
life.

Chapter Nine:

Burr and Burton

The more Bill read, the more he wanted to read. He had read about Horatio Alger and Thomas Edison. He read *Heidi* and the family encyclopedia and, of course, the Bible. Every week a buckboard would come up from Manchester loaded with books for Rose Landon's lending library. Bill became a reading addict, staying up all night while the rest of the Griffith house slept. With his kerosene lantern sputtering, he would drape his long body over the bed and down to the floor, where he rested the book he was reading. He was determined to absorb as much knowledge as possible. Remembering what he read was easy for him. If he learned enough, he thought, he would be able to control the course of his life. Not only would he know how everything worked, but he could avoid disasters like the one that had already shattered his family. In reading, he also escaped, becoming a sailor on a whale ship or a boy trapped on a desert island or a captain on a Mississippi River boat.

Bill had heard about Harvard and Yale, but for him the epitome of education was the graceful spire of Burr and Burton Seminary. It was the school on a hill. With its pale grey limestone walls and white trim, it was housed in one of the most impressive buildings set above impressive Manchester Village. On the slope of the mountain behind the Equinox Hotel, where presidents had slept, the seminary was backed up against the steep ledges, with views of the town and the Batten Kill Valley below. Begun in 1829 as a training school for ministers, Burr and Burton had become one of the finest private coeducational boarding schools in Vermont by the beginning of the twentieth century. Burr and Burton boys wore tweed trousers and jackets with little belts in the back. Burr and Burton girls were all beautiful. Burr and Burton students went on to Harvard or Yale or the Massachusetts Institute of Technology.

Sometimes on a summer evening Bill would pass by one of the dances given by the people he had learned to call "old money." Under the fragrant trees young women in bright dresses, moving to the music of a sublime dance band, were danced back and forth across polished floors by handsome young men in suits who seemed to know exactly what to do. These young men were never shy. They were never awkward. Some of them went to Andover and St. Paul's, and some of them went to Burr and Burton. Still going to the local two-room schoolhouse, Bill assumed that he would graduate with his peers and find work in the farms or quarries or mills as they did. Slowly, however, as he began to see the difference in the way he thought and read and reasoned, he began to wonder if that would be enough for him. As it was, if it weren't for Mark Whalon, he would have no one to talk with.

At the same time, his grandparents were worried about him. He was beginning to look like his father, and women seemed to warm to him and he to them. He was only interested in impossible dreams, not the ordinary dreams, like the dream of being a farmer or even a congressman. After consulting with Emily, Fayette Griffith applied to Burr and Burton for his grandson. In true Yankee fashion, he didn't ask Bill about the application, and he didn't tell him. Finally, when the boy had been admitted, his grandfather told him to plan to start eighth grade at Burr and Burton in the fall of 1909. He would board at the school during the week and be expected to come home on weekends to help around the place.

Burr and Burton was only seven miles away—a five-mile train

trip and a two-mile hike—but it might as well have been a thousand miles from the narrow parlor and tiny bedroom that was Bill Wilson's home at the Griffith house. The first floor of the school was taken over by a huge, light-filled chapel with high arched windows looking out over the valley and the green mountains beyond. There were classrooms on the second floor and, on the third floor, two sets of dormitory cubicles, with the boys on the left and the girls on the right. Each student had a window, bed, and desk. In this monastic, simple, and beautiful setting established for the education of Vermont youth, Bill saw that he had a second chance at life. At Burr and Burton he could reinvent himself and leave the past behind.

It wasn't easy. By East Dorset standards he had been a fair athlete and a crack shot. During his first sally out onto the Burr and Burton baseball diamond, he learned exactly what that meant. He was playing with boys who had never had to work at anything but sports, and they threw and hit and pitched with a grace and abandon that he could only imagine. He missed his first catch and the ball hit him in the head and knocked him down. He got laughed at.

Singing along on a bus trip with the rest of his class, he noticed that those near him had stopped singing and started moaning at his flat rendition of the song. The next day he knocked on the door of the office of the headmaster's wife and asked her to give him singing lessons. Wilson was as determined and stubborn as he was clumsy and out of tune. At last he had found a place where his energy, his defiance, and his refusal to be labeled became assets. Slowly, he began to shine. He found a Victrola and listened to music, and decided that he would develop his fiddling talent until he could join the Burr and Burton orchestra as a violinist. He practiced and practiced.

By the spring of 1912, Bill Wilson's second year at Burr and Burton, he was a promising student who was one of the school's best pitchers, a talented high jumper, the captain of the football team, and the school's best punter and dropkicker. His grades were erratic, but he often scored in the 90s, and he was also an accomplished actor who appeared in the school's theatrical productions. Then, in his junior year, he became the lead violin in the school orchestra. He was voted president of his class. There was no prize that seemed to elude this brilliant and gifted boy.

Then he got the girl. Although he thought of himself as gawky and ugly, in fact he was a tall, handsome, athletic boy with a thoughtful way of approaching everything. It was no wonder that many of the Burr and Burton girls began to take an interest in him. One in particular, Bertha Bamford, a popular, pretty, brown-haired girl and the daughter of Manchester Village's Episcopal minister, seemed to single him out. Bertha was the class treasurer and president of the Y.W.C.A. That spring they fell completely in love.

Bertha's family also liked Bill, and welcomed him into their house in Manchester. Now he was at the dances he had once watched longingly from across the grass. He and Bertha were a handsome couple, and with her he knew just what to do. She gave him a kind of confidence he had never had before. He made new friends, people like the Thachers, whose son Ebby was at Burr and Burton with him, and the Burnhams and the Shaws. He had been transformed from the awkward outcast to a young prince of the most beautiful place on earth.

The two towns where Bill Wilson grew up—East Dorset and Manchester Village—have been oddly preserved almost as they were a hundred years ago. Neglect has preserved East Dorset, tucked in a hollow off the new main road from Manchester to Danby. Wealth has preserved Manchester Village. The Equinox Hotel is a vast structure that has been added on to, burned down, lived through bankruptcy, and grown some more. It's on a different scale from anything in East Dorset. Everything in Manchester Village is capacious and airy, as if summer would last forever, as if the Vermont seasons were nothing to worry about. Everything in East Dorset is built for practicality: the steep roofs deflect the snow, the small rooms are easy to heat, the sheds where the animals live are roomier than the rooms where the people live.

Everything in Manchester Village is built for pleasure. East Dorset is the fiddle; Manchester Village is the violin. East Dorset is baked beans and bacon; Manchester Village is a crown roast of lamb with new potatoes. East Dorset is Ethan Frome; Manchester Village is Ethan Allen. In his own mind Bill sometimes confused the two places, as if it were Manchester Village where he really belonged, and not dear old East Dorset. He told a biographer that his grandfather had often taken him to visit the War Memorial in front of their village church. The War Memorial is not in East Dorset, where there is only thin grass in front of the small church. The War Memorial is an impressive monument topped by a Minuteman and surrounded by engraved names at the head of Main Street in Manchester Village.

Burr and Burton is still there too, although the high-ceilinged chapel has been divided into offices, and the school has spread into other buildings. The limestone for the original school came from local quarries, but when the school wanted to build again, the quarries were exhausted. A geologist found a branch of the same vein of limestone in Canada, and that's what they used. The school is still tucked into the side of Mount Equinox, with views of the valley below, and it echoes with the voices of students changing classes, clanging lockers, murmuring over their books.

The summer and early fall of 1912 were one of the happiest periods of Bill Wilson's life, he often said. He had been through the fire. He knew what pain felt like. Yet with his own energy and intelligence he had worked and thought and played his way into a life that, as a young boy, he could barely have dreamed about. It had

paid off! All those hours of determined practicing, of doing whatever it was again and again that his sister and his grandmother called
stubbornness, had all paid off. Bill remembered how he had taught
himself the fiddle by taping paper with the notes on it to the neck of
the instrument. It had seemed impossible at the time, but he had
been able to learn, and now he was a master of the violin.

After the day when he walked out of the East Dorset church, he
had never really returned to Christianity. Bertha insisted, of course.
Bill felt that if there was a God at all, he was only for emergencies.
Bill hadn't needed God's help, and he had overcome the hardships
God had sent him. Yes, he had built a boomerang. Yes, he had built
a world for himself. "I'm going to make quite a point of an easily
understood triad of primary instincts which result in primary
drives," he said in dictating his autobiography forty years after this
happy summer. "The drive for distinction and power; the drive for
security, physical, financial and emotional; and the desire to love
and be loved, romantically or otherwise. Well, you see at this period
now that I am in love I am fully compensated on all these primary
instinctual drives. I have all the prestige there is to have in school. I
excel, indeed I am number one where I choose to be. Consequently
I am emotionally secure. My grandfather is my protector and is
generous with my spending money, and now I love and am loved
fully and completely for the first time in my life. Therefore I am
deliriously happy and am a success according to my own specifica-
tions."

Chapter Ten:

Bertha Bamford

On the long weekend of November 18, a few weeks before Bill's seventeenth birthday, the Bamford family traveled to New York. Bill and Bertha had said a loving goodbye, although they knew they would see each other in a few days. They could hardly bear to be apart for an hour, so the weekend stretched ahead like an eternity. Bill busied himself with reading and doing chores back in East Dorset. Although no one talked about it, the trip had been arranged so that the seventeen-year-old Bertha could visit Flower Hospital on Fifth Avenue to have a small tumor removed.

Now it was Tuesday morning and Bill burst into the morning assembly held in Burr and Burton's downstairs Chapel. His eyes scanned the rows of friends and students, squinting against the sun that poured in through the high east-facing windows. He couldn't find Bertha. Where in the name of heaven was she? Everyone was singing. *For still our ancient foe doth seek to work us woe; his craft and power are great.* When the hymn was over, the headmaster, Mr. James Brooks, stood up behind the lectern at the front of the room. He took a yellow piece of paper out of his pocket, and for a moment he hesitated as if he had been given a job he didn't quite know how to do. He looked at Bill and then out at the slopes of the mountain, golden in the morning sun. The yellow piece of paper was a telegram from New York, and it said that Bertha Bamford, a student at the school, had died of internal hemorrhaging from surgery in New York over the weekend.

The whole world seemed to stop turning for a minute. Then the next hymn began. *Jesus calls us; o'er the tumult of our life's wild restless sea.* Some students burst into sobs; others turned to look at Bill. Most of them slowly took up the singing. *Day by day his sweet voice soundeth, saying, "Christian, follow me."* "It was a cataclysm of such anguish that I've since had but two or three times," Bill wrote later. Security had been snatched away again, and the whole thing—divorce, loss, death—seemed to crash down on him.

Bertha's funeral was on Friday, and instead of spending the day as they had planned, sitting on her family's porch and talking about their future, Bill spent that day as a pallbearer. Even fifty years later when he wrote his autobiography, he didn't want to talk about the pain of that week, a time when he sank into a depression and could hardly speak. If Bill's life had seemed difficult before, he had been able to recover. Resilience was a Yankee characteristic, and through hard work, brains, and sheer tenaciousness he had come out on top. Now he had lost his bearings, and his life and his feelings seemed to spiral out of control.

He seemed to hate his former success. Along with destroying his health and his peace of mind, Bertha's death erased any vestiges he might have had of belief in God or any other supreme being. What on earth was the use of believing in anything? He quit all sports—baseball, football, high jumping. He had trouble talking to his old friends and got grades of forties in classes where he had once been the teacher's pet. He wasn't going to graduate. He didn't even seem to care.

His grandfather treated him to a trip to the battlefield at Gettysburg for the fiftieth anniversary of the Civil War battle. They heard speakers and walked the muddy fields, and Fayette Griffith showed his broken grandson the sloping hillside where Vermonters out-flanked Pickett's charge and helped decide the outcome of the battle. Fayette Griffith tried to tell the boy about his own suffering and his own resilience. Bill didn't seem to be listening. They stayed in a tent city put up by the State of Pennsylvania and the War Department, crowded on the anniversary with thousands of aging Union and Confederate soldiers. On the Fourth of July, President Woodrow Wilson gave a speech. Nothing, however, seemed to reach the boy.

The whole thing made Emily Griffith Wilson angry. What had happened to her successful son? Where were the accomplishments that seemed to suggest that whatever she had done as a mother had been the right thing for her children? She steamed up from Boston and confronted James Brooks. No one knew what to do, he said. She knew what to do. She took her spiritless son back to Arlington, outside of Boston, where she was living, and enrolled him in the Arlington High School. He had failed German; he would make up German.

Emily had a plan. No one was going to derail her Bill. He would graduate from Arlington and go to the Massachusetts Institute of Technology. He would become a brilliant engineer. "Success, success, success!" They were Griffiths from a proud and important family; she wasn't going to let her son's no-good Wilson blood ruin his life. For once, though, her son was unable to oblige. In the grip of a nervous breakdown, he couldn't focus and he couldn't study. He flunked the M.I.T. entrance exams.

Desperate, Emily arranged for her son to visit his father—a man he hadn't seen in seven years. The teenaged boy took a train to Montreal and then another train out to British Columbia, where Gilman was the manager of the Marblehead quarries of the Canadian Marble Works. He traveled alone. While he was there, Bill wrote obligatory travel descriptions to his Grandmother Wilson back in East Dorset. "Everything is ragged and angular showing marks of sudden and violent changes," he wrote, describing his first look at the Rocky Mountains. He might have been describing his life. He wrote about the train trips and the mountains, the oil and gas fields, and the city of Medicine Hat.

Gilman Wilson had a new quarry to run, a new life, new friends, and a new woman named Christine who would soon become his wife. He was welcoming to his only son, but he was distracted. He wasn't a resentful man, but his clear opinion was that the failure of his first marriage was his wife Emily's doing. In characteristic Wilson fashion, his good-natured solution to the problem was to move on. Within a year Bill would have a new sister, Helen, who later became one of the many people he took care of.

Now, though, Bill chose not to write about what it was like to see his father again after all those years. His letters read like the letters of an incidental tourist, not a son in search of his vanished father. There are no letters pouring out his feelings, feelings that would come to the surface later in the presence of a sympathetic listener. His father had started over. Back in East Dorset after his trip, Bill had the opposite experience. Nothing had changed. The farmers went out to sow and reap as always; the quarriers lived by the foreman's whistle. His life came to a painful standstill.

CHAPTER ELEVEN:

LOIS BURNHAM

Miss Lois Burnham, an educated and wealthy young lady from Brooklyn, and a graduate of the Packer Collegiate Institute, was part of a family that owned two of the tall shingle houses called camps at the edge of the Emerald Lake. For years the Burnhams had picnicked at the lake, traveling from their house in Manchester Village with horse-drawn wagons filled with plates and flatware as well as the food for an outdoor feast. One summer they were horrified to find that someone had built a peak-roofed shingle house on their favorite picnic spot at the south end of the lake. Dr. Clark Burnham, Lois's handsome father, sauntered over and bought the house. The next summer, staying in their new camp, the family was again upset to see another new house nearby. Dr. Burnham bought that one too, and it was always called, with a chuckle, "the other house."

Lois's father was a popular and wealthy man who was part of the New York community of Swedenborgians. His own father had been a minister of the Swedenborgian Church in Lancaster, Pennsylvania. The New Church, or the Church of the New Jerusalem, is based on the teachings of the eighteenth-century Swedish scientist and nobleman Emanuel Swedenborg. Swedenborg, a respected philosopher, devoted the last part of his life to psychical and spiritual research and wrote interpretations of the Bible including *Arcana Coelestia,* a book that divides understanding into a series of steps. Although Swedenborg didn't intend to found a religion, his followers did, and American Swedenborgianism with its humanistic overtones and its faith in an afterlife was the belief of choice for many successful professionals and wealthy businessmen at the turn of the century.

The Burnhams had their own buggy, pulled by horses Jerry and Bess, and their own convertible Stevens-Duryea in which Lois's brother Rogers liked to tool up and down Route 7 and through the surrounding green summer countryside. They were friends with Robert Lincoln, the president's son who had built Hildene, and his wife, and the Burnham children played with the Lincoln children.

Lois was twenty-two years old that summer, old enough to be called an old maid. More and more, she understood—although she never talked about it—that the perfect outward surface of their family life hid some imperfections.

Their Manchester summers were lovely, for instance, but although Dr. Burnham liked to say that his patients loved him so much that they followed him to the country, sometimes Lois wondered if it wasn't more a case of the doctor following the patients. Could he have afforded a summer without them? Her mother came from an old New England family, and the Manchester Village house had been the Spelman house before her father bought it from his in-laws and it became the Burnham house. Her mother's cousin, Laura Spelman, her own Aunt Laura, had married John D. Rockefeller, and Lois was a favorite with the Spelman women. As a girl, she remembered a visit to the Rockefeller mansion, Kykuit, in Pocantico Hills, where she slept in a trundle bed and caught a glimpse of the wizened great man of Standard Oil—John D. Rockefeller—holding forth in his own endlessly long living room. She remembered the way he leaned on the mantelpiece and the way everything was decorated in green and gold.

*   *   *

During the summer of 1913, the Burnhams brought a trim little skiff from New York with an attachable mast and sail, and dressed in the latest sailing costumes, Miss Lois Burnham liked to practice sailing in the mild, gusty winds of Emerald Lake. She carefully tacked around the lake's small island as she had been taught to do by her brothers, taking a broad reach toward one of the stands of white birches on the shore.

Lois hadn't really been introduced to the Wilson family, whose son occasionally camped at the other side of the lake, but she knew who they were. Her brother Rogers knew Bill Wilson, a rawboned eighteen-year-old who seemed to know a lot about machines and hunting. They liked to talk about cars. She had met Bill and his sister, Dorothy, but they seemed very young and very local. She knew the Wilsons' parents had been divorced, and that Bill and Dorothy lived with their grandparents three miles down the road in East Dorset. Rogers seemed very enthusiastic about the Wilson family, but Lois couldn't figure out why.

Lois had a lot on her mind that summer. With no suitors in the wings, her future seemed to offer little more than a secretarial job and a bedroom in her parents' house. In sailing she forgot all about those problems. Out on the little lake, she could look over the gunwale and see fish swimming slowly in the weeds. The wooded island and the sheer mountains on either side of the lake seemed to comfort her.

The lake winds were unpredictable, and one afternoon as she came about, sedately moving from one side to the other under the mainsail boom, she found herself racing with a tall boy who had rigged up a homemade sail on one of the lake's leaky public rowboats. To her well-bred amazement, he sailed better than she did even in his rickety craft. It was Bill Wilson. Later, when the boats were anchored in the green water, they sat on the beach in front of the Burnham camp, and he told her that he had learned how to sail by reading his grandfather's encyclopedia. He didn't mention that they were near the spot where his mother had once taken him and his sister for a picnic he would never forget.

Bill Wilson knew the name of every part of the boat and the name and purposes of every piece of rope. Lois Burnham was only four years older than Bill Wilson, but she was almost another generation from this ragtag local teenager whose principal education, in spite of Burr and Burton, was from the school of hard knocks. She had graduated from college, and he couldn't seem to graduate from high school. She was a summer visitor, and he was what some of her friends slightingly called a native. Still, she found him teaching her something. They spent sunny summer days racing each other up and down the little lake. There was something about Bill Wilson that intrigued her even though he was a teenager and she was a young lady. Was he letting her win?

That fall Lois went back to Brooklyn and Bill managed to get enough accreditation from Burr and Burton to enroll in Norwich University, a military college in Northfield. He was miserable. The forward momentum provided by his own will and by his mother's will was not enough to overcome his emotional deadness and inertia. He was still in grave mental trouble. On the train to school he suffered a massive anxiety attack. "The sensation that I was going to die increased," he remembered. "I began to be seized with terrible shortness of breath, and frightful palpitations. It seemed as though I just couldn't get enough air and to the surprise of the conductor I left the coach and eventually laid down in the vestibule with my nose to a crack in the floor to see if I couldn't get air." Bill made it back to school, but his heart palpitations and his fear kept him from going to class. At the school infirmary they told him there was nothing wrong.

At Norwich, Bill didn't get a single fraternity bid. He was on no sports teams. He flunked algebra. Then, in his second semester, he fell and injured his elbow. He insisted that he be sent to his mother in Boston. After a few days she packed him back to East Dorset, where he lay in bed day after day in the Griffith house, crying and chattering through palpitations. The doctor came again and again. His diagnosis—nothing. "Some days I can eat nothing," Bill wrote his mother, explaining that he didn't feel he could survive a trip to Boston to see her. "It makes me mad to think I am scared, but I am scared just the same."

Late that spring, Fayette Griffith got the idea that he might become a car salesman. Many of the wealthier residents of the area had cars, and Fayette—who had seen the possibilities of the spruce on empty land, who had the idea of importing Canadian labor—thought he had once again landed ahead of the curve. He would link up with one of the big automotive companies—Ford or Packard—and become the agent for sales in the area. When he talked about this at dinner, Bill suddenly perked up. The idea of cars, his beloved engines, seemed to bring his grandson temporarily back to life.

Suddenly, it seemed as if there was nothing Bill cared about more than cars. He knew how they worked. He knew all about how everything worked. He could talk about them better than anyone in town. There were only a few thousands of cars in the whole country, and he and his grandfather would be getting in at the beginning of something huge. He and Mark Whalon spent hours talking about cars and which ones they preferred and which ones ran the best and which ones would be the easiest to sell. Bill knew that his passion for engines could be translated into a compelling sales pitch. He had a glimpse of a future in which his own love and conviction could be powerfully persuasive tools even to people who resisted whatever he was trying to tell them.

He dropped by the Bamfords' house to tell the people who had once been his family about his new idea. They were enthusiastic and promised to buy a car from him as soon as he had one to sell. This showed him how convincing he could be as a salesman. What would it be like to have a car to drive, as a salesman surely would? What would it be like to tool up Route 7 to Emerald Lake in a bright red Pierce-Arrow? He imagined the way he would bump across the railroad tracks at the foot of Morse Hill and soar past the cemetery and over the crest of Beech Ridge and through Manchester Center.

Bill wrote his mother the first positive letter she had gotten in a long time. Didn't she remember Rogers Burnham's Duryea, and how interested he was in that? He had already practically sold a new car to the Bamfords without even trying. Emily wrote her son back forbidding him to have anything to do with the proposed automobile agency. His job was to get through school. He was a student, not a salesman. What about his education? Furthermore, he was still suffering from the aftermath of a nervous breakdown, she reminded him. Would it be safe for him to drive a car in his mental condition?

Her son argued with her as if his life depended on it. Yes, education was important, but he wasn't planning to give up on his education. He even argued that he wouldn't have to drive the cars; he could just sell them. She was adamant. She let her father know what she thought too. Everyone who knew Emily knew that it was useless to argue with her. In the end, Fayette didn't get the car dealership, but the prospect of it had given his grandson a moment of good health. He began eating again. His spells and chattering and dizziness disappeared. Something, some enthusiasm for the romance of automobiles combined with the intrigue of the combustion engine, had finally pierced the nineteen-year-old's caul of despair.

Chapter Twelve:

New York City

The next summer, circumstances seemed to conspire to entangle the now twenty-three-year-old woman from Brooklyn and the brokenhearted kid from East Dorset. By this time Lois had graduated from Packer and had completed two years at the New York School of Applied and Fine Art (later, the Parsons School of Design). She was working in the employment department of the Y.W.C.A. and waiting for her life to begin. The oldest of six children, Lois knew that some of her sisters were married and established as head of their own family.

One suitor, Norman Schneider, had appeared, but she didn't much like him, at least not in the way that he wished she did. They had met at a church convention, and she knew that he was ready to propose to her. He was from a wealthy family, and he would want her to move to Kitchener, Ontario, where he lived and where they would work together on church business for the rest of their lives. She loved her family, and even a man she loved would have had trouble convincing her to move so far away from them. She was desperate, but she was not quite that desperate.

Lois's sister Barbara had a series of beaus. For a while one of them was Bill Wilson. Then Barbara was going with someone else. Lois's brother Rogers was courting Bill's sister, Dorothy. At dances and baseball games and everywhere Rogers and Dorothy went, Lois and Bill found themselves together, and they found themselves talking.

One awkward night Bill grabbed her and tried to kiss her, but Lois resisted him. She remembered that she was a young lady from Manchester Village and he was a native from East Dorset. After that disastrous encounter, they started a relaxed friendship that they both enjoyed. There was no self-consciousness between them. They could be friends without wondering how they could benefit each other. Bill was still suffering from anxiety and depression, and Lois listened to him for hours. He would tell her that he was no good, and she would reassure him.

"Lois came along and picked me up as tenderly as a mother does a child," Bill wrote in his autobiography. Later, when he had learned to take better care of himself, he wasn't quite so patient with Lois's maternal tendencies. "At the unconscious level I have no doubt she was already becoming my mother, and I haven't any question that was a very heavy component in her interest in me," he said.

That summer, the summer of 1915, Lois, ever the lady, had the idea of building a tea arbor for travelers from Manchester to Danby or even Montreal who might find themselves in need of a little light refreshment. On a hill above Otter Creek at the north end of Emerald Lake, visible from the road, she had an arbor constructed of evenly spaced birch poles, rustic chairs, and handmade maple tables. There Lois brewed tea for what she hoped would be a stream of thirsty visitors. Business was slow, very slow. At the same time, Bill, still disappointed over the failure of the automobile venture, was peddling burners for kerosene lamps from village to village as his summer job. His business was also slow. The fire that had him selling cars even before he had any to sell did not translate into the selling of kerosene burners.

Bill got in the habit of heading north on old Route 7 and stopping on the way. The tea arbor was almost always empty. Lois was always there and ready to listen and reassure. She was from a different world; she didn't know how different. Bill wasn't about to tell her about how people where he came from used the back steps as a bathroom. He didn't want her to know how many times he had watched from a distance as the Burnhams and their friends partied and danced on the perfectly manicured lawns of Manchester Village.

Now often, as evening fell, Bill would walk Lois back to the Burnham camp and end up staying for dinner. If only for a few hours he felt like a member of a family again. The Burnhams joked and laughed with each other, Bill and Rogers were already friends, Lois was always listening, and even the younger Burnhams, Kitty and Barb and Lyman, seemed to be part of the family's enchanted atmosphere. Barb still seemed to be interested in him, and sometimes Bill found himself kissing her and hugging her. The real attraction was the way he felt when he was with the whole family. He remembered how to tell a story and relished the happy pleasures of an audience.

Dr. Burnham liked to talk about patriotism with his young guest, and both men agreed that this was an exciting time to live in the United States. Margaret Sanger was in jail. Germany was at war with France, but in spite of that far-off rumbling, life was good. Robert Frost's first poems had just been published, and there were exciting new novels like Somerset Maugham's *Of Human Bondage* for the ladies to read. As the summer wore on, Norman Schneider came for a visit to the Burnham camp at Emerald Lake. Norman and Lois talked and went sailing as people who were courting might, but Lois didn't feel like being someone who was being courted. Faced with a handsome, smitten prospect, she found herself missing the quick wit and encyclopedic knowledge of her nineteen-year-old friend.

"I was longing every minute to be with Bill," she wrote later. Near the end of his visit, Norman asked her to marry him; she told him maybe. When she took him to the Emerald Lake train station to catch the train back to Montreal, the train seemed to take forever to come. She didn't want to turn down her only suitor, but she didn't want to move to Canada either. Under the circumstances, every minute with Norman became more annoying. Finally, the train came down the single track from East Dorset and Manchester. As Norman got on, waving sadly, who should swing off the train on his way to Emerald Lake but Bill Wilson.

Bill and Lois walked back to the lake together, and naturally Lois talked to her friend about Norman Schneider and the good work he was doing. She confided in Bill that Norman had asked her to marry him and come and live with him in Canada. Bill's reaction was immediate and thrilling. "It was as if all summer he had been standing in the sunlight, and now a great pit was opening and he was going to be pulled back into it," Robert Thomsen wrote in *Bill W.,* the biography he based on interviews with Bill. Without Lois, he would once again be alone, abandoned, a nobody. Overwhelmed by those old feelings, he instinctively reached for her—and she was there. This time she didn't reject his advances. She had faith in him and in their future. By about midnight that same night, when Bill turned to walk down the railroad trestle, home to the Griffith house, he was engaged to Miss Lois Burnham.

For a while they kept their engagement a secret, and Bill confided only in Mark Whalon. "She loves you because you are Bill Wilson," Mark said, and that sounded like a very wise statement. At the end of the summer the lovers were parted. Lois went back to her secretarial job at the Young Women's Christian Association in Brooklyn, and Bill went back to Norwich University, which had been a kind of compromise choice brokered by his mother and grandparents. He had hoped to visit Lois before Christmas, but he was in trouble at school again. Angry at his mathematics teacher, he had taken the trouble to learn more than the teacher knew. This earned him a failing grade. At the same time, he got a job chopping wood and began to put together some savings.

Soon enough he was in trouble with Lois, who had confided her feelings to Barb and apparently been told a thing or two about her beloved Bill Wilson. In letter after letter to Lois, Bill tried to explain away his flirtation with Lois's younger sister. He was nineteen and Barb was seventeen. Lois was twenty-three. Barb was just a kid, he wrote to Lois in one letter. Barb was not to blame. His flirtation with Barb had been a long time ago, earlier in the summer. In another letter he came up with a different story. He had been continuing to flirt with Barb, he said, so that she wouldn't guess that he was secretly engaged to Lois. Lois managed to visit Vermont in October, and a visit with Bill at the Emerald Lake camp in the lovely autumn air seemed to calm her fears. Yet, in November, Bill was still writing letters making excuses, still telling Lois he felt cheap and that he was trying to be honest about his sexual history.

In Vermont at the turn of the century, there were many different cultural attitudes toward sex. Bill Wilson came from a quarry family, and his father had defined masculinity through sexual activity. In a letter to Lois at this time, Bill straightforwardly shared his sexual history. He began young, he confided. His first sexual experience occurred when he was thirteen, and it was with an older girl who worked at the hotel. Continuing his letter, he wrote about a girl named Anna Davidson whom he had taken on a straw ride and a girl named Gertrude McClure who embraced him one night after hearing him play the fiddle.

These letters to Lois are startlingly eloquent, and they set the pattern for their long marriage. Bill was passionate, and abashed by his behavior; Lois was forgiving and comforting. This was long before he had begun to drink. By January he had told his mother and grandparents that he was going to marry Lois; she had told her parents. All was well. Soon Bill was on the train to New York to visit his girl and buy a ring. He was wearing a new suit, overcoat, and hat, and he had $25 in his pocket.

He was amazed by the way the Burnhams lived in what seemed wonderful luxury at 182 Clinton Street in Brooklyn. In East Dorset, a house was a shelter from the elements, but the Clinton Street house was a series of rooms with colors and furniture chosen to please the eye and comfort the body. He felt supremely awkward. He was sure he looked like a country boy who had already grown out of his still-new clothes. Lois thought he looked wonderful and she said so. Her family didn't seem to notice how clumsy he was, or how impressed he was by what they thought of as normal life. He pretended; they accepted. It was a big day when he and Lois took the subway to Manhattan to go shopping for their engagement ring. Lois took him to a series of wholesale jewelers on Maiden Lane. Bill examined the rings for sale there, but he was just being polite. He had heard that Tiffany & Co. was the best jeweler in the city, and so to Tiffany they must go. He had to have the best. Lois was worried, but Bill was determined.

Finally, they hurried uptown through the winter twilight and got to the store at 37th Street and Fifth Avenue just as it was about to close. Lois was terrified, but Bill's luck held as it often did. At Tiffany they found the perfect ring—a simple amethyst set in gold that fit Lois perfectly. Bill Wilson from East Dorset proudly peeled off $25 to secure the hand of Miss Lois Burnham. She gave him her Packer Institute class ring in exchange.

Later, when Bill's drinking was tearing them apart, Lois lost the Tiffany ring that meant so much to both of them. They were driving home from Montreal from another failed business venture in 1930. On a bridge over a deep ravine, Lois pulled off her gloves with a little more strength than was necessary. Glove and ring sailed out the window and down into the abyss. Much later, four years after Bill's death, Lois's friends decided to replace the ring; she drew a picture of it, and Tiffany made a new one for the 1983 cost of $2,765. In researching the new ring, Lois's friends discovered the Greek myth about Amethyst, the young woman whose corpse was drenched with wine by a vengeful Bacchus, and then turned to a glowing purple stone.

*   *   *

Back at school, Bill was soon in trouble again. This time it was a hazing incident. A freshman had been savagely dunked in the university pool, and Bill refused to tell the authorities what he knew about it. Something about the manner of his refusal caused tremendous trouble. Could it have been that edge of defiance and stubbornness creeping into his voice? His entire class was suspended for a term. In the larger world, however, more significant events were about to shape Bill Wilson's life, for by this time it was becoming clear that the United States would have to have a part in the war in Europe.

In many ways Bill Wilson and Lois Burnham were made for each other, and their fifty-three-year marriage endured tremendous strains with astonishing grace. At the beginning they were both lonely: the rube who had never been anywhere, and the young sophisticate who spoke French; the older woman who was ready to comfort, and the raw, desperately hurting boy who needed to be comforted. Lois was a woman who would never play around, who would never leave, who always—when Bill gave in to his doubts and fears—was there with a reassuring word. Her father was a doctor, and she in turn practiced her own kind of healing.

It's interesting now to read Bill's version of the events of those two summers in his autobiography—with the country on the brink of war and these two people locked in their own story—and contrast it with Lois's version in her autobiography. He writes that he was barely holding on; in her story he's a dashing young sailor, a man she just plain fell in love with because she wanted to be with him. In his story he's a messed-up dropout. In hers he is unjustly blamed for others' crimes because of his sense of honor. He is always down and out and she is always there to defend him.

We understand our lives by telling ourselves stories about what happens to us. Happy marriages are often based on two people telling the same story about their life together. Bill and Lois didn't have the same story, but they had ideas that complemented each other. It's tempting in hindsight to diminish what happened between them in the summer of 1915. It's tempting to say that his nervous breakdown and her desperation as an aging spinster converged and provided them both with a simple solution. Sometimes, later in life, Bill wrote as if this was the case.

But the truth about this marriage—about any marriage—is much more complicated and mysterious than the needs which may or may not draw people together. Lois and Bill had an extraordinary marriage, a marriage that continued to be passionate and that continued to serve and sustain both of them for decades, through disasters and triumphs, through sickness and health, through poorer and even poorer. They loved each other in a way that was more old-fashioned than what we now think of as love, in a way that was as much about practicality as about the pleasures of the eye and the comforts of the body.

Chapter Thirteen:

New Bedford and the First Drink

In many ways World War I came to Bill Wilson's rescue. Things seemed to be taken out of his hands. Everyone was getting engaged. Everyone was getting married. The war was a great leveler and provided tremendous emotional momentum. Decisions were easy to make. Men who were going off to a foreign country from which they might never return had a sudden new freedom and latitude that went far beyond anything known in the college classroom. Grades and disciplinary problems faded into unimportance as a generation prepared to face the war. Bill was still in trouble at Norwich, but here too the war saved him.

In 1917 all classes were canceled, and students automatically became members of the United States reserve forces. Bill was catapulted from being a naughty boy to being a man with serious responsibilities. Choosing to join the Coastal Artillery, he was sent to officers' training camp in Plattsburgh, New York, where he learned how to fire a machine gun with a 26-inch telescopic site and a 400-shot-a-minute capacity, a weapon so heavy it had to be carried by ten men and three mules. Vermont has a strong military tradition, and the hours of hunting and shooting with which Bill had whiled away the lonely afternoons paid off. He was still a great shot and completely at home with guns and ordnance.

Nonetheless, the sense of inferiority, the feelings of failure that had driven Bill to excellence and then had sabotaged him after the death of Bertha Bamford, were still seething just below the awkward surface. Here he was, a second lieutenant in the 66th Coast Artillery Corps preparing to be shipped out for the war in France. Yes, he was engaged to a proper young woman who loved him, yes he was an officer in the United States Army. But in his mind he was a coward for joining the heavy artillery and a reject whom only an excessively maternal woman could love. The fact that he had joined the Coastal Artillery, one of the safest units in the Army, ate away at him. Did this mean he was yellow? What would his grandfather think if he knew the truth? Some nights he lay awake, shivering with fear of death. True soldiers were never afraid, he believed. Obviously, he wasn't a true soldier.

In 1917, Bill was stationed at Fort Rodman in New Bedford, Massachusetts, and the fort's neighbors in New Bedford and neighboring Newport, Rhode Island, opened their houses to the young officers who were going abroad to fight. Thus, Bill Wilson from East Dorset, the son of a divorced quarryman, found himself invited to many elegant dinner parties.

One Sunday night he went with his commanding officer to a dinner featuring rarebit—cheese laced with beer and poured over toast. Given by a mother and her daughters, the party was a revelation for Bill Wilson. The women were wealthy and attractive, but they smoked and drank, a display of feminine sophistication that shocked and thrilled him. As he described the scene in a letter to Lois, there was a beer at each place at the table and beer in the rarebit. Bill felt the only polite thing to do was to drink a glass of beer and eat his rarebit. The drink didn't seem to lead to anything awful, he explained to his wife. He sang a song or two after dinner, and everyone said he had a lovely voice.

Another dinner party a few weeks later found Bill a guest of the wealthy Grinnell sisters. Emily Grinnell's young husband was already fighting in Europe, and her sister Catherine had lost her husband in France, so the Grinnell women had a special feeling about men in uniform, a special need to take care of them. Like their neighbors, they opened their mansion to the soldiers from Fort Rodman. Bill had never seen a mansion like the Grinnells'. The Wilson House itself could probably have fit in the main hall, and the glowing rooms and fragrant gardens beyond were filled with people chatting, drinking, and laughing. Bill didn't see anyone he knew. The few familiar faces there were those of senior officers, men he didn't dare approach. Then there were the socialites, the men in evening clothes, and the butlers circulating with silver trays of glistening cocktails. Bill Wilson had never seen a butler.

Secretly writhing, he began to think about making his escape when one of the Grinnell sisters appeared next to him. He tried to smile and avoid saying anything stupid. Then someone put a cocktail in his hand, a Bronx cocktail, it was called. The sweet drink made of gin, dry and sweet vermouth, and orange juice shimmered in its glass. This was the new drink from New York, a pretty girl standing next to him said. She knew that he would love it. Bill Wilson was a man who had decided again and again that he would never drink. "I'd been told how many of my ancestors went down with it," he remembered. Standing there, a tall young soldier in uniform with a full-scale war going on inside his head, he somehow didn't feel as if he had a choice.

Bill compared this situation to the rarebit dinner and decided that the beer hadn't seemed to hurt him. So now the man who had said he would never drink, the man whose life had already been ruined by others' drinking, gratefully accepted the Bronx cocktail. This was different from the beer, though. This time its effect was unmistakable. It tasted wonderful, sweet and airy at the same time. Orange juice and gin are a time-honored drink because of the way they combine to relax and energize. It tasted so good that it was gone in what seemed like a moment.

The second Bronx cocktail was what really did the trick. Suddenly, the gawky soldier felt completely at home in this fancy crowd. The pretty girl, his new best friend, guided him around, introducing him to her friends. Bill laughed and relaxed and told stories. Everyone laughed with him. Soon he was one of those people he had been so impressed by, one of those men who seemed to belong exactly where he was. "That strange barrier that had existed between me and all men and women, even the closest, seemed to instantly go down," he remembered.

The scene went from being a nightmare to being beautiful. "I could talk well. I could actually please the guests." Bill had ascended into the top ranks of society with just a few drinks, and he thought he had found the elixir of life. After he had been invited to return another time, and made many plans with his new friends, he stepped out into the driveway of the house, enthralled. Behind him he could hear soft saxophone music. As he walked down the drive through the fragrant summer night, he moved as easily as if invisible chains had fallen away. He felt a new kind of freedom. "I was part of things at last," he remembered. "Oh, the magic of those first three or four drinks."

For a while no one really seemed to notice that Bill was drinking. He was a new man, a happy man. He had a drink or a few drinks whenever they were available. He had thought for so long that he would never drink. He had always looked down on boys who drank. Yet, here he was drinking, and he discovered that he loved it. He found that in situations where he couldn't drink, the old inferiority and discomfort would come flooding back. He found himself avoiding those situations. Even sitting with his new family at the dinner table at Clinton Street was agony without a drink.

PART TWO

Drinking

Chapter Fourteen:

France

I try to be a good boy. Grandpa says I am," Bill Wilson wrote to his mother when she had gone to Boston and he was living at the Griffith house. "I guess you will not know me when you come home. When are you coming home?" He signed these notes "your little son Willie." But Emily never responded with the warmth and love and encouragement he was crying for—she couldn't. In Bertha Bamford he had found a woman who cared about him, but that had been snatched away. Now, at last, in Lois Burnham he found a woman who was usually encouraging and rarely critical. Lois didn't say anything about what was happening to her fiancé. As always, she was loving and supportive. Into their old age together she referred to him as her little Willie.

Lois and Bill were great letter writers. When they were apart, as they were when Bill was posted at Fort Rodman before their wedding, they wrote letters back and forth, sometimes more than once a day. These hundreds of letters, which range from romantic love letters, to letters that plead with Bill not to drink and letters filled with his promises to change, to businesslike exchanges of information, tell the story of their marriage. Stored in boxes, they are in the Stepping Stones Archives in the basement of a house that Lois built in Bedford Hills, New York, next to the house where she and Bill lived for thirty years.

Soon after the party at the Grinnells', Bill's letters to Lois brought up something that had suddenly become very interesting to him, the subject of alcohol. Drinking had never been part of their relationship, but now Bill wrote Lois wondering if they should change their minds. "Should we be teetotalers?" he asked. When they were married, he pointed out, they would entertain, and it might be convenient to have liquor in the house. What did she think? Lois didn't respond to these questions. Bill persisted. Now that they were about to be a married couple, he wrote, perhaps they should change their attitude toward drinking. He was out in society now, far from poky old East Dorset, and he had noticed that sophisticated people always served liquor.

While Bill had found another love, cocktails, he was still anxious to please his fiancée, still sure that she was somehow too good for him. As Bill struggled to control his alcohol intake, he was again and again besieged by the old feelings of self-loathing and inferiority. "Where did she get that one?" he imagined people in the Burnhams' circle asking derisively when they met him.

The voices in his head were lifted right from his letters from his mother Emily, who was called Dr. Emily even by her own family. She preached success, but she was convinced that made her unpopular. "They don't like it here if anybody goes off and makes a success of themselves," she wrote from East Dorset. Was she writing about her own experience, or warning her son off potential accomplishment? "They want you to stay in East Dorset and if you don't want that kind of life, they think you are highbrow, you know." The Burnhams were definitely highbrow. But his Lois was always 100 percent positive. Even though Bill had never graduated from college and had no real job except the Army, everyone loved him, she said.

Everyone was on edge in the Army. No one knew when they were going to be called overseas. There was a rumor that Bill's unit was going soon, so Bill and Lois decided to get married as soon as possible, on January 24, 1918, instead of February 1, a date they had decided on earlier. They changed the invitations to announcements.

The wedding took place in the Swedenborgian Church in Brooklyn, and they had their reception at the house at 182 Clinton Street in Brooklyn, which would become the center of the second chapter in Bill Wilson's life. Rogers Burnham was Bill's best man; Lois's sister Kitty and four girls from Packer were bridesmaids. Dr. Emily had a sudden attack of the flu and was unable to attend, and Bill's sister, Dorothy, stayed to nurse her. None of Bill's family was there, but that didn't matter. Had they ever really been there? He had a new family now.

Their wedding day was cold and overcast, and Bill was in uniform. The fact that he was soon to be shipped overseas lent poignance to every moment. He was twenty-two and his bride was twenty-six—a big difference in age. At twenty-six in those days, an unmarried woman could already expect to become relegated to the pathetic fringes of society. Lois never stopped being grateful to Bill, and he had many, many reasons to be grateful to her. Their marriage was certainly one of the things that enabled Bill Wilson to help invent, found, and structure Alcoholics Anonymous. Still, when these two people, Bill towering over his bride, stood in front of the round marble fireplace in her father's parlor and took their solemn vows, they could hardly have imagined what those vows would mean in the amazing lives that lay before them.

The newlyweds took an upstairs apartment in New Bedford, two simple rooms sparsely furnished with an oak desk and chairs, and began married life in a state of near ecstasy. They became each other's world. They made love. For the first time in a long time Bill felt he might become the man he had dreamed of being. They entertained often—Lois cooked and there was always plenty to drink. Bill's views on alcohol in their marriage had prevailed, at least for the moment. They went out often too, stepping out as a married couple to parties that were beyond anything they could have imagined in elegance and abundance. At these parties, Bill always drank, and he often became the center of animated attention as he hit on one amusing story after another. He was astonished to find himself in demand. He was amazed at how easily he could make people laugh.

Sometimes when he got home with Lois, he was sick, or sometimes he just passed out and called it going to sleep. Sometimes after the party they went to together was over, he would hear about another party. He'd want to go on. He didn't want to stop. He had someone else take Lois home. At one party she was shocked to hear two of his friends tell a story about dragging Bill home one night and putting him to bed. Lois saw that Bill was growing into his body, putting on weight and learning to use his height and his voice to command the men under him. Bill saw that Lois was very good at explaining things. According to her, everything was always absolutely wonderful.

By the spring, Bill had been transferred to Fort Adams in Newport, and he and Lois joined another couple for a farewell dinner before the men were to ship out. "A tremendous pall of gloom settled over all of us," he wrote. "But Lois bore up." Finally, he and Lois were alone together watching the sunset on the cliffs above the sea. Once again Bill's fear and foreboding were dissipated by the glorious show provided by nature and by the loving support of his wife. Out over the water they could see battleships anchored and the harbor alight with yachts and pleasure boats—some like the little skiff Lois had sailed across his bow on Emerald Lake. As the sky darkened, Bill felt a calm that he couldn't understand. In his wife's eyes he saw reassurance; in the scene before them he saw some kind of greater power. In the morning when the troops boarded the train, he waved goodbye still wrapped in this odd sense of calm.

On board the old British troop ship *Lancashire,* Second Lieutenant William G. Wilson discovered both brandy and courage. As
the ship steamed south of Iceland on the way to Great Britain, the
air grew cold, and the crew—packed into bunks on every deck—
grew fearful. The fear mounted as they turned southeast into the
Irish Sea, which was infested with German submarines. One night,
Bill was on watch belowdecks, down near the keel, where the men
would be the last out in any kind of emergency. The air was icy and
smelled of salt and sweat. He was trying to stay awake, watching the
glimmer of dawn appear in the hatchways, when there was an ear-
shattering crash and a huge thud. Always a country boy, he said later
that the sound reminded him of the time he had put his head inside
a bell and another kid had hit the bell with a rock. The ship trem-
bled and shook, and men started the rush from the bunks. It was
Bill Wilson's job to keep the crew from panicking, although he and
the rest of them thought they were about to die. He drew his pistol
and stood at the door to the deck, threatening to shoot the first man
who tried to pass him. He didn't have to raise the pistol; he used his
voice to calm them. It worked. He felt a wave of confidence and ex-
altation. The crash turned out to be an American depth charge—
called an ash can—dropped by a nearby destroyer in an effort to hit
a passing German sub. There had never been any real danger, but
there had been real courage. By the time the ship landed safely, Bill
was a hero in his own mind, a true leader of men.

After they landed, Bill's regiment went by train to a camp outside
of Winchester. One day, feeling depressed, Bill and a friend from
the camp went to visit the city's famous cathedral. It was midsummer and there were other soldiers wandering around the grounds.
Looking up at the arched nave and the stained-glass windows of the
great church, Bill was suddenly suffused with a feeling of peace.
"The atmosphere of the place began to possess me and I was lifted
up into a sort of ecstasy," he wrote. Bill didn't believe in God, but

there was some force right there, just for that moment, that made him know that everything was going to be all right. This was a sacred space, a place where he could feel a power outside the efforts of men and women. "The notion of God kept coming to my mind," he remembered.

Bill was a connoisseur of marble in general and of tombstones and their carving in particular, so he entered the churchyard for a closer look. There he happened on the gravestone with an inscription that would come back to haunt him, which he would use in later years to tell his story in the book *Alcoholics Anonymous,* and which would therefore become a touchstone for generations of recovering alcoholics. As he remembered this epitaph, it read: "Here lies a Hampshire Grenadier who caught his death drinking cold small beer. A good soldier is ne'er forgot, whether he dies by musket or by pot." (The epitaph actually reads: "Here lies in peace a Hampshire Grenadier / who caught his death by drinking small cold beer / Soldiers be wise from his untimely fall / and when yere hot drink strong or none at all / An honest soldier never is forgot / whether he dies by musket or by pot.")

Bill thrived on being in the Army, where no one was a failure and no one was highbrow and everyone drank whenever they could and whatever they could. He liked traveling through England, and later going from village to village in France setting up gun emplacements and breaking them down and practicing and moving on. His regiment was never near the front lines, although he yearned for combat as much as he feared it. As he traveled with them through the countryside from Cherbourg to Limoges, he began learning French, and he started writing his letters home to Lois in French. He loved the way the French drank . . . all the time. He couldn't understand why they weren't always drunk. They drank and drank and drank, yet they never passed out or got sick or embarrassed themselves.

One morning in the French farmhouse where he had been billeted, he watched a grandmother pour a few fingers of rum for a little girl. Wine was everywhere. Another farmhouse where he was billeted was run by a grandmother who had the care of her five-year-old grandson. One cold morning Bill crawled out from his bed and came downstairs to find the five-year-old boy pointing at a bottle of rum on a shelf. "Ça!" commanded the boy. The grandmother obliged. She told Bill that the rum was being administered for medicinal purposes.

Bill's regiment was in a tiny mountain village when the armistice was signed and the whole town partied for days. Bill went to Paris and then south to Bordeaux, boarded a troopship, and crossed the Atlantic without incident. A happy Lois met him at the piers in Hoboken when the ship landed.

Chapter Fifteen:

The Edison Test

In a way, the war was easy for Bill Wilson. In uniform he was a natural leader. Everyone was friends with everyone else. They all had a common purpose—to stay alive and to win the war. Coming home was hard. At home in Brooklyn, because Brooklyn was home now, Bill found himself frightened of everything. The subway under the East River terrified him. Suddenly, everything familiar was weirdly unfamiliar. He was surprised when the guards on the subway system failed to salute him. "I fancied myself a leader," Bill wrote later, "for had not the men of my battery given me a special token of appreciation? My talent for leadership, I imagined, would place me at the head of vast enterprises which I would manage with the utmost assurance."

Out of uniform, he was just another vet—a vet with no college degree and no marketable skills. Finally, a Burnham brother-in-law got him a lowly clerking job in the insurance department of the New York Central Railroad, in a grim office located on lower Broadway. This was a huge comedown from being an officer, and Bill let everyone know that. He flubbed the books and blew off the management tasks that were assigned him. It was a nothing job, but he got fired anyway.

By this time, Bill Wilson was a man with a drinking problem. In its simplest terms, his story is the story of a man who was destroyed by drinking and who, in finding a way to stop drinking for himself, also hit on a way to help other people stop drinking. At the same time, Bill Wilson's drinking problem, like anyone's drinking problem, was as individual as he was. There are as many kinds of alcoholism as there are alcoholics. Until this time—the spring of 1919—life had happened to Bill Wilson in a series of happy and unhappy ways. He had no part in causing his parents' divorce or the death of Bertha Bamford. Now, Bill Wilson began to happen to life. Instead of surviving terrible events and bringing triumph from disaster, Bill Wilson began to bring disaster out of triumph.

The New York Central job was followed by more low-level jobs. Bill drove spikes on the New York Central piers. He decoded telegrams for an export company. When he was out of work, Lois tried to make the best of their situation. They took a walking trip from Portland, Maine, through New Hampshire and Vermont, camping in an old Army pup tent and living off what they could pick and catch. They caught a huge eel in Lake Winnepesaukee in New Hampshire and ate sections of it cooked over their campfire. They heard a whippoorwill at Newfound Lake and bought new sneakers in Alexandria, New Hampshire. Both of them loved these trips; they shared a passion for nature, and they both had young, athletic bodies. Lois was happiest with Bill in sight and out of trouble. Bill, a consummate fisherman and woodsman, was happiest doing what he was good at.

On another camping trip they stayed in East Dorset for a month, and Bill picked up a new enthusiasm for pursuing a career in law from conversations with Fayette Griffith and Mark Whalon. Back in Brooklyn he enrolled in night classes at Brooklyn Law School. Through the men married to Lois's friends, many of whom were already making money in the postwar boom on Wall Street, he landed the promise of another job as an insurance investigator for United States Fidelity & Guarantee.

Now important things began to happen, and a pattern of self-destruction combined with compensatory brilliance begins to emerge from the facts of Bill Wilson's life. In the spring of 1921, Bill had answered a blind want ad in the newspaper asking for "Young men capable of close observation. No particular scholastic requirements." That was him. As a result, one day he was summoned to the Edison Laboratories in East Orange, New Jersey, for a test.

Thomas Alva Edison was a hero of Bill's, the god of American invention. He was a man who had substituted intuition for education, a man who had brilliantly played his own hunches. Bill had read Edison's biography, and he could quote Edison at length and knew all the details of the old man's life. He understood the "Edison effect" in the way electricity passed through a filament. He had tried and retried many of Edison's own experiments with radios, with electricity, and with automobile engines. He knew that Edison was capable of flying into a temper as well as experiencing flights of genius. It was Edison who said that the secret of success was to hustle while you work.

Along with a group of other young New York City hopefuls, early one morning he took the train out through the tunnel under the Hudson River to New Jersey. A manager picked out a dozen men—including Bill Wilson—from the forty who had shown up, and the chosen few went into another long brick building and up a flight of stairs into a room with rough tables and chairs lined with drains and sinks and lab equipment. In one corner, at a small desk, obviously lost in thought, was Thomas Alva Edison. At seventy-three, the old man was already world-famous for his dozens of inventions. He had been awarded the French Legion of Honor and his methodical scientific methods, which included extensive reading, had been universally adopted and admired. He was famous for saying that genius was 2 percent inspiration and 98 percent perspiration. On that day, Edison's clothes were worn and stained with chemicals, and across his cheek was the scar that Bill remembered had come from a failed experiment with nitric acid.

At each chair was a set of papers that turned out to be a test with 286 questions. There were questions about the diameter of the moon, the overtones on a stringed instrument, and the kind of wood used for barrel staves. Wilson could feel his brain engaging with the test, and his sharp memory retrieving facts from his obsessive reading and from his own experience. The test was meant to measure powers of observation, and few people were as observant as the second lieutenant from East Dorset, Vermont. First Bill answered all the questions he could. Then he went back to unanswered questions and started to estimate. It took hours, and as evening fell, Bill was the only man still working on the test. Edison wandered over as he finished and asked if Bill thought the examination was hard. Bill said yes, he did. Scanning Bill's test, Edison told the young man he was impressed.

Edison's ad had also attracted a huge amount of negative attention from the press. The old man's contention that education made men stupid rather than smart caused an uproar. The press got hold of some of the questions on Edison's test and had a field day with them. How could knowing what tires were made of or how Cleopatra died be a gauge of intelligence? A *New York Times* editorial excoriated Edison for his attitude toward education; a *Wall Street Journal* writer accused him of trying to "calibrate the human soul."

These days it's commonplace to administer tests which, by testing general knowledge, actually test powers of observation, memory, and ability to learn. In fact, what Edison had come up with was an early version of the S.A.T. tests that are such a large part of our contemporary world. Like the inventors of the S.A.T. two decades later, Edison was looking for a test that would create a meritocracy of intelligence, a test that would bypass class, wealth, looks, and even education, and deliver a score that actually meant something about a person's ability to think.

In 1921 this approach to measuring intelligence was heresy. It was a heresy tailor-made for Bill Wilson, though. Wilson often compared his mind to his grandfather's toolshed, a place where random objects could be stored "that might one day come in handy." The day of the Edison test seemed to be that day.

When, after some time, Bill hadn't heard anything from Edison, he started work at another job doing investigations for Fidelity & Guarantee, and he took the subway back to Brooklyn for law school classes at night. Lois was working as an occupational therapist at the Brooklyn Naval Hospital, and with her salary and his combined, the two of them moved to a three-room apartment in a pretty brownstone on Amity Street, around the corner from the Burnham house on Clinton Street. They were delighted by the apartment and by their Syrian landlords who lived downstairs, and after they painted it and installed a few pieces of furniture from Clinton Street, it really looked like home. They had three rooms on the top floor under the roof, and when it rained, the roof sang with the noise.

One evening the bell rang and it was a *New York Times* reporter looking for a Bill Wilson. Wilson had been one of the high scorers on the Edison test, and the great inventor was offering him a job in his own laboratories. Bill didn't know what to say. Suddenly, he was a news story. Furthermore, this connection to Edison was the realization of a childhood dream. Instead of working at low-level jobs and trying to stay awake while law professors droned on about *McKee vs. Shallo* and other boring cases, Bill could work in Edison's laboratories under the guidance of a childhood hero. His test results had revealed his knowledge of music and sounds. In the apartment on Amity Street, Bill had even built some radio sets that could pick up stations as far away as Los Angeles. Edison offered him a job in acoustics, a great opportunity for the young man from Vermont, a job that could lead anywhere.

Bill didn't respond to this dream come true. Perhaps he was already in love with Wall Street and didn't want to leave. Lois's old friend Elise was married to an important Wall Street man named Frank Shaw, who seemed to like Bill. Or perhaps Bill told himself that he had promised Fayette Griffith that he would go to law school. Or perhaps he just didn't feel like commuting to East Orange. Or maybe he was irritated that Edison had waited so long to anoint him. Whatever his reasons, the brash twenty-three-year-old never worked with his hero Thomas Edison. He was supposed to travel back to New Jersey to take the job; suddenly, that was too much to ask.

In January, the Eighteenth Amendment to the U.S. Constitution became law, and drinking became illegal. Bill found ingenious ways to get around the law. He became a regular at the local speakeasies. He bought grapes, which he fermented in huge crocks. Sometimes he drank the stuff before it was completely ready. He couldn't wait.

In the fall of 1922, after failing and retaking two courses, and after three years of classes, Bill Wilson finally completed the course requirements for graduation from law school. Another childhood dream that he had spent so many hours discussing with Fayette and with Mark as the seasons passed in East Dorset was now a real possibility. He was a lawyer at last; all he had to do was take the final exam. On the day of the exam, though, one thing led to another and Bill Wilson was too drunk to be there. Although he took the exam again the next fall and passed it, he was required to attend commencement the following spring to receive a diploma. Again, that was too much to ask. The young man who had wanted to be a lawyer more than anything, who read Clarence Darrow between the milking chores and picking the corn, had become a man who never got around to picking up his law degree.

Chapter Sixteen:

Brooklyn

The stock market was booming. Skirts were shorter and women got the vote. Prohibition was a joke. The whole country seemed to be on a spree. Bill's drinking, however, had become a problem that he and Lois could no longer ignore. On their long camping trips, Bill was able to control his drinking or even to stop drinking altogether. Yet, when they returned to Brooklyn, and to the nine-to-five job that Bill hated, the drinking would begin again.

More and more often, Lois arranged camping trips in the hope that this charismatic husband of hers would find a way to drink as little at home as he did when they were on the road and he was under her supervision. They took the train to Croton-on-Hudson and walked back along the aqueduct. They picnicked in Van Cortland Park and sailed a rented rowboat on the Hudson River with a bath-towel for a sail and an oar as a mast. They camped in New Jersey under a favorite oak and swam naked in a nearby brook. They took the train to Northport, walked out on the sandy neck of land in Long Island Sound, dug clams and caught fish, cooked over a bonfire, and camped on the beach. Together they whooped and hollered like kids and thoroughly enjoyed themselves. Each return to the city dashed Lois's hopes; as soon as they got home, Bill's drinking resumed.

Lois had saved some money from her job—about $1,000—and

when Bill asked for it, she turned it over without questions. Hope returned when he invested it in securities, including two shares of General Electric that quickly became worth ten times what he had paid for them. Maybe he wasn't so bad after all. Maybe his drinking was just a way of connecting with information he needed to play the market. With Lois's salary they had more than enough money to live comfortably. It was at this point that the couple decided to have children.

That summer Lois got pregnant, the first of three heartbreaking ectopic pregnancies she would have in a year. (In an ectopic pregnancy the impregnated egg grows outside the uterus.) From their first loving letters to each other, even from the moment of their engagement, Bill had often talked about the children they would have. He liked to imagine coming home to a family, and the family they would have was a favorite subject in his letters to her. He hoped their children would have Lois's eyes, which squinted when she laughed, as well as her sweet nature.

Lois recovered from the first ectopic pregnancy, but the second one was originally misdiagnosed and required surgery performed by one of her concerned father's colleagues at Brooklyn's Skene Sanitarium. When she failed to recover, Bill called his sister Dorothy's husband, Dr. Leonard Strong, who diagnosed an ovarian cyst, which also had to be surgically removed. This was the first time that Leonard Strong's friendship and medical instincts saved Bill and Lois, but it would not be the last.

Dorothy and Leonard had married and moved to Tarrytown, New York, and they already had a child. Their life seemed to be moving on, while Bill's was somehow stalled. That December he went back to East Dorset for a last visit with Grandma Griffith, who died on New Year's Day. Then, in May of 1923, Lois suffered a third ectopic pregnancy. This series of medical disasters effectively ended the Wilsons' hopes of having children, a devastating disappointment for both Lois and Bill. During these episodes he was often too drunk to get to the hospital for visits.

The couple's inability to have children seemed to distress them both equally, but in different ways. After a while they decided to adopt a child and made a halfhearted attempt through the Spence-Chapin agency. They were turned down, and later Bill said he thought someone had written to the agency about his alcoholism. They had been married four years, but at this point they had to reconstruct the assumptions that held them together, a difficult task under any circumstances, made even more difficult by Bill's drinking problems.

Perhaps Lois was to blame for the couple's childlessness. Perhaps Bill was to blame. Perhaps the Burnham genes were involved; oddly, none of Lois's four brothers and sisters ever had children. "I knew I had done nothing to prevent our having children," Lois wrote later. "Yet somehow I could not help feeling guilty. So how could I blame him for the increase in his drinking?" The pattern of Lois's suffering and Bill's remorse was set by Christmas of 1922, when Bill wrote a promise to her on the flyleaf of the family Bible. "For your Christmas I make you this present: No liquor will pass my lips for one year." Of course, it was a promise he couldn't keep, a promise he would make many, many times over the next decade. In the face of Bill's drinking, Lois was dogged by the guilt, sorrow, and waves of love that characterize life with an alcoholic.

When Bill didn't keep his promise to stop drinking, Lois would move from the apartment in Amity Street back to live with her parents in the house on Clinton Street, leaving him a letter saying that she would return when he had gone two weeks without a drink. He would write her there at her parents' house, begging her to come home, beginning a letter with neat apologies at the top of the page and then writing in larger, sloppier scrawls as the booze and his feelings took over. "The remonstrances of my friends terminated in a row and I became a lone wolf," he wrote later in telling his own story for the book *Alcoholics Anonymous.* "There had been many unhappy scenes. . . . There had been no real infidelity, for loyalty to my wife, helped at times by extreme drunkenness, kept me out of these scrapes."

When he was sober, Bill poured most of his energy into the stock market. Lois clung to the hope that the Bill she enjoyed on camping trips was still the real Bill. The couple took a loan of $100 from Lois's mother to buy a Harley-Davidson three-wheeler motor bicycle with a sidecar, and in this three-wheeler they traveled to Vermont to see Fayette Griffith, and then toured all over New England.

It was this vehicle as well as Bill's sporadic astuteness that gave him what would turn out to be a wonderful, prescient idea, an idea which—almost—saved everything. In observing the stock market, and what made people buy and sell, Bill had noticed that people bought stocks without knowing much about the companies that sold them. If he were a farmer, he would never buy a horse or cow without examining it, so why should people buy shares in a company without examining it first? Essentially, Bill had hit on the idea of market research long before there was any such thing as market research.

Chapter Seventeen:

Motorcycle Hobos

From the time he married Lois in January 1918, until April 1939, when the mortgage company foreclosed, the Burnham house at 182 Clinton Street, with its long front stoop and pretty back garden dominated by a huge old sycamore tree, was the heart of Bill Wilson's world. It was here that Lois had grown up and gone to school; it was in this neighborhood, on State Street, that the young couple had their first apartment, a dingy room in a house around the corner from the Burnham house. Later, when they both had jobs, they moved to a three-room apartment two blocks away on Amity Street, and, still in the neighborhood, they finally lived in the sumptuous, large apartment in one of the new apartment buildings, called the Colonial, on Livingston Street.

When the market crashed, it was back in the Burnhams' house as reluctantly welcomed guests that Bill and Lois lived out the worst years of his drinking, years when it seemed that the only conclusion to their sad story would be when Bill finally ended up in an institution or sanitarium. When Bill finally did stop drinking during his third hospitalization, he returned to the house on Clinton Street. In its front parlor, with wide windows and a view of the church, the first meetings of what would become Alcoholics Anonymous stutteringly, haltingly took place.

The neighborhood, streets of brick houses with long entrance

staircases and wrought-iron balustrades, is at the border of Brooklyn Heights and Cobble Hill, a few blocks from the hustle of Atlantic Avenue and the bars where Bill often stopped for a drink on
his way back from the Schermerhorn Street subway stop. These
days, it's very much as it was seventy years ago. You emerge from the
subway onto the leafy sidewalks of Schermerhorn Street and walk
past the back of the old Macy's where Lois once worked and past the
buildings of the Brooklyn Law School and turn right onto Clinton
Street where the Burnham house, with its graceful lintels, still dom-
inates the end of the block. In the distance, down State Street and
Atlantic Avenue, there is the water, the broad expanse of New York
Harbor, and the heavy machinery of the docks.

   Brooklyn has always been the civilized alternative to living in
Manhattan. It is the thinking person's New York. Although it spans
a huge plot of land, Brooklyn has always been a small town with
small-town loyalties. With its hefty literary tradition and generous
spaces, it has been welcoming to immigrants of all kinds, even ambitious kids from Vermont. There is no plaque on 182 Clinton
Street to mark its historical significance, and visitors are rare enough
that the family who live there are happy to show the garden and the
living room and the basement.

*   *   *

But Bill began to feel constrained by the Burnhams' hospitality, and
by the graceful life into which he had fallen like a rogue into a tub of
butter. As his drinking increased, Lois's worry increased. Their
evenings were more and more often spoiled by Bill's drunkenness.
Bill would promise not to drink, and then decide to have just one.
Inevitably, this led to two or three drinks, which quickly became
five or six drinks. Sometimes he staggered out to the nearest bar. If
they were already out, there were nights when Lois had to half carry

him home. Then there were the long, remorseful, absolutely futile talks they had the next morning, and the contrite promises that Bill kept until it happened again.

They agreed that the answer was travel. On their Harley, Bill decided, he and Lois could travel around the country doing market research, gathering information about companies at first hand. They would start with General Electric in Schenectady. His Wall Street friend Frank Shaw said he thought it was an interesting idea, but he was not willing to advance money on it. Lois, of course, thought it was a great idea. Out of the city meant out of harm's way. So in April of 1925 they gave up their Amity Street apartment, said goodbye to their Syrian landlord, and packed the sidecar with a tent from Sears Roebuck, sleeping bags made from sewing army blankets together, food in waterproof bags, a radio, a gasoline stove, an army locker filled with clothes, a set of four Moody's Manuals on industry, and $80 in cash.

With tremendous excitement and high hopes, the couple tied their duffle onto the side of the motorcycle and took off up the parkway with Lois at the wheel. The first night they stopped in a field beside a brook near Poughkeepsie. They built a fire and cooked supper, and as night fell, they listened to the radio and read by the tent's light, which Bill hooked up to the motorcycle's battery. They took their time over breakfast the next morning, enjoying the yellow and blue violets in the field in front of the tent and white bloodroot on the hillside. Then they headed north again for Emerald Lake.

During the next twenty-four months Bill and Lois rode up and down the Atlantic Coast. They traveled as far west as Pennsylvania and as far south as Florida. They slept on the ground and bathed in brooks, only occasionally treating themselves to a cheap hotel and the luxury of hot and cold running water. They visited Bill's mother,

Emily, who had married a doctor named Charles Strobel and was living on a houseboat on the Florida Gulf Coast. Sometimes they stayed with friends. When they ran low on money, they took odd jobs. Once they spent a month picking apples.

The Harley-Davidson broke again and again; its engine skipped, its starter blew out, its tires went flat, the spokes fell out of its wheels. Sometimes Bill, the man who everyone said was such a talented engineer, could fix the problem, but more often he could not. Worse, they often had accidents, once swerving off the road in a mishap that injured Bill's collarbone and Lois's knee.

In all the accounts of the trip—the one that Bill confided to biographer Robert Thomsen, the one in Bill's autobiography, and the one in Lois's memoir and in her letters—there is no complaining by Lois. "Well, of course everybody thought we were utterly out of our minds," Bill remembered years later. "Meanwhile the drinking got worse and worse and although I couldn't be impressed with its seriousness, except now and then when there was a humiliating episode, Lois was greatly bothered and worried and she thought something like this might get me out of it." Lois came from a tradition of unquestioning loyalty to a husband, but she also seemed to be an amazingly good sport. Bill's harebrained, adventuresome brilliance and Lois's willingness to go along were the engine of their affection for each other, an engine that purred along a lot more evenly than the Harley.

Their journey started in Schenectady at the General Electric plant. What happened there set the pattern for much of Bill's future research. First he dressed up in a suit and tie and presented himself at the plant, saying he wanted to do research for the purposes of evaluating the stock. He was met courteously. All his questions were answered, but he learned nothing. He walked away knowing that he was wasting his time. Because he and Lois had run short on money, they took a job cooking and farming with a local family.

As the month they spent there came to an end, Bill wandered into a bar in the little nearby town of Scotia. He struck up a conversation with the men drinking there, and it turned out they worked for General Electric. A few more beers and they were best friends. A few beers after that and the G.E. workers decided to make their point by showing Bill where they worked. Thus he was granted a full tour of the General Electric research laboratory, and a preview of future plans for G.E. products, including the next generation of radios, and an inventory of equipment at the plant—invaluable information. The next day he sat down and wrote a detailed report on General Electric for Frank Shaw.

In Egypt, Pennsylvania, Bill set his sights on Giant Portland Cement. By this time he had learned his lesson. Instead of dressing up and going to the top, he started at the bottom. He applied for a job at the plant and got it. Because of what he saw inside the plant —new equipment, how much coal was burned to make a barrel of cement, and how efficiently the work was done—he realized that Giant Portland stock was drastically undervalued at $15 a share. He called Frank Shaw at Rice & Co. Rice bought 5,000 shares, they bought Bill 100 shares, and the stock increased in value from $15 to $75. Bill and Lois took his system—get a job, talk to the workers, evaluate the company, buy or sell the stock—to phosphate companies and iron and rubber factories.

By the time Bill and Lois came back to New York for good to attend Kitty Burnham's wedding at Clinton Street, it was 1927 and Bill Wilson was a made man on Wall Street. He and Lois had outgrown the Harley. They bought a Dodge and then turned it in for a Packard. He still drank a lot, but didn't everyone?

Partly in deference to Lois, and partly because he wanted his new colleagues to understand what a serious man he was, Bill made it a rule to not take a drink before the stock market closed at 3 P.M. Sometimes he'd leave the office after the closing bell with a wad of money in his pocket, start uptown, and get a drink or two along the way. Of course, what started out as an innocent whiskey to unwind on the way home became another and then another. By the end of the day, he'd be so broke he had to slide under the turnstile to get back to Brooklyn on the subway.

Chapter Eighteen:

Manchester Airport

Bill consolidated the reputation he had made as a shrewd analyst. No more motorcycles for Lois and him. Now when they went off to investigate a company, they traveled in style and stayed at expensive hotels. Bill combined his flair for market research with a penchant for lucky buys on margin. He invested heavily in a small molasses company named Penick & Ford, and its stock obliged by doubling and tripling. Calvin Coolidge was president. The stock market was thriving. Even Coolidge, who never seemed to say anything, said that the business of America was business.

As his financial fortunes soared along with everyone else's in the extended bull market of the Roaring Twenties, Bill Wilson's life at home started to sink. Sometimes he could drink normally, but more often, a few drinks led to disaster. Night after night, he crawled home with little memory of where he had been. At other times he turned on people, using to terrible effect his instinct for finding the jugular. Lois did whatever she could to stop this downward spiral. She scolded and she wept. She threw his shoes out the window so that he couldn't go out drinking. She wrote him dozens of pleading letters. She left him and moved back to Clinton Street.

In return, Bill wrote her more letters filled with morning-after contrition. Nothing worked. Bill's brother-in-law, Leonard Strong, his sister, Dorothy's, husband, had a serious talk with him about alcoholism. It was progressive, Strong told Bill. Unless he managed to stop, it would only get worse.

Bill respected Leonard, but from a distance. No one could possibly understand how much he needed to drink, or how much he wished he didn't need to drink. Sometimes when he was drunk, he felt that his anger was part of the real Bill, some essential self that had been hidden under layers of respectability all these years. *In vino veritas.* Other times he drank to calm his nerves. The first sips always filled him with a wonderful glow. He also drank to counter the anxiety attacks and fits of depression that seemed to be stalking him. At these times it was the old dread from boyhood days, making his heart race and his stomach churn and telling him he was about to die. Fear came flooding back, but only a few drinks would make it go away.

At work, at the offices of Tobey & Kirk on Broad Street where Frank Shaw had taken a job and brought Bill with him, Bill was a dignified, respected presence. He was famous for never taking off his hat; he always seemed to be on his way to somewhere very important. His knowledge of business, and his ability to understand the behavior of companies and their stocks, had won him tremendous respect. In the summer of 1927, Bill got interested in Cuban sugar. On a resulting visit to Cuba he and Lois were treated like royalty. At Havana's luxurious and expensive Hotel Sevilla they settled into the style to which Bill felt he should be accustomed. He visited sugar plantations during the day and drank all night.

When Frank Shaw wrote expressing concern about Bill's drinking, Bill characteristically fired off a letter from Havana promising never to drink again. He did that a lot in those days. "It has always been a very serious handicap to me," he wrote Shaw, "so that you can appreciate how glad I am to be finally rid of it. It got to the point where I had to decide whether to be a monkey or a man."

More and more, of course, Bill was a monkey, but now he was a very rich monkey. After he mailed this letter to Shaw, his resolve lasted less than a day.

Back home in Brooklyn, he and Lois rented the apartment on Livingston Street. The apartment wasn't grand enough for Bill, though, so they rented the apartment next door and knocked down the walls, creating a huge living room and giving the apartment two bedrooms, two baths and two kitchens. Bill expanded his business, doing research for another Wall Street trader named Joe Hirschhorn.

In October of 1928, just a year before the stock market was to crash, Bill wrote yet another pledge to Lois in the family Bible: "To my beloved wife who has endured so much, let this stand as evidence to my pledge." By November he was renewing the broken pledge with another pledge: "My strength is renewed a thousandfold in my love for you." By January 1929 he was pledging again on the Bible's worn pages: "To tell you once more that I am finished with it."

Early in 1929, on his way to Vermont, a place that still represented solace, he stopped off in Albany to visit his old Manchester Village friend Ebby Thacher. The two of them started drinking and made their way to the Albany airport. After uproarious deliberations, lubricated by a bottle, they decided that instead of taking the train to Manchester, Bill should fly. The Manchester airport hadn't opened yet, but that was a small problem for these inebriated great minds. Bill and Ebby found a pilot who wanted to fly the first plane into the new Manchester airport.

The three men and their bottles took off from Albany, hovered shakily north across southern Vermont, and landed bumpily in snowy Manchester on a cold day to find a distinguished welcoming committee there to celebrate the airport's first arrival. Manchester Village had turned out for her home boys. Mrs. Orvis, who owned the Equinox, was there and the town band was playing. When the plane landed, Bill and Ebby, thanks to the drinking, were barely semiconscious. They slid out of the cockpit and lay, unable to speak, at the feet of the welcoming committee. The next day Bill couldn't stop crying. He wandered around in a haze of remorse.

Nevertheless, by springtime he had decided that Manchester would be his salvation. The hero's welcome had its effect. He decided to move north and quit being in business with Frank Shaw. He would go on his own. Why should he have to share the profits of the hard work he did? He would be a lone wolf, a singular genius. In Vermont he took up golf and pursued it with the passion of the lost. When he wasn't golfing, he was gloating. Here he was, backwoods Bill, cultivating the kind of tan rich people have and walking the fairways at the Ekwanok. There was a kind of revenge in being a big man in a town he had once seen from the rattling buckboard borrowed from the East Dorset general store. Penick & Ford was at $55 a share. All was right with the world.

CHAPTER NINETEEN:

MONTREAL

In the spring of 1929 the stock market began to slip, and Bill took action. He bought more shares of Penick & Ford to inflate the price, even persuading his mother, Emily, to buy 900 shares. When the first market wobble appeared on October 23, Bill was not alarmed; this was what he had prepared for. On the next day, Black Thursday, 13 million shares across the board changed hands and prices began to slide. Everyone thought the market had hit the bottom. The next week, on October 28 and 29, 16 million shares were put up for sale with a loss of $30 billion in the price of common stocks. Penick & Ford slid to $32 a share.

In a few days Bill Wilson had gone from being a stock whiz at the top of his game to being a man with $60,000 in debt and no ready cash. Alcoholics love a challenge, and Bill put in a call to an old brokerage friend, Dick Johnson, at Greenshields & Co., a firm in Montreal. The depression hadn't hit Canada in the same way, and in the past Bill had worked with Johnson on many lucrative transactions.

Soon enough he and Lois had moved to Montreal, and Penick & Ford was at $55 again. They rented another grand apartment, this one with a view down the St. Lawrence River and south into the mountains of Vermont. On a clear day it almost seemed as if they could see their own history. Bill played golf. Bill drank, and then stopped drinking and promised never to drink again, and then drank again. At first, things went well at Greenshields. "I felt like Napoleon returning from Elba," Bill wrote.

By the fall of 1930, Dick Johnson had had enough of Bill's drinking, with its inevitable results: missed deadlines, angry scenes, drunken disappearances. Bill got fired. Bill was outraged at being left high and dry in a strange city after only ten months of work. He and Lois were forced to borrow money to get home. When Lois lost the amethyst wedding ring Bill had bought her at Tiffany's, it seemed like an omen. Lois wrote her mother asking for financial help, and Bill cashed in on a life insurance policy.

Lois headed home to Brooklyn, but Bill stayed behind in Montreal to close up the apartment and sell the couple's Packard. He decided not to drink. The more he decided not to drink, the more irresistible drink seemed to become. It was time for him to head home, but days seemed to slip away. After a few more drinking sprees, he woke up one day in the Burnhams' camp at Emerald Lake in Vermont with a stranger he didn't remember befriending and his pockets empty. With the blessing of Lois's parents, Bill and Lois moved back into their old bedroom at 182 Clinton Street. It was a terrible time for the family; Lois's mother was dying of bone cancer. Even Bill's love for the woman who had become his surrogate mother couldn't keep him from drinking. Lois's mother's sickness, death, and funeral were all vaguely discerned scenes in one long drunken haze.

Although Bill and Lois didn't know it, Dr. Clark Burnham's financial situation was also shaky. Through it all, Bill drank. He got drunk at Joe Hirschhorn's parties, and drunk at the Ekwanok Club, and drunk at the $100-a-week job that he finally landed in Manhattan at Stanley Statistics. After work he often stopped for a drink on his way to the subway, and once he got in a brawl with two thugs. Slowly, he realized that he didn't remember much of what happened when he drank, and that he could commit any crime imaginable and have no memory of it the next morning. This knowledge terrified him. But the more he struggled to stop drinking, the more he seemed to drink. Lois got a job at R. H. Macy's a few blocks away, near Borough Hall. She worked in the furniture department demonstrating folding card tables, and she brought home $19 a week. Every day on her way to work she walked by their old Livingston Street apartment.

In 1932, when blue-chip stocks were selling at prices that Bill realized were far below their worth, he decided to try and form a buying syndicate. With the help of Kitty Burnham's husband, Gardner Swentzel, and two other Wall Street big shots, Arthur Wheeler and Fran Winans, Bill started having meetings again about which stocks to buy. Wheeler and Winans were impressed with Bill's Wall Street record, but they were also impressed with his record of being drunk on the job. Before joining the syndicate, they made him sign a contract that spelled it out. If he drank, he would be fired and lose his interest in the group. He was happy to sign. The comeback kid was making another comeback.

For a while it worked beautifully. Bill didn't drink and the syndicate made money. Once again he was a Wall Street player. Lois got her hair done and bought a few pretty dresses. They seemed to be falling in love all over again. At dinner Dr. Burnham turned to Bill to ask about his day and the state of the market, and he and Lois listened enthralled as Bill spoke volubly about business and life. Other people seemed to be happy to welcome the smart man back into their own ventures. Bill branched out, taking another job where he was paid for stock analysis. He was doing what he was good at. Even in these bleak times, when there were breadlines everywhere and trainloads of desperate hobos coming into New York every day, Bill was back in control.

In Bound Brook, New Jersey, on an overnight trip with a group of brokers to see the new photographic process at the Pathé Laboratories, Bill was offered a jug of applejack in a card game. No thanks, he said, he had had enough to drink for a lifetime. That was the line he used. There's a lot of bluster to alcoholism. Even on their worst days many alcoholics proudly pull themselves together, take long showers, and dress up so that they look flamboyantly normal. An alcoholic has something to hide, so he or she is often cleaner, quicker, smarter, better dressed, and just plain more alive than most people. There is energy in secrets. On this particular evening, well launched on his fifth miraculous comeback, Bill Wilson heard someone mention that the applejack was not just ordinary applejack—it was something called Jersey lightning.

"I'm afraid my first twenty years as an adult were less than distinguished," he wrote his friend Margaret Haven in East Dorset in 1958, "though I must say I am grateful for this period, too, for it was the one in which I was subjected to the pains and defeats which finally led to the formation of A.A." The pains and defeats of Wilson's New England childhood, the divorce of his parents, the death of Bertha Bamford, seemed to have extended themselves into his thirties.

On that night in New Jersey he was closing in on forty, a man who had already ridden a roller coaster of ups and downs for four decades. Still, he thought, he had never had a drink of Jersey lightning, and he reached for the jug. He woke up the next morning blinking from the sun. His colleagues had gone off to investigate the photographic process. Looking across the room, he spotted a jug with an inch of liquid still there. He finished it off and called for the bellboy to get some more. It was three days before he made it back to Brooklyn.

"I made my way back over to Wall Street, but all my friends were sorry, so sorry," Bill wrote later. "Nothing could be done. Sometimes now, I got drunk in the morning even while trying to transact business. When I was crossed, I abused the very people on whom I was trying to make an impression. Sometimes, I had to be led out of offices." It was 1933 and Prohibition was repealed; Bill just shifted from speakeasies to bars. Lois's father had remarried and moved out, deeding the house on Clinton Street to Bill and Lois, but Bill hardly noticed. He slid from humiliation to humiliation. It was all his mother's fault; it was all his father's fault. He went golfing and was gone for days. He ended up at the flea-bitten Naomi Hotel in Harlem and finally wound up in jail. Sometimes it was all Lois's fault. He threw a sewing machine at her and went around the house kicking out door panels.

In the summer, he and Lois headed for Vermont, where they spent several months in his sister Dorothy's house—the Strongs were away on vacation. Even here, in the kind of gorgeous isolation with nature that had proved to control his drinking in the past, Bill was out of control. He considered himself to be a Vermont Thoreau. During the day he did farmwork. He stayed up all night drinking and writing furious letters to Franklin Delano Roosevelt. The wrong Roosevelt was president and this made Bill Wilson angry. He also wrote angry letters to Joseph Hirschhorn and everyone else he could think of. Lois got to the letters before they could be mailed, and many of them are still in the archives at Bedford Hills, unaddressed to anyone except historians. The mortgage company was ready to foreclose on the house, but Roosevelt's New Deal—against which Bill liked to rant and rave—had passed a mortgage moratorium, which enabled Lois to pay the monthly stipend on her salary from Macy's.

Once they were back in Brooklyn, Bill's drinking got worse. He stole from Lois's purse to buy drinks and often thought of throwing himself out the window. One night Lois found him dragging a mattress downstairs to the first floor. He was afraid to sleep on a higher floor because he thought he might jump. Life didn't seem worth living. By the fall of 1933 the situation seemed hopeless. Leonard

Strong proposed a solution. He had another long talk with Bill about alcoholism, and Bill convinced him that he genuinely wanted to change. In fact, he genuinely *did* want to change. He just couldn't. Leonard Strong said he would pay the bill if his brother-in-law would check himself into Charles B. Towns Hospital, the expensive drying-out clinic on Central Park West.

Bill agreed. His first visit to Towns Hospital seemed to have succeeded in nothing more than drying him out for a few weeks. In November 1934, he got a call from Ebby Thacher that has become a famous part of the Bill Wilson story. Bill invited Ebby over to Brooklyn expecting a congenial drinking companion. They could relive their glorious descent on Manchester Airport. Sometimes events that were humiliating in life became lovely stories. But Ebby, who was living at the Calvary Mission in Manhattan, had been going to meetings of Frank Buchman's Oxford Group. He had stopped drinking.

A Christian group that later became Moral Rearmament, the Oxford Group recommended meditation, adherence to Christian principles of behavior, belief in a God of the believer's understanding, and adherence to what they called the six tenets:

1. Men are sinners.
2. Men can be changed.
3. Confession is prerequisite to change.
4. The changed soul has direct access to God.
5. The age of miracles has returned.
6. Those who have been changed must change others.

It was in the spirit of this sixth tenet that Ebby Thacher found his way to the kitchen of the house on Clinton Street.

By the time of his visit from Ebby, Bill Wilson had retreated from the Burnham family and from his disappointed wife, and spent much of his time in the basement kitchen at 182 Clinton Street. To welcome Ebby, he had poured a pitcher of pineapple juice and rescued his bottle of gin from the overhead tank of the toilet in the downstairs bathroom. Ebby Thacher's involvement with the origins of Alcoholics Anonymous goes as deep as its roots. Ebby had been one of Bill Wilson's best drinking buddies. Now he brought with him the word that sobriety was possible.

The man who had brought Ebby into the Oxford Group and shepherded him into sobriety, beginning with making a deal with Ebby's parole officer, was Rowland Hazard. During the summer at an Oxford Group house party at Rowland's summer home near Bennington, Vermont, Rowland learned that his old friend Ebby Thacher was about to be committed to the Brattleboro Retreat, the Vermont Asylum for the Insane. He and another Oxford Grouper decided to take Ebby on as a prospect.

Rowland himself had been an alcoholic who couldn't stop drinking. He had tried almost everything, including traveling to Switzerland and putting himself under the care of a famous Zurich psychiatrist named Carl Jung. During his unsuccessful treatment of Rowland, Jung told him that most alcoholics are hopeless cases. He added that the only cures he had seen with alcoholism were through spiritual experiences.

Still in the grip of alcoholism, Rowland had returned to New York, where he had joined the Oxford Group, had a conversion experience, and been able to stop drinking. Now this idea, that drunks were hopeless unless they had some kind of life-changing conversion experience, was relayed to Bill by Ebby Thacher. Later, in 1961, in his role as cofounder of A.A., Bill Wilson would write to Jung that Jung's treatment of Rowland "was to become the first link in the chain of events that led to the founding of Alcoholics Anonymous."

Although Ebby's conversation with his friend Bill in the Clinton

Street kitchen appeared to be a failure, it was actually a success beyond either of their wildest conjectures. Over the years Ebby relapsed and got sober again and again, and finally died penniless after Bill had rescued him many times. But his fresh-faced enthusiasm that night had a far-reaching effect for millions of other people. At the time, though, Bill was horrified at Ebby's newfound sobriety. "I was aghast," he wrote. "So that was it—last summer an alcoholic crackpot; now, I suspected, a little cracked about religion." Bill had walked out of church when he was eleven and had never lost his hatred and distrust of religion. Sitting at the small enamel kitchen table, which now stands in the kitchen of Stepping Stones, the Wilsons' house in Bedford Hills, New York, Ebby added something critical to Bill Wilson's understanding of reform and redemption— an understanding already in place from his New England childhood.

Chapter Twenty:

Towns Hospital

Towns Hospital at 293 Central Park West, in an ornate Victorian stone and white brick building, was a fashionable and famous clinic for treating alcoholics in the 1920s. Its founder, Charles B. Towns, was a proponent of gymnastics, a health nut with a heart, whose Towns-Lambert treatment, as it was called, consisted of belladonna (deadly nightshade), combined with ingredients like dried bark of prickly ash and henbane, followed by castor oil. For calming the nerves, Towns prescribed pills that were principally chloral hydrate. Towns was only for people who could pay in advance or had a financial guarantor.

The chief of staff was a Princeton graduate with a medical degree from New York University named William Duncan Silkworth. Silkworth had lost all his savings in the 1929 crash and had come to Towns on a mission—he would help alcoholics. Later, Bill Wilson called him "the little doctor who loved drunks."

It was on his second visit to Towns that Bill Wilson, already a desperate case, heard Dr. Silkworth's theories about alcoholism. Silkworth believed that alcoholism was not a failure of willpower or anything else. He believed that certain people had an allergy to alcohol. This allergy created the "phenomenon of craving," Silkworth believed, whenever the alcoholic took a drink. "These allergic types can never safely use alcohol in any form at all; and once having

formed the habit and found they cannot break it, once having lost
their self-confidence, their reliance upon things human, their problems pile up on them and become astonishingly difficult to solve."
It all sounded familiar to broken-down Bill Wilson. Silkworth explained that since alcoholism was an allergy, it could no more be de-
feated by willpower than tuberculosis could be.

Bill thought he had found his salvation. Now that he knew he
was allergic to alcohol, he thought that he understood everything.
Of course, he couldn't drink safely, so he wouldn't drink. Lois also
thought that their problems were over. She filled the house with
flowers and cooked all Bill's favorite foods. The smell of roasting
chicken and Indian pudding wafted up the stairs from the kitchen.

This time Bill stayed sober for a month or two. When he started
drinking again, Lois quit her job at Macy's in order to take him back
to Vermont where he always seemed to get better. This time he didn't
get better. He went fishing and found a fisherman with a bottle. He
went to the dentist and, on the way, spent the money for the dental
visit on a bottle, which he shared with the cabdriver.

By July of 1934 he was back at Towns Hospital. Once again a series of talks with Dr. Silkwood convinced him that he couldn't
drink. This time the doctor told him that if he continued he would
have to be confined in an asylum, probably before the end of the
year. Bill remembered driving past the asylum in Brattleboro with
Grandpa Griffith when he was a boy. The inmates were on the other
side of a fence, shuffling miserably along in a light rain or just sitting, staring into nothingness. This time Bill swore he understood
what alcohol would do to him if he drank. He was sober for a few
weeks and Lois went back to work at Macy's.

On Armistice Day of 1934, Bill decided to spend the day on
Staten Island playing golf on the public course. On the way he met
a man who suggested they stop for a drink together. Bill declined

and explained himself to his new friend over lunch. As the stranger listened, Bill laid out the disease theory of alcoholism and then for good measure threw in Dr. Silkworth's allergy theory and a little bit of Oxford Group doctrine. But when the bartender came around with a drink on the house to celebrate Armistice Day, Bill took it. The stranger was horrified. Early the next morning Lois found her husband passed out in the areaway of the house on Clinton Street, bleeding from a head wound and still clinging to his unused golf clubs.

Now sunk in a cycle of binge drinking and desperate remorse, Bill had more visits from Ebby and his friends Rowland Hazard and Shep Cornell. All three men had become members of the Oxford Group. Ebby was living at the Calvary Mission at 246 East 23rd Street operated by Dr. Sam Shoemaker's Calvary Church, which was located at Fourth Avenue and 21st Street. The men suggested that Bill Wilson come to a service. He refused.

A few days later, in the grip of murderous remorse and the splitting headache and nausea of a bad hangover, Bill Wilson decided to wander down to the Calvary Mission to see what it was like. On his way down 23rd Street he stopped at a number of bars, at one of them starting a conversation with a Finn named Alec who seemed infinitely wise and attractive. Bill Wilson and Alec arrived at the Calvary Mission only to have the man in charge try to deny them entry. They were outraged. Finally, Ebby Thacher appeared and welcomed them, suggesting that the three of them share a meal of a plate of beans and some coffee. After the meal, the three men trooped into the mission for a meeting. There on the hard wooden benches were dozens of men in various states of dereliction. The room smelled of sweat and alcohol.

After a few hymns and prayers, the preacher called for all those who had been saved by Jesus to come to the rail of the church. Unaccountably, before Ebby could stop him, Bill jumped up and started forward. Half drunk, he launched into a testimonial about salvation and the way he had given his life to God. Afterward, Bill felt sober, and a great weight seemed to have lifted off him. On the way home he walked right by the bars on 23rd Street that had earlier been so irresistible. Perhaps this was it, he thought, the cure he had been wishing for and praying for; perhaps he was released from his need for drinking.

That night he and Lois stayed up talking about what had happened. Lois was impressed by the story. They fell asleep feeling hope, and Bill slept well without a drink or any alcohol in his system. The next morning he expected a huge hangover, but instead he seemed fine. He woke at dawn. Perhaps he did have a slight hangover. He watched Lois sleep, happy in the knowledge that her husband had solved his drinking problem. He didn't want to disappoint her. He had a couple of slugs from the gin bottle, but rinsed his mouth out with mouthwash. Everything seemed fine. When Lois left for work, a few more drinks seemed like a good idea. By the time she got home that night, her husband was drunk and passed out on their bed.

Still, something had changed in the way Bill drank. He thought about the formula that Ebby had claimed got him sober: you admit you are licked, and what was the rest? First, because he knew he was going to stop drinking this time, he drank for another two or three days. He set out for Towns with a few cents in his pocket, but on the way he managed to buy four beers on credit. He met Dr. Silkworth in the hall, waving a bottle and preaching the good news. The good doctor was horrified and sad.

As usual, Dr. Silkworth gave Bill belladonna and barbiturates, and as the alcohol wore off, Bill sank into a deep depression. Ebby visited him again and went over the points from the Oxford Group that he said had helped him to stop drinking: admit you are licked, get honest, talk it out, make restitution, give of yourself, and pray. Bill listened, but the darkness of his mood seemed to close in on him. He reached some kind of bottom. Although he didn't believe in God, although he believed only in the power of his own mind, he found himself begging God for help. "If there be a God, let him show himself!" he cried. The response was amazing. "Suddenly my room blazed with an indescribably white light. I was seized with an ecstasy beyond description. Every joy I had known was pale by comparison," he wrote later. "Then, seen in the mind's eye, there was a mountain. I stood upon its summit where a great wind blew. A wind, not of air but of spirit. In great, clean strength it blew right through me. Then came the blazing thought, 'you are a free man.'"

Later that afternoon he talked with Dr. Silkworth. Perhaps, Bill Wilson thought, he had really gone over the edge. He thought he heard the voice of God! Perhaps he was finally ready to be locked up. But Dr. Silkworth, after hearing about his patient's experience, disagreed. He had heard of such sudden epiphanies, he said, and he sensed a change in Bill that he hadn't felt before. No, Dr. Silkworth thought that Bill had had a genuine conversion. Lois agreed. She said when she saw her husband the next morning, she knew he had changed and she somehow was sure he would never drink again.

In the next few days Bill was further reassured by reading William James's *Varieties of Religious Experience*, brought to him by Ebby. The book is rich with examples of alcoholic conversion, and it is James's belief that transforming spiritual experiences often follow calamity and collapse. This must certainly have gotten Bill's attention. In his descriptions of conversions, James writes eloquently about the necessity of surrender and "letting go," and teaches that "the only cure for dipsomania is religiomania."

In the intervening years, it has often been suggested that this experience, so like the ones in *Varieties of Religious Experience,* was also buttressed by the chloral hydrate in Bill's system. It is also strangely like the experience Bill's own grandfather had had four decades earlier at the summit of Mount Aeolus. When Bill started drinking, alcohol made him feel a free man. Fourteen awful years later, the promise that he could stop also made him feel a free man. It really doesn't matter. Bill said that after that experience, he never again doubted the existence of God. At any rate, there is proof that some profound change took place in him that afternoon. The proof? He never drank again.

In the years between his first and last drink, the years between when he was a twenty-year-old army officer and 1934 when he was a down-and-out drunk, Bill cycled through an entire alcoholic career, from the first euphoric moments to the last desperate beers. If the story of these years has a theme, it is the enormous power of alcohol over an alcoholic. Most alcoholics can't stop, ever. Most alcoholics die of alcohol-related accidents and diseases. Bill Wilson was an extremely intelligent man, a man with a great deal of personal experience with alcoholism and its path of destruction. He knew at first hand what drinking could do, and as a result, he had often said he would never drink. Yet he drank. When he began drinking, he saw almost at once what a toll it took on his young marriage. In a family of doctors, he was often told what the effects of alcohol might be on his brain, his liver, and his ability to hold a job. He lost job after job. Yet he drank.

His wife's misery, her heartbreaking ectopic pregnancies, his mother-in-law's death, the Great Depression—all came and went as he promised again and again to stop drinking, and yet went on drinking. Bill knew as well as anyone can know how insidious and fatal one stop at a speakeasy could be. Yet he kept on drinking. His pledges in the family Bible became a joke; his morning-after promises were laughable. He did everything he could to hold a job. His work in the stock market had become his identity. Even after he had signed a contract with partners promising that if he drank he would lose everything, he reached for that jug of Jersey lightning.

What's even more striking is that even after he was visited by Ebby Thacher and had the benefit of being spoken to by another alcoholic, Bill kept on drinking. Even after his second stay at Towns Hospital, after Dr. Silkworth had explained to him that he had an allergy to alcohol, Bill kept on drinking. Each time he visited Towns and heard Dr. Silkworth's explanation, he swore that he would never drink again. Yet he kept on drinking.

By 1934, Bill had experienced almost everything that would later form the basis of his program for alcoholics. He had heard from another drunk—a man who had been his drinking partner and was now sober. He had gone to Oxford Group meetings and been to the Calvary Mission and felt the power of the group. He had come to understand from Dr. Silkworth that alcoholism is a disease, an allergy combined with a phenomenon of craving that was activated by the first drink. Yet still he drank.

Ebby and Shep were asking him to give up the attribute of which he was most proud. The single thing that set humans above the animals—the inquiring rational mind. Although there wasn't much left of this mind, and although he knew that his next stop was probably a storehouse for the mentally deranged, Bill still clung to the idea that his own power might help him. His drinking story is a vivid testament to the power of alcohol. Nothing, apparently, could stop this man from drinking. Yet he did stop.

The message of Bill's story is clear. The difference in his behavior, the moment that defined before and after, was not when he heard from another drunk nor when he felt the power of the group, nor even when he understood that his drinking was a disease like any other disease. It was when his mind and heart were suddenly opened to the power of God. "So this is the God of the preachers," he thought that day.

Bill Wilson was always adamant about the fact that each person was free to develop a God of his or her own understanding. Alcoholics are told that their God can be a radiator, or the power of the group—G.O.D. can be an acronym for Good Orderly Direction, or even for Group of Drunks, they are told—or anything they like. But in Bill Wilson's story it is clear that alcohol is astonishingly powerful and that the only thing which can stop its course for an alcoholic is an experience of God, a spiritual awakening, a surrender of the rational mind.

*   *   *

The history of religion in America is entwined with the history of drinking. The pilgrims, who were religious refugees from England and came to the New World looking for the freedom to worship the God of their understanding, were also drinkers. They had not planned to land on Plymouth Rock in Massachusetts, but had hoped to sail down the coast toward a warmer, easier climate in Virginia. However, they ran out of beer and decided to try to fashion a life on the rocky coast of New England because it was closer at the time. No hardship could be as great, presumably, as continuing to sail without the sailors' and passengers' daily ration.

As the cofounder of Alcoholics Anonymous, Bill Wilson was careful to distinguish between religion and spirituality. Although both he and Robert Smith were devout Christians in their own way, and at different times in their lives, Bill Wilson sensed that divorcing his movement from the official church was imperative. As Ernest Kurtz, the author of *Not-God*, has written, by the mid-1930s, most alcoholics had more than enough of some preacher or other trying to sober them up in the name of Christ or some other belief system. The Protestant church had been a huge force in the temperance movement, and with his extraordinary intuition about what drunks would and would not tolerate, Bill Wilson stepped away from the ancient battle between religious morality and excessive drinking.

Nevertheless, in many ways, Alcoholics Anonymous is a religious program—although this statement would no doubt provoke howls of protest from most group members. Kurtz, in tracing the development of Alcoholics Anonymous, puts all religious beliefs into the category of "pietist" belief—that man is limited and separated from God and that "salvation" is an end to human alienation. Pietists believe that salvation comes from the divine, a powerful and distant being. Salvation is a gift from God, not an achievement of any single man. In contrast, humanist belief, that somehow God appears through people and people's activities, focuses on human participation.

"Both these approaches have shaped religious thought in America, and both appear in the fellowship and program of Alcoholics Anonymous," Kurtz writes. Of course, both of these approaches were also alive and well in the New England of Bill Wilson's childhood, as the humanist approach favored by Emerson and his band of transcendentalists made inroads into the old-fashioned Calvinist approach, an approach that required ritual conversion and salvation.

It's no coincidence that 1934, the year Ebby visited Bill Wilson in Brooklyn and started a chain reaction that would lead to Bill Wilson's sobriety later in the year, is an important year in the history of American religion. Theologians from Kurtz to H. Richard Niebuhr hail it as the moment when the strains of the old and new religions merged into a kind of neo-orthodoxy in which God becomes simultaneously beyond, beneath, and above human possibility. Bill Wilson often referred to himself as a brilliant synthesizer.

He was fond of saying that no one founded A.A. but that it had grown organically from the needs, ideas, and solutions of dozens of men and women. Nevertheless, this synthesis began at a time in the history of American religion when ideas and traditions had an unprecedented flexibility, a flexibility and fluidity that made the synthesis possible.

PART THREE

Alcoholics Anonymous

CHAPTER TWENTY-ONE:

THE OXFORD GROUP

Perhaps the visit from Ebby Thacher to the kitchen at Clinton Street was the crucial element in Bill Wilson's epiphany. Or perhaps it was the Oxford Group, of which Thacher was a new member. Others credit William James. It was an opportune moment in religious history. Bill Wilson was a man steeped in temperance education. He was a businessman who had always been a talented salesman, and someone who had grown up with Vermont libertarian principles. He was attended in the hospital by a doctor who also believed that alcoholism was a disease, and who had experience with the effects of spiritual and mystical revelations on human psychology.

Whether Bill read William James the day before his spiritual experience, the day after, or when Ebby brought him the book two days later, is also open to question. James and Jung also met and spent two evenings together at a conference in 1909; probably the treatment of alcoholics was a subject of their discussions. "This Harvard professor, long in his grave, had without anyone knowing it, become a founder of Alcoholics Anonymous. Dr. Jung, Dr. Silkworth, and the Oxford groupers had already set candles upon the table around which our society was to arrange itself. William James had lighted still another," Wilson wrote of the impact James's book had on his ideas.

James, the scion of an Albany family, the brother of the writer

Henry James, who was a professor at Harvard, had given the Gifford series of twenty lectures at Edinburgh University in 1901 and 1902, and these became *Varieties of Religious Experience.* James understood the destructive power of alcohol and also recognized its enchantments. "The sway of alcohol over mankind is unquestionably due to its power to stimulate the mystical faculties of human nature," James told his learned audience at Edinburgh, in his lecture on mysticism. "Sobriety diminishes, discriminates and says no; drunkenness expands, unites and says yes." Reading this, as his body began its physical recovery from his last binge and he heard the traffic as it hummed by on Central Park West outside the windows of the hospital, Bill Wilson felt he was understood.

"At this point my excitement became boundless," Bill wrote prematurely of his discovery that he could stop drinking. "A chain reaction could be set in motion, forming an ever growing fellowship of alcoholics, whose mission it would be to visit the caves of still other sufferers and set them free. As each dedicated himself to carrying the message to still another, and those released to still others, such a society could pyramid to tremendous proportions."

When he got home to Brooklyn from Towns Hospital, Bill and Lois began regularly taking the subway across the river to meetings of the Oxford Group at Calvary Church, where discussions were often led by the charismatic Reverend Sam Shoemaker. Over and over again, Bill and Lois heard testimonials from people whose lives had been changed by practicing the Oxford tenets: the four absolutes of Purity, Honesty, Unselfishness, and Love. The Oxford Group made a practice of never interfering with a member's religious beliefs. They put heavy emphasis on one-to-one personal work, a kind of confession of past sins that they called "sharing," and a practice of making amends which they called "restitution." Problems were solved through "quiet time," a meditation by the individual or in a group in which God's guidance was sought for every one of life's problems, from marriage and family to social life.

At the beginning of the 1930s, the Oxford Group, modeled on first-century Christians and led by Pennsylvanian and former Lutheran minister Frank Buchman, was at the height of its popularity. The group held fashionable open meetings at good hotels or in the homes of the wealthy, and well-dressed speakers stood and told their stories of surrender, restitution, and serenity in a new life. Buchman had met Sam Shoemaker in China where both were working with Christian missionaries, and the two men helped spread the movement among America's upper classes as well as abroad. Like the Swedenborgian movement that had been such an integral part of life in the Burnham family, the Oxford Group aimed itself at the educated and elite, managing to recruit members like Henry Ford, Mae West, Harry Truman, and Joe DiMaggio.

The Oxford Groupers who interested Bill Wilson were the recovering alcoholics. He knew how hard it was to stop drinking, and he saw that a dozen members of the Calvary Church Oxford Group seemed to have managed some degree of sobriety. The Oxford Group formula for dealing with alcoholics was called "guidance for others." A team of nonalcoholic Oxford Groupers would sit down with an alcoholic. After an imposed quiet time during which God's guidance was sought, they would come up with precise instructions as to what the alcoholic should do in every area of his life. Many of these alcoholics got sober. They went to meetings. They talked with each other. They adhered to the tenets.

At the same time, some leaders of the Oxford Group were turning against the alcoholics in its membership. They had made the mistake of offering some of the alcoholics free housing. One of the drunks, whose hold on sobriety was slipping, threw a shoe out the window, breaking one of the stained-glass windows in the church across the street. In general, the alcoholics made trouble, especially when they started drinking again. As the Oxford Group leadership became impatient with alcoholics who couldn't get sober, many of those drinkers found their way to a tall member who parted his hair down the middle, maintained a wide smile, and was never impatient with them. Bill Wilson, already on a mission which at its outset had saved his life and which would become his life, grabbed alcoholics wherever he could find them, at the mission or at Towns Hospital when Dr. Silkworth let him come and work there. As soon as he could sit an alcoholic down, Bill would try preaching *his* new gospel of surrender and recovery. He formed a group of alcoholics within the Oxford Group who met regularly at the mission and at Stewart's cafeteria nearby.

With his newly open mind, Bill learned the techniques and structure of the Oxford Group and applied them to his alcoholic followers with the systematic interest of a laboratory technician. He saw the usefulness of Buchman's slogans: phrases like "sin binds and sin blinds" which were hard to forget. He saw the importance of Buchman's leadership, although he was always suspicious of evangelical authority. Sometimes he thought that Frank Buchman's power might well be eroding the very movement which provided it.

Bill also came to see that alcoholics needed latitude to find their own way almost as much as they needed his help. They didn't want rules: they wanted compassion. Although the Oxford Group method worked for a while, many of the men who got sober began drinking again. This discovery—that rules and regulations do not work in the treatment of alcoholism, and that each alcoholic has his or her own drinking story and his or her own road to sobriety—is at the heart of Alcoholics Anonymous and is one of the principal reasons why A.A. has survived while many similar groups, like the Oxford Group and the Washington Temperance Movement before it, have not.

In his first months of sobriety, Bill Wilson was so high on his own discovery and so grateful that he was not drinking that he didn't notice that what he was doing was not working very well. In spite of his efforts, most drunks stayed drunk. When he confided his discouragement to Lois, she reminded him that his program was working well for one alcoholic in particular—himself. He continued preaching at Oxford Group meetings, describing his own spectacular experience and meeting afterward with the men who were attracted to him, but unfortunately he was not getting anyone sober for long. They listened to his story, agreed that they would stop drinking, and then went out and got drunk. Bill understood this process all too well. Dr. Silkworth gently suggested that he might do better if he talked about the disease of alcoholism. "Stop preaching to them!" he said.

It was at this point, as an Oxford Group member with some sobriety behind him, a resolve to be less preachy, and a series of sharp observations about what did and didn't work gleaned from watching the Oxford Group, that Bill decided to explore a business opportunity in Akron, Ohio. Through an old connection on Wall Street he had heard about a proxy fight taking place over a small machine tool company there. Imagining that this might be his sober comeback, Bill read up on the company, and in April—after five months of sobriety—went to Grand Central Terminal and boarded the train to Akron to make a bid for control of the National Rubber Machinery Company.

Bill and his team from Wall Street, all of whom backed the takeover bid, checked into Akron's Mayflower Hotel. For the first few days it looked as if the company would be theirs. The newly sober businessman from New York had plenty of time to imagine the life he would lead as a board member of a new company. Lois would be able to quit her new job at Loesser's department store. The two of them could pay off the mortgage at Clinton Street and save the family house.

In the end, the Wall Street team was double-crossed. For the moment it looked as if they had lost the business. Everyone went back to New York except Bill, who was left to see what could be salvaged. Alone in a strange city, with $10 in his pocket and the familiar taste of failure in his mouth, he badly wanted a drink. The bar of the Mayflower Hotel cast a rosy glow into the hallway that he passed through every time he left his room.

Chapter Twenty-two:

Akron, Ohio

Bill Wilson stood in the posh lobby of the Mayflower Hotel, with its wood paneling and patterned Axminster, and found himself slowly drifting toward the bar. He wasn't going to drink. But perhaps he might find some friends in the bar, some society to keep him company and dispel the bitterness he felt about the loss of his dream. This was what he had always done for comfort. A tall man from New York with a long face, a felt hat, and a suit that—as always—seemed to have been made for a slightly shorter man, Bill paced back and forth. His long stride took him from the entrance of the bar, past the local newsstand where all the headlines were about farm programs and droughts and the other government programs that President Franklin D. Roosevelt had instituted, to the other end of the lobby where a heavy wooden telephone booth was advertised with a brightly lit sign. On the side of the booth, Bill noticed a Church Directory with a list of local clergymen. Walking back and forth, he reviewed everything he knew about his situation. There was his own experience and the Oxford Group slogans. If he could help someone else to stop drinking, perhaps he would feel better.

Instead of heading for a soda at the bar—where there were plenty of drunks—he wandered over to the Church Directory list where he picked out the name of Reverend Walter Tunks. Maybe he picked it because in Vermont vernacular they say "taking a tunk" instead of taking a walk. Lois thought he picked it because he liked funny names. Walter Tunks was a strong Oxford Grouper, and when Bill called, he immediately gave him ten names and telephone numbers where he might find a "drunk to talk with." Now his stubbornness kicked in. Bill's tenacity was what had earlier enabled him to build the boomerang and had helped teach him to play the violin. He knew how to persist. Working from the top of the list Tunks had given him, Bill called all ten names.

In fact, Akron at that time was a center of Oxford Group activity. A huge rally featuring Frank Buchman himself had been held there in 1933. Billed as a dinner-jacket revival, and held at the Mayflower Hotel, the Oxford Group's brand of personal evangelism had attracted a crowd of thousands of Akron natives. Akron's ministers, including Walter Tunks, had turned over their pulpits to the Oxford Group members and their new way of preaching the Christian Gospel. Four hundred women had gathered in the Mayflower ballroom for a special women's meeting. Unlike the New York Oxford Group, the Akron group had experienced a great deal of success with alcoholics, and they were very proud of the effect of the Oxford tenets on its hard-drinking members.

One of the men Bill Wilson reached that day, Norman Sheppard, said he knew a woman named Henrietta Seiberling who was trying to help a certain friend who was prominent in Akron and who had a terrible drinking problem. "Call her!" he advised Bill. But Bill Wilson didn't want to call Henrietta Seiberling. He recognized her name and assumed she was the wife of Frank Seiberling, a Goodyear tire magnate who had known Bill slightly when he was on Wall Street. "I could hardly imagine calling up his wife and telling her that I was a drunk from New York looking for another drunk to work on," he said. What would her husband think when he heard that his erstwhile respected business colleague had become what he would probably think of as a traveling snake-oil salesman? What Bill didn't know was that Henrietta was not Frank Seiberling's wife.

She was his daughter-in-law, who had divorced her husband and been banished from the Seiberlings' mansion, Stan Hywet Hall, and given the small gatehouse in which to live and raise her children. At any rate, by this time Bill's urge to join the drinkers at the Mayflower Hotel bar had passed.

Finally, later that afternoon, Bill did call Henrietta Seiberling, as difficult as it was. He mentioned that he was a member of the Oxford Group, and as it happened, so was Henrietta Seiberling. Just a few weeks earlier, a man in her Oxford Group, Dr. Robert Smith, had confessed to the group that he was a secret drinker in terrible straits. Smith's wife, Anne, seemed to be at the end of her rope. "You come right out here," Henrietta Seiberling told Bill. But the meeting between Bill Wilson and Bob Smith was delayed because Smith had, unfortunately, passed out. They rescheduled it for the next day, Mother's Day.

Dr. Robert Smith was also from Vermont. Fifteen years older than Bill Wilson, he was another lanky Yankee kid who had been the bright son of a prominent family and who had just about destroyed his career through drinking. He had grown up in St. Johnsbury, northeast of East Dorset, the son of a local judge, and he had gone to Dartmouth College just across the river in New Hampshire. Although he started getting into trouble with drinking as an undergraduate, he managed to get to medical school in Chicago and set up a practice as a proctologist in Akron, Ohio. He had married his childhood sweetheart, Anne, had a child also named Bob, and adopted a daughter named Sue. By now the children were teenagers.

For years, his routine had been that he didn't let himself drink while he was at the hospital. Then he had medicated himself with sedatives from his own store. Occasionally, he had spent a week drying out, but his sobriety never lasted once he went back to work. Recently, all deterrents and all remedies had stopped having an effect. He had lost his post at the Akron City Hospital and was trying to make a living through a fading general practice. He knew that he wouldn't be able to perform surgery much longer. Still, he loved to drink. He couldn't stop drinking. "I just loved my grog," he told Bill Wilson. The Smiths had joined the Oxford Group, but Bob continued to drink. When the meeting with Bill Wilson was finally arranged, Smith agreed to meet for fifteen minutes at five in the afternoon, and he brought his wife and seventeen-year-old son along for protection. They stayed for dinner, and talked until eleven o'clock at night.

The Stan Hywet gatehouse (*stan hywet* is a Welsh phrase meaning "rock is here") is a tiny half-timber Tudor cottage with cozy dormers under big trees and surrounded by pretty gardens. It's at the edge of the Stan Hywet estate, the home of the Frank Seiberling who caused Bill so much apprehension. It was here that Bill Wilson met Bob. What happened that night? Armed with the knowledge of his previous failures and the sharp memory of his recent need to drink in the Mayflower Hotel, Bill Wilson told Bob that he wasn't there to help him. He, Bill Wilson, needed help, he said, and he could only get it from another man with a drinking problem. He hoped *Bob* could help *him*.

At the beginning of their conversation Bill was confronted with a surly, barely sober Vermonter, a type with whom he was deeply familiar. He probably knew more about surly Vermonters than anyone on earth. He talked about himself, about the physical aspects of drinking, and the psychological aspects that followed from them. Bob listened. "You see, our talk was a completely mutual thing," Bill Wilson wrote later in *A.A. Comes of Age*. "I had quit preaching. I knew that I needed this alcoholic as much as he needed me. *This was it.*"

Bob Smith heard this man from New York and agreed to stop drinking. Within a week Bill Wilson had moved in with the Smiths and was calling his new friend "Smithy," and they were laying plans for staying sober forever and taking their show on the road. Of course, that isn't what happened. They both decided that Bob was well enough to travel to Atlantic City for the annual meeting of the American Medical Association.

They were wrong. Bob left for Atlantic City brimming with confidence, but his newfound sobriety could not stand up to decades of drinking. Bill Wilson and Anne Smith waited anxiously for a call from Bob, but days passed without a word. Finally they heard. Bob was staying at his own nurse's house. He had called her from the station, drunk, and asked her to pick him up. Bill Wilson and Anne brought him home, put him to bed, and endeavored to get him sober. They tapered him off gradually, detoxed him, brewed pots of coffee, and sat by his bed day and night. He had scheduled a surgery in three days, and suddenly everything seemed to depend on his ability to perform that surgery. His patients had forgiven him in the past, but they wouldn't be willing to forgive him again. But Bill and Anne were successful. As Bill let Bob out at the hospital on the day of the surgery, he handed him a bottle of beer to steady his hands. That was Bob Smith's last drink and also the official date of the founding of Alcoholics Anonymous, June 10, 1935.

Chapter Twenty-three:

182 Clinton Street

Bill Wilson had a halcyon summer in Akron, staying near Stan Hywet at the nearby Portage Country Club, or with other wealthy Oxford Group members, and finally moving back into the shingled, dormered house on Ardmore Avenue with Anne and Bob Smith. He spent some time working on the proxy fight for the National Rubber Machinery Company, but most of the time he played golf or went with Smithy to talk to drunks at Akron City Hospital. During this time his attitude toward National Rubber Machinery Company changed, part of the change of heart that Bill Wilson began to see as a condition of his new sober life.

He stopped trying to engineer a takeover that would put him and his backers in power, and started trying to make peace between the warring factions of the company. He wrote Lois that his job was to do what was best for all concerned. When Bill Wilson finally did win the proxy fight, he declined to become president of the company. Instead he supported the candidacy of another businessman, Paul Frank. They lost the battle, but a few years later Frank succeeded in getting the company back, and he was its president for twenty-five peaceful and prosperous years. By that time Bill had more important things to do.

The Oxford Group welcomed him, and he and the Smiths regularly attended meetings at the house of T. Henry Williams and his wife, Clarace. Williams was a descendant of Roger Williams, and he freely gave whatever he had to the higher purpose of the Oxford Group. The Williamses' living room was a perfect place for meetings, with its long flowered couch, easy chairs with antimacassars, and Mission-style rockers.

Throughout Bill Wilson's story, the issue of class surfaces and resurfaces. Bob Smith was a well-respected doctor who had gone to Dartmouth College and on to medical school. Bill Wilson had grown up in a small rural backwater. He never really graduated from either high school or college, and although he had taken years of night courses at Brooklyn Law School, he hadn't managed to pick up his law degree. For all his efforts, his sense of inferiority and his rawboned nervousness often gave him away. True, he had married an upper-class woman, but Lois just didn't seem to notice, had never seemed to notice, that the two of them came from different worlds. The Burnhams' generosity extended to a kind of class blindness that surprised and eventually changed their small-town son-in-law. Other people, including Henrietta Seiberling and later Oxford Group leaders, were not so blind. Henrietta Seiberling later admitted that she was put off by Bill Wilson's mannerisms when she met him: he laughed too loud and too often, she complained, and when he smiled, he showed too many teeth.

Alone with Bob Smith in Henrietta Seiberling's library, Bill Wilson clearly changed from a small-town boy feeling awkward to a recovering alcoholic who could describe alcoholism in a way that no one else could. His conversion made him eloquent. Bob Smith, who had read everything he could find and heard everything there was to hear about alcoholism, had never heard another drunk tell his story. Afterward, he would say that it wasn't so much what Bill Wilson said that reached him, but it was that Bill Wilson, another alcoholic, said it.

Under the aegis of Anne and Bob Smith, Bill Wilson was provisionally accepted in Akron high society, and he wished he could stay forever. In July, Lois took the train out to join him, and she too was enchanted by the prairie landscape, the big sky, the comforts of the wealthy Midwest, and the sweetness of the Smiths. Bill and Bob spent many hours hammering out the best ways to talk to alcoholics.

The two men came from the same tradition of practical Vermont independence. They both understood that no one can tell an alcoholic what to do, but that another alcoholic could tell his own story and that sometimes this reached even the most desperate cases. Together they hit on the twenty-four-hour concept. No drunk wants to hear that he or she can never drink again, they realized. But if a sober life is broken down into days or even hours, it often becomes bearable. "One day at a time," they told each other. "We only have to stay sober for today." By the end of August, when Bill Wilson and Lois left Akron to go back to Brooklyn, they had attracted five or six alcoholics who actually seemed to have a shot at staying sober.

Back in Brooklyn, Lois went back to her job in the furniture department at Loesser's department store, and the couple resumed regular attendance at the Calvary Mission Oxford Group meetings. Knowing that helping other alcoholics helped him, Bill Wilson trolled the meetings for potential converts, and Dr. Silkworth sometimes called him from Towns Hospital to ask if he could come up and talk to someone in trouble. Two early successes, Fitz Mayo and Hank Parkhurst, became close friends and allies in what was slowly becoming a movement.

Hank had been an executive at Standard Oil, and now he decided to start an automobile dealership in Newark, New Jersey, called Honor Dealers. He rented an office and hired a secretary, Ruth Hock, and these offices became the unofficial center of the new unnamed organization that was being built around Bill Wilson, Dr. Bob Smith, and their methods for working with alcoholics.

The Burnham house at 182 Clinton Street, with its elegant wrought entryway, became a haven for all kinds of drunks, those who were sober and those who were struggling to be sober. Money remained scarce, and the mortgage company was still accepting a token payment each month. Dr. Burnham had sold the camp and the other house at Emerald Lake, and in 1936, at the age of eighty-one, he died after a short illness. In the possession of his daughter and son-in-law, his once grand house became a flophouse of sorts, with two rent-paying sisters on the top floor, Lois and Bill Wilson in the second-floor apartment built for Mrs. Burnham when she was ill, and every other order of drunk, half-drunk, and total drunk packed in rooms from the basement to the garden.

On Tuesday nights Bill Wilson held meetings in the parlor-floor living room with its rounded marble fireplace, comfortable sofa, and a circle of chairs dragged from other rooms. Sometimes strangers showed up. "My name is Bill," Wilson would say to introduce himself. "I'm an alcoholic." A few times people who liked the meetings didn't leave; one drunk stayed for a year. The Wilsons' dress clothes and practically everything else that was portable were stolen. One afternoon Bill came back from a trip to find that a resident had committed suicide, filling the house with the awful smell of gas. All this helped to keep him sober. Besides the rent from the Carlin sisters upstairs and a few Wall Street jobs that Bill managed to find, Lois's income was all that kept the mortgage company stipend paid and food on the table.

Nevertheless, Bill was happy. One account from this time has him driving down Park Avenue in Manhattan in Hank's convertible late at night. In the story, Hank stands up in the moving car and shouts out, "God Almighty! Booze was never this good!"

Lois was not so happy. A supremely practical woman with a truly great heart, she found herself increasingly irritated at Bill's euphoria. One night, when he asked her to hurry so that they wouldn't be late for an Oxford Group meeting, she threw a shoe at his head. Forced to look at her own behavior, she came to realize that she was jealous. She had spent years trying to cure her beloved Bill. She had supported him through thick and thin, and even thinner. Now a group of ragtag homeless men had done what she couldn't. In this flying shoe was the idea that later became Al-Anon, a program for people who are bothered by others' addictive or recovering behavior.

Because of financial pressure, Bill was thrilled when Charles Towns offered to take on the whole alcoholic movement. Bill could have his meetings at Towns, treat his drunks right there on the spot, and be a successful lay therapist, Towns suggested. Towns Hospital had fallen on hard times. Charles Towns saw a way to end Bill Wilson's financial problems and his own at the same time.

At first Bill was ecstatic. On the way home on the subway he thought he heard the voice of God congratulating him on what had happened. The phrase "the laborer is worthy of his hire" kept sounding in his head. It was Tuesday night, though, and in what was really the first Alcoholics Anonymous business meeting—meetings that are famously obstreperous and effective—the drunks gathered at the meeting to tell him that he couldn't take the Towns job. If he became a professional, they pointed out, if he took money for what he did, his ability to help drunks would be drastically curtailed.

Reluctantly, Bill Wilson saw their point and declined Charles Towns's offer. This is the first example of what Alcoholics Anonymous calls "group conscience," the will of the group of recovering alcoholics by which the program is still run today. Although millions of people now do alcoholic counseling professionally, Bill understood that he couldn't. He must remain nonprofessional. He also saw that when he heard the voice of God, it was often just the voice of Bill Wilson. The principle of checking with another human being before assuming any kind of higher guidance also arises from this story. Although Bill had to decline this important opportunity, it has repaid him and millions of recovering alcoholics a thousand-fold.

Chapter Twenty-four:

Not Maximum

The shabbiness and desperation of many of the drunks made them less and less welcome in the Oxford Group meetings of the Calvary Mission. Their secondhand rags didn't go with the Oxford Group's dinner jackets. It wasn't just that Bill Wilson was broke, or that his wife worked in a department store, but the people they attracted also tended to be rowdy and uneducated. The Oxford Group, on the other hand, and its founder, Frank Buchman, were attracted to celebrity, wealth, and all the trappings of the American upper classes. Buchman gave many house parties at the homes of the wealthy where he recruited impressive "key people" for his movement. He was extremely proud of his famous members. His pride, in a way that he couldn't have known at the time, was teaching his follower Bill Wilson a lot about the value of anonymity.

The Wilsons' break with the Oxford Group started in 1935, when the Reverend Sam Shoemaker's secretary told a few of the Calvary Mission members that they were not allowed to attend the Wilsons' Tuesday night meetings on Clinton Street. This effectively ended the cooperation of the Oxford Group with the movement that would become Alcoholics Anonymous. The Wilsons were "not maximum," the secretary implied, using an Oxford group phrase. The Wilsons had no desire to change their ways—quite the opposite. As Bill's focus became more and more on helping alcoholics and less and less on what he could do to help the Oxford Group, relations frayed even further.

Later in his life, Bill was always quick to say that the Oxford Group had saved his life, and that Alcoholics Anonymous owed a great deal to the Oxford Group. In 1937, at the time that Bill's fledgling group finally broke with the Oxford Group, no one had heard of Alcoholics Anonymous; it did not even exist yet. What Bill Wilson had was no money and a ragged group of drunks in a mortgaged house being supported by a woman's salary. Often the drunks who got sober at Clinton Street went out and drank again. The Oxford Group members told each other that it wasn't even certain if Bill Wilson's methods were actually helping anyone. The Oxford Group, on the other hand, was world-famous, with tens of thousands of members and coffers overflowing with contributions.

In Akron, members of the Oxford Group were still welcoming the alcoholics who were trying to get sober with the help of Dr. Bob Smith. Perhaps Akron was a friendlier place, or perhaps Dr. Smith's credentials were better than Bill Wilson's. At any rate, the cooperation that was working in Akron was not working in New York. Shoemaker was weary of Bill Wilson and his drunks. The break was painful but inevitable. By this time, Bill didn't think twice about leaving the Oxford Group. In hindsight, he left just in time.

In 1936, Frank Buchman had started recruiting in Germany. Buchman, originally a Lutheran, felt drawn to German culture and German landscapes. In Germany he met with the men in power, the members of the fast growing Third Reich. He publicly thanked God for the existence of Adolf Hitler and met with Himmler. He said that he thought Hitler would make a great "key person" for the Oxford Group. Hitler was "maximum." Back home, many members remembered the role of Germany in World War I and feared the possible role of Germany in any world war to come. Buchman's pronouncements were extremely unpopular.

The Oxford Group began to lose members. It took the Akron members of Dr. Robert Smith and Bill Wilson's group longer to make the break with the Oxford people, but eventually they did, in 1941. By then even the Reverend Sam Shoemaker and the Calvary Mission disowned the Oxford Group. Eventually, Oxford University asked Buchman to change the group's name.

At the end of 1937, Bill decided to travel west looking for work. He had picked up a few Wall Street jobs, but the time he spent with alcoholics had taken over the time he might have spent working. The trouble was that it didn't pay. This trip also gave him an excuse to visit Dr. Bob and the Akron group. He boarded the train at Grand Central and read and slept in his coach compartment as the engine crossed New Jersey and into Pennsylvania, then cut through the western Pennsylvania oilfields and the Allegheny Mountains and emerged in Ohio on the midwestern plains. The country seemed to be healing, although Bill was glad that Congress had kept President Roosevelt from increasing the number of Supreme Court justices from nine to fifteen just so that he could have his way. He hated the New Deal and the Social Security Act; government money meant government power.

With the eyes of a man who hadn't had a drink in three years, he felt calm about Roosevelt, though. He wouldn't be writing any more of the furious letters that had characterized his last year of drinking. If he stayed sober, perhaps government would take care of itself, he thought as day turned to night and the train clacked peacefully over the rails. Also, the farms seemed more prosperous than they had been the last time he looked out the windows of the train two years before.

He read in the news that Szent-Gyorgi had won the Nobel Prize for discovering the effects of vitamins on cell development, and wondered if vitamins could help alcoholics. There were rumblings of war from Japan and Germany. As the train pulled past Canton and into Akron, he realized how different he was now from the man he had been two years earlier, a man trying to take over a company. Now he really had something to sell.

Although Bill Wilson and Dr. Bob Smith had communicated through dozens of letters, sitting down together again after almost two years turned out to be an astonishing experience. When they compared notes in person, they realized that they had actually found something that doctors and laymen had been searching for as long as anyone could remember: a way to help alcoholics get sober that actually worked. Between them they counted forty men who hadn't had a drink in more than a year.

In talking with his own mentor, Bob, Bill Wilson began to see that, as time passed and he didn't pick up a drink, he was learning something every day. Frank Buchman taught him about the perils of one-man leadership and the problems of courting money and fame. Charles Towns had taught him, inadvertently, about the strings that might be attached to money and professional opportunities, and in the bargain he had been forced to understand that God tended to speak more clearly to groups than to individuals—even when he was the individual. He had absorbed the ideas of group conscience and the importance of being self-supporting as well as the idea of the power of anonymity.

Buoyed by this success, the two men decided that it might be time to expand. They could raise money and start special hospitals, and they could run educational centers. They could have paid missionaries who spread the word. They should have leaflets and books to spell out their program both as a means of spreading the word and as a means of being sure it didn't get distorted as it passed from person to person. They also needed money for more personal reasons. The Smith house was about to be foreclosed on by the bank to which they owed $3,000, and Bill Wilson was still living in a mortgaged house and being supported by his wife's small salary.

Excited by what they had discovered, the two men called a meeting, summoning eighteen Akron recovering alcoholics to the Smith house on Ardmore Avenue to hear Bill Wilson state his case. This was the second Alcoholics Anonymous business meeting, although no one knew it at the time. Even now, A.A. business meetings are famous for their ability to deflate egos.

The eighteen recovering alcoholics meeting in the Smiths' living room were grateful to Bill Wilson and Dr. Bob, but they did not share their excitement about building sober empires. They thought the idea of sober hospitals would invite all kinds of trouble. They wanted to know why Bill Wilson had split with the Oxford Group. They wanted to know what Bill Wilson had done with the money he collected when he passed the basket at his house in Brooklyn. To Bill these questions seemed absurd. He and Lois were barely making it. He stayed calm.

When Bill returned to New York, back across Ohio and Pennsylvania and New Jersey, he had a reduced mandate from the group. They had given him permission to start trying to raise money. They had said that he could start writing a book about the program. His other, more ambitious plans would have to wait. This tension between the zeal of the founders of Alcoholics Anonymous, especially Bill Wilson's wild energy and appetite, and the go-slow attitude of the members of the fellowship began that winter in 1937, and persisted to the end of Bill Wilson's life.

Chapter Twenty-five:

John D. Rockefeller, Jr.

When he got back to Brooklyn, Bill Wilson started trying to raise money right away. He called everyone he could think of to ask for money. He called Frank Shaw and Leonard Strong. He hadn't known it would be so difficult. His cause was brilliant, and it was obvious to him that he and Dr. Robert Smith had hit on something that men had been searching for since the beginning of time. People wanted proof. People wanted statistics that showed how his program worked where others had not. People had already committed their money to other worthy causes, like cancer research or homes for orphans. Sometimes he even got the feeling people thought that drunks had only themselves to blame.

In 1937 his mother's husband, Dr. Charles Strobel, died and his mother came to visit Clinton Street. Emily also made it clear that she thought her son's situation was not what it should be. Bill didn't seem interested in the kind of success that was important to her. "She was a very brilliant and forceful woman, with perhaps more love for ideas than people," wrote Lois. More and more, Emily's anger seemed to rule her nature. "Neither Dorothy nor I have ever stood in quite the right relation to mother in spite of our efforts," Bill Wilson wrote a few years later. "While she doesn't know it, mother is a person of moods so far as the family is concerned. Sometimes she thinks we are wonderful, and sometimes she thinks we are lousy."

Still, it would always be his mother who understood what things cost Bill Wilson. It was always to his mother that he complained when things went wrong, whether he had stomach problems or money-raising problems, or whether he was hit again with his old enemy, the black depressions that had paralyzed him when he was a teenager before he drank, and that would paralyze him again now that he had stopped drinking.

Dorothy's husband, Leonard Strong, once again came to the rescue. He remembered that he knew a man named Willard Richardson who worked for John D. Rockefeller, Jr. Called Mr. Junior, the son of John D. Rockefeller spent most of his time giving away money. The Rockefellers were famous for their wealth, but what was more remarkable and less well known about the family was the vast amount of money they gave away. John D. Rockefeller, Sr., was a devout Baptist who thought that tithing to the church—giving 10 percent of one's income—was insufficient. Even when he was an Ohio stock clerk making less than $50 a week and helping to support his mother and siblings, John D. Rockefeller found a way to give a large percentage of his income to his beloved local Baptist church.

As John D. Rockefeller's wealth increased, his philanthropy also increased. He single-handedly built the University of Chicago, financed medical research that cured hookworm and made important inroads against cancer, and continued to support the church. Rockefeller was never popular with the press, but toward the end of his life he was making money so fast that giving it away became expensive and time-consuming. He surrounded himself with men versed in philanthropy and the different ways in which money could be turned into good works. John D. Rockefeller, Sr., had just died in 1937 and left his son John D. Rockefeller, Jr., to carry on his philanthropies. (In fact, the Rockefellers were cousins of the Burnhams through Lois's Great Aunt Laura.)

Because the Rockefellers supported temperance and prohibition, they seemed the perfect supporters of Bill Wilson's new cause. Strong telephoned Richardson in October 1937 to ask if he would be interested in meeting Bill Wilson. He would. Bill and a few of his drunks and Dr. Bob then met with a panel of Rockefeller men, including Frank Amos and Albert Scott, in John D. Rockefeller's private boardroom. The meeting went well. Both Amos and Scott seemed convinced that the program was just the kind of thing Mr. Junior would like to support. Amos traveled out to Akron and met with the group there, even investigating possible sites for a hospital or recuperation house. Amos wrote a thorough report and recommended that Rockefeller give the fledgling movement a grant of $50,000.

Mr. Junior was worried about the recommendation. He knew more about money and its effects on human nature than most people. He thought that a grant of that size would hurt the movement. He said no to the $50,000 grant, which Bill had already spent in his mind. Instead he established a $5,000 drawing account at the Riverside Church to pay off Bob's mortgage and give Bob and Bill Wilson each a $30 weekly stipend. Bill Wilson was bitterly disappointed. At the same time, Rockefeller offered other kinds of help. The Rockefeller Board, including Amos, Richardson, and Scott, helped Bill Wilson and Bob set up the Alcoholic Foundation, a tax-free foundation that would enable other people to make donations.

Bill Wilson and Dr. Bob and a few alcoholics had ideas about who should be on the board, however, that made the Rockefeller men shake their heads. They insisted that the new foundation should have two classes of trustees: alcoholic and nonalcoholic. Frank Amos and the Rockefeller attorney John Wood wanted to know how they were proposing to define alcoholic? If an alcoholic stopped drinking, was he still legally an alcoholic for purposes of board membership? What if an alcoholic started drinking again? The board was finally formed with three recovered alcoholics and four nonalcoholics.

In the hours he spent with the Rockefeller advisers and lawyers, Bill Wilson came to see that Mr. Junior had given them something much more valuable than money. Through talking with these wise men who had handled millions of dollars both as they were earned and as they were taxed and given away, Bill Wilson got a lesson in money management that would shape the way A.A. handled its money in years to come.

At the same time that Bill Wilson was trying to raise money, he decided to start work on the book that would allow their program to reach men who couldn't get to meetings or find a fellow alcoholic. He began drafting notes for the two opening chapters, "Bill's Story," a condensed version of his own autobiography as a drinker, and "There Is a Solution," a version of his own recovery story.

In May of 1938, with three and a half years of sobriety behind him, he sat down in the Newark offices of Honor Dealers and started dictating to Hank Parkhurst's secretary, Ruth Hock. Hock remembers him smoking and pacing as he spoke the paragraphs. He would walk back and forth and then spout a few sentences. Then he hovered over her as she typed. Each paragraph was reworked while he was still thinking about the ideas it contained. To her he seemed eloquent, as his version of problems and solutions were spoken and respoken in his deep voice, with its clipped accent. She acted as his audience as well as his typist.

The first two chapters were copied and sent out to some backers, including Eugene Exman at the publishing house Harper & Brothers, who offered Bill Wilson a $1,500 advance. After some excitement and discussion, the group decided to publish the book themselves. As each chapter was finished, it was read for discussion to the New York group, where every paragraph was picked over again and again. "It got a real mauling," Hock remembered. Then

Bill and Ruth went back to work rewriting it. It was sent to Akron for comment. Back in Newark it was rewritten again, and then edited by a variety of people that included former *New Yorker* and *New York Daily News* editors who had gotten sober through the program. When he got to Chapter 5, the heart of the program, Bill Wilson sat up in bed in the Clinton Street house one night with a pencil and a scratch pad. He had a template of six steps that had been modified from the six tenets of the Oxford Group.

"I set out to draft more than six steps," he wrote, "how many more I did not know. I relaxed and asked for guidance. With a speed that was astonishing, considering my jangled emotions, I completed the first draft. It took perhaps half an hour. The words kept right on coming. When I reached a stopping point, I numbered the new steps. They added up to twelve."

Charlie Towns lent the organization $2,500, and a business plan was drawn up for Works Publishing Co. In the meantime, members in Akron and New York began writing their stories for the second half of the book. When it was all finished, there was still no title. Some wanted to call it *100 Men;* others wanted *Dry Frontiers, The Empty Glass,* or *The Way Out.* For a few embarrassing days, Bill thought his book should be titled *The Bill Wilson Movement.* At the same time, one of the men, a former *New Yorker* writer, came up with the idea of calling the book *Alcoholics Anonymous.* Finally, the choices were narrowed down to two: *The Way Out* or *Alcoholics Anonymous.* By this time Bill was overwhelmingly in favor of the latter, but he knew his enthusiastic endorsement sometimes backfired among his members. He suggested a check at the copyright office to see which of the two titles had been used before. The check showed many other books titled *The Way Out.*

Alcoholics Anonymous was published in April of 1939 with an initial press run of fewer than 5,000 copies.

Chapter Twenty-six:

Stepping Stones

In 1939 the mortgage company foreclosed on the Burnham house. For a few glorious years after Dr. Burnham's remarriage, 182 Clinton Street had belonged to Bill and Lois, but as they had found out the hard way, sobriety doesn't always bring money. Bill had devoted himself to expanding and defining the program of Alcoholics Anonymous, and Lois continued to work. Still, between them they couldn't afford the grand house that had been at the center of so much of their life together. The day Bill Wilson stood on the sidewalk and watched the movers take everything from the house and ship it off to storage was a hard one. He could hardly bear to watch the men load into their truck the old curved sofa that had been the center of so many meetings, or the big wooden bed where Lois had been born. He barely had the money to pay the movers. In the next two years Bill Wilson and Lois were essentially homeless. They moved fifty-four times, staying with many friends and, incidentally, spreading the word of Alcoholics Anonymous.

They spent summers camping on Emerald Lake and staying in East Dorset or at the nearby Londonderry Inn. By 1941 they were living in a few small rooms on the second floor of the 24th Street offices of Alcoholics Anonymous in Manhattan, paying $20 a month to keep their furniture in storage. The book called *Alcoholics Anonymous* had begun to sell, but the debt incurred to publish it hadn't yet been paid off. People who had lent money to finance it, including Charles Towns, were getting impatient.

Two years passed after the mortgage company foreclosed on 182 Clinton Street, before Bill and Lois finally found another place to live. In the winter of 1940 a wealthy woman named, coincidentally, Helen Griffith turned up at Alcoholics Anonymous meetings and became friends with Bill. Mrs. Griffith liked to buy and fix up houses, and she was appalled to find Bill and Lois living above the office. She offered to sell them a shingle house on a ridge in Bedford Hills. But there was no money. Bill Wilson and Lois were even behind in paying their storage bill. Still, as it happened, one afternoon when they were visiting another A.A. friend in nearby Chappaqua, the subject of the house came up. On a sunny March day, with patches of snow on the ground and a few buds on the maple trees, they all drove over to the little house in Bedford Hills to take a look.

Bill liked it right away. To him the house looked like an old East Dorset house. Set modestly at the edge of an expanse of grass, it looked out into the Westchester woods where sycamores and maples grew along the rocky terminal moraine that sloped downhill toward Long Island Sound. With its dormer windows and white chimney it was both cozy and imposing at the same time. By this time Bill Wilson had a taste of fame, and so he was also taken by the way the house was up off the beaten path and hard to find. They broke into the house through a back window and were enchanted by the huge open front room with its large stone fireplace, the three bedrooms on the ground floor, and the second-floor master bedroom. "The interesting, brown shingled hip-roofed dwelling stood among trees on a hill," Lois wrote later. "We were charmed."

Lois thought it was an impossible dream, but Bill Wilson's knowledge of miracles and, of course, Mrs. Griffith's generosity as well as collateral from another A.A. member came together to provide the couple with the home they would live in for the rest of their lives. Mrs. Griffith offered to sell them the house and the land around it for $6,500, with no down payment, and a payment rate of $40 a month. Lois was stunned, and concerned that it was too much money, but Bill Wilson pointed out that they were already paying $20 a month in storage.

In the month of May, with the lilacs in bloom, the Wilsons moved into the house they called Bil-Lo's Break. Bill Wilson bought a secondhand Stutz car for $30 from another A.A. member, and they were home, albeit a home with no furnace, a small water pump, unpainted upstairs rooms, and a ceiling that needed scraping and painting. A set of rough stone steps set into the hill below the house led to the garage. Because of the steps and because of the steps of the program of Alcoholics Anonymous, the couple renamed the house Stepping Stones.

Over the years the garage has been moved, and you can drive into Stepping Stones from the road now. The driveway has also been paved, but in many ways the little house remains exactly as it was when Bill Wilson and Lois moved in. The Burnhams' best furniture is arranged in the big living room behind the porch, and the shawl that Lois draped over the piano and the swags she put against the windows are still there. In the kitchen the coffeepot looks ready for Bill Wilson to pour, and the worn white porcelain kitchen table from Clinton Street still stands in the middle of the room. Bookshelves line the walls. Bedford Hills is the suburbs now and new houses cluster at the bottom of the road, but Stepping Stones, as well as the small study that Bill built for himself at the top of the hill, and the matching brown shingle house that Lois built later for her secretary, make an enclosed little world, a world where nothing has changed in the last thirty or forty or even sixty years.

*   *   *

The Bedford Hills house was empty the first time I drove up, on a whim, really, with a car filled with children—my own and their cousins. It was a summer afternoon; the family at the end of the road had a Kool-Aid stand set up, and we stopped for a drink and to ask the way. Once we pulled into the driveway behind Stepping Stones, the rest of the world vanished and we were looking at the brown shingle house trimmed with blue. No one was around, but I didn't want to break in as Bill had.

Later, I was at Stepping Stones in the winter when snow was heaped around the house and my son rode an ancient toboggan on the hill that sloped down to the road. Bill Wilson's spirit certainly survives in the hundreds of thousands of meeting rooms of Alcoholics Anonymous, where his words are read aloud each day in dozens of languages, in voices inflected with the educated drawl of the Ivy League and voices that stumble over the simplest words. Bill Wilson believed in spirits. There is a "spook" room downstairs in Stepping Stones where he, Lois, and other like-minded recovering alcoholics tried to visit the spirit world and communicate with the dead. The archives have folders of the automatic writing he did when he and Lois would use their Ouija board to invite the spirits to join them.

Standing in the Westchester County woods looking in through the windows of the house, you definitely feel that someone is there, that someone has just been working there or reading on the couch and has gotten up for a moment to pace back and forth out of view, or to make coffee in the kitchen at the back. You can almost imagine a curl of smoke from a cigarette left in a metal ashtray, or hear the sounds of a violin playing square-dance tunes coming from the room at the other side of the house as the afternoon fades and darkness seeps through the trees.

*　*　*

Bill Wilson was always more at home in the woods than he was in the house where he lived, whether it was the small gray house on the north side of the East Dorset village green or the shingled house on a ridge in Westchester. His first refuge as a boy was the woods. The Vermont forest, with its stands of birches and ferny swamps, provided a place he could go and be by himself—although in the woods he never felt alone. He knew the woodland creatures intimately, as a friend and as a hunter. He could tell the difference between a chipmunk hole and a black snake's lair, and the larger holes where red foxes hibernated in the winter and emerged with their cubs in the spring.

In the 1800s, the Vermont woods had been cleared for pastures by the homesteaders who thought they could grow anything anywhere. They chopped down trees for their houses, pulled out stumps with their oxen, plowed and replowed the stony fields to plant corn and wheat and vegetables. In the woods around East Dorset there were foundation holes where houses once stood, where proud farmers had come in from the fields for dinner and sat somberly with their wives and children to say grace at the table.

The woods of Westchester were different; there were no abandoned stone walls or crumbling barns or old foundations, no air of the ruined past. Instead of moss and ferns, Bill Wilson walked over myrtle and pachysandra, low green cover that grew on the rocky soil built up into the ridges around his house. In northern Westchester, glacial formations are so extreme that the landscape sometimes seems like a maze, a series of ridges and counterridges, where great trees grow among the boulders. There he could see deer and woodchuck and other woodland animals, although Bill Wilson was no longer a boy out hunting with a gun, but rather a distinguished looking man on his way to the train station headed to the city on important errands.

Still, like Henry David Thoreau, another strange Yankee who felt that the woods held the secret of living deliberately, and who wrote that in the woods a man would be able to find the answers to why he had lived, Bill Wilson felt restored by the great trees, with their miraculous thick, abundant greenery in the summer and their strange skeletal shapes in the winter. Other people looked into the woods and saw nothing, but for him there was always the trace of life, a deer path that he knew would lead to water, a fallen log gnawed through to make a home. The woods still comforted, for while his life had changed in ways that he had never dreamed of, the trees were centuries old and the woods were always the same.

Chapter Twenty-seven:

334 ½ West 24th Street

The year 1941 marked a turning point. Until then Bill Wilson, Robert Smith, and their followers were hanging on through stubbornness or, in most cases, because they had nowhere else to go and nothing else to do. Bill had been sober for more than five years; he had traveled to Akron and founded a fellowship with Dr. Bob Smith. He had held hundreds of meetings and welcomed dozens of drunks into his home. He had written a book outlining the program of recovery he had helped to create, so that men and women who couldn't get to meetings might take advantage of its ability to heal. He had shepherded the book through a group editing process that reduced it to a quarter of its original length. Still, the book wasn't selling, the program was heavy with debts, and most of the books were stored, unsold, in a warehouse.

Money to publish the book had been borrowed from Charlie Towns and others, partly on the basis of *Reader's Digest* editor Kenneth Payne's remark to Bill and Hank in an interview at the magazine's offices in Pleasantville that he thought it might be the kind of thing that would interest the *Digest*. In raising money Bill Wilson and Hank had used the words Rockefeller and *Reader's Digest* as often as possible. But when they triumphantly visited the elegant *Digest* offices again, walking up the hill from the railroad station to announce that the book was ready, Kenneth Payne had forgotten all about them. With sinking hearts, they reminded him. He dimly remembered that the editorial board had turned the suggestion down. Too controversial? Too unreliable? It was a memory from so long ago that he couldn't even recall exactly why the editors had decided they weren't interested.

Bill Wilson knew that he had a program that worked. He also knew that there were thousands of people who had problems with alcoholism. Nevertheless, the crowds of drunks and their families begging for help that Bill Wilson and his friends knew would materialize were just not there. Two plus two was not equaling four. It wasn't happening. They had finagled some publicity for the program and the book through radio broadcasts and newspaper articles, with little result.

One new prospect turned out to be a friend of Gabriel Heatter's. Heatter was a prominent radio personality whose program, *We the People,* was one of the most popular in the country. They had persuaded Heatter to let the new member tell his story. The new member was so excited by the prospect that he had a few drinks. Bill and Hank had to foot the bill for a hotel room in order to keep him sober in the hours before the broadcast.

Working day and night, Bill Wilson, Hank, and Ruth Hock had sent out 20,000 order blanks to coincide with the radio show. They rented a post office box in Grand Central Terminal to hold the replies. It all seemed to pay off. The new member, who proclaimed himself a recovering alcoholic who had been saved by Alcoholics Anonymous, was brilliant on the show. He told his story and explained how the program worked. Gabriel Heatter himself plugged the new book. They had it made! Three days after the show came off perfectly, they went uptown to the station with a suitcase. Inside the post office box there were twelve letters; only two of them contained orders. Sales continued to be minimal.

At the same time, the book *Alcoholics Anonymous* was attacked by a group of doctors in the *Journal of the American Medical Associa-*

tion. Although many medical professionals now recommend Alcoholics Anonymous to patients who have drinking problems, the relationship between A.A. and the medical profession was less than friendly at first. With some exceptions—Dr. Silkworth and later Dr. Harry Tiebout—doctors resisted the idea that alcoholism could be cured by some kind of spiritual awakening, or even by meetings with other alcoholics. Traditionally, alcoholics had been hopeless medical patients. It took a long time for that attitude to change.

The New York members of Alcoholics Anonymous had once again expected the breakthrough to come when Dr. Leonard Strong brought them to the attention of the Rockefellers. Instead of money, they got help, but they still needed money. In February of 1940, John D. Rockefeller, Jr., announced that he would give a dinner for Alcoholics Anonymous at New York City's Union Club. Although in the end he was unable to attend, his son Nelson and dozens of his closest business associates—four hundred guests in all—were there to hear Bill Wilson describe the program. Dr. Harry Emerson Fosdick spoke in praise of A.A., and some invited recovering alcoholics answered questions from the floor. Reporters and great men were there. The mood in the room was elegant and encouraging. Bill Wilson's heart lifted. Surely now at least their financial problems would be taken care of.

Then Nelson Rockefeller stood and explained his father's belief that the last thing the new movement needed was money. The wealthiest men in the nation nodded in understanding. After dinner, a billion dollars' worth of American capitalists walked out of the club without donating a cent. Then John D. Rockefeller, Jr., himself wrote a letter to every guest, explaining that he supported the program and was writing a check for $1,000. The money was badly needed, but other donors from the dinner seemed to calibrate their gifts according to the size of their fortunes in relation to Rockefeller's. There was even a check for $50. Still deeply in debt,

Bill Wilson was angrily disappointed. Later he saw the dinner in a different light. "Only much later did we realize what Mr. Rockefeller had really done for us," he wrote. "At the risk of personal ridicule, he stood up before the whole world to put in a plug for a tiny society of struggling alcoholics. . . . Wisely sparing of his money, he had given freely of himself. Then and there John D. Rockefeller, Jr., saved us from the perils of property management and professionalism. He couldn't have done more."

After the Rockefeller dinner a few more orders for the book *Alcoholics Anonymous* trickled in. There was some additional press coverage as well, but the situation hadn't changed much. The office moved from Newark to a cubicle on Vesey Street in lower Manhattan, and finally in February of 1940 to a former stable behind some buildings at 334¹/₂ West 24th Street. It was there that Bert T. and Horace C. found a small building with a long hallway leading in from the street that came to be known as "The Last Mile." They guaranteed the rent. A retired firefighter came with the place as a caretaker, and although at first the fellowship suggested to him that he should work for nothing, he insisted on being paid. Bill and Lois, who had been living in other people's houses for more than a year, moved into two tiny rooms on the second floor. They often had to take up a collection to pay the $20-a-month fee for the storage of their furniture.

Then as if his professional reverses weren't discouraging enough, Bill Wilson ran into problems with Hank Parkhurst, one of his oldest friends and fellow members, and with Ruth Hock who had become the group's indispensable secretary and who had been Bill's assistant in writing the book *Alcoholics Anonymous.* Hank was the first man whom Bill Wilson had actually been able to keep sober. The two men had shared all the ups and downs of the early years. Now their friendship and fellowship was ending.

Throughout his life Bill Wilson provoked passionate feelings in men and women. Sometimes men who had been close to him turned on him; sometimes there were women involved. Hank decided that he was in love with Ruth and wanted to marry her. Ruth declined his proposal, and Hank believed that somehow Bill was to blame. Bill had a charismatic way with women, and this seemed to provoke other men's jealousy and anger. Hank's wife was angry too, and she was suing him for divorce. Hank had been in charge of the business side of Works Publishing, the company they had formed to publish *Alcoholics Anonymous,* but it now appeared that he had no records and no accounting system, or if he had had them, they were lost. He began to rail against Bill, accusing him of all kinds of things, including seducing Ruth and keeping her from marrying him. Soon Hank started to drink again.

One rainy night, alone in one of their small rooms on 24th Street, Bill Wilson sat despondently, discouraged and nursing a stomach pain that he imagined might be an ulcer. It was all useless. He was going to die soon, he thought. There was a knock at the downstairs door, and Tom the custodian announced that there was a crippled old bum from St. Louis downstairs who wanted to talk about the Twelve Steps. The bum was a Jesuit father named Edward Dowling who had noticed the parallels between the exercises of St. Ignatius and the exercises of a man in New York named Bill Wilson. He had decided to take the train to New York. Dowling's directness and his unquestioning faith somehow pulled Bill's spirits up that night. His message was that saintly men are not happy men. When Bill whined about wanting contentment and asked if there was ever to be any satisfaction in his life, Dowling replied no, that there never would be. Ironically, it was the most cheering thing Bill had heard in a long time.

In a way, the eventual spread of Alcoholics Anonymous was helped by the fact that many of its newly sober members were salesmen. They had an understanding of how to persuade and connect with other men—especially other men who happened to be alcoholics. Bill Wilson had always had a talent for selling. The idea of selling cars had pulled him out of a depression. His ability to sell information on Wall Street had made him a small fortune. Selling A.A. took patience, but gradually more and more pins indicating A.A. groups went up on the map of the United States that Bill kept in his office.

It's hard to know what made Bill and his fellow A.A. members persist through these discouraging years. For one thing, they were all seriously broke, and essentially unemployable. Most of them had used up any resources they may have had. In other words, they didn't have a choice. In retrospect, of course, it's clear that if their big break had come any earlier, they wouldn't have been ready for it.

Curtis Bok, publisher of the *Saturday Evening Post*, had been hearing about Alcoholics Anonymous from two friends of his who were doctors, so he assigned a tough investigative reporter named Jack Alexander to check out the story. Alexander had just finished a story busting the New Jersey rackets, and he wasn't interested at first, saying that self-help didn't sound like his kind of thing. Then he heard that the Rockefellers were somehow connected to this strange religious group, and that its leader, Bill Wilson, was regarded as a saint by many of its members. Perhaps there was some muckraking to be done after all. He took the train to New York to see for himself. At first Bill Wilson's honesty about the program and his own difficulties put him off. Later he wrote that he had thought Bill Wilson was either incredibly naïve or a bit stupid.

Bill suggested that he give the reporter a tour of the groups as well as a series of interviews. By this time the program was ready for such scrutiny in a way that it would not have been earlier. Together the two men traveled around Pennsylvania and Ohio and on to Chicago, staying with A.A. families and going to A.A. meetings. In each city they were greeted by clean-shaven, well-spoken recovering alcoholics who were eager to show them local meetings and welcome them. They had lunch with lawyers in Cleveland and visited Doctor Bob in Akron and watched A.A. members visit an alcoholic patient in the psych ward of Philadelphia General Hospital.

When he saw how well Alcoholics Anonymous worked, and when he heard people talk over and over again about their salvaged lives and their redeemed families, Alexander slowly became a convert. His *Saturday Evening Post* article appeared on March 1 of 1941, with a cover line on the Norman Rockwell drawing showing a sophisticated model with the body of a schoolgirl with a lapful of books. The issue also included an installment of Clifford Dowdey's serialized novel *Sing for a Penny*. The *Post*—which cost a nickel at the time—had more than 3 million subscribers, and Alexander's article seemed to finally get national attention for the movement.

"To an outsider who is mystified, as most of us are, by the antics of problem drinking friends, the results which have been achieved are amazing," he wrote admiringly in the story titled "Alcoholics Anonymous: Freed Slaves of Drink, Now They Free Others." "Many doctors and staffs of institutions throughout the country now suggest Alcoholics Anonymous to their drinking patients. . . . According to A.A. estimation, 50 per cent of the alcoholics taken in hand recover almost immediately; 25 per cent get well after suffering a relapse or two, and the rest remain doubtful. This rate of success is exceptionally high. Statistics on traditional medical and religious cures are lacking, but it has been informally estimated that they are no more than 2 or 3 per cent effective."

The article was 7,500 words of praise, it said just what Bill Wilson and Dr. Bob wanted it to say, and it was fascinating reading. It told readers that two men—Bill Wilson and Bob Smith were referred to by pseudonyms, Mr. Griffith and Dr. Armstrong, to protect their anonymity—had found a method that actually worked to keep alcoholics from drinking. It didn't work perfectly. It didn't work all the time. But it worked often and fairly well, which was worlds ahead of anything else that has been thought of to combat addiction before or since.

The *Post* article signaled the end of the A.A. leaders as struggling pioneers, desperately trying to spread their message beyond a few friends. Within a few weeks the little office in the 24th Street clubhouse was hit with an avalanche of 6,000 letters, as well as hundreds of desperate telegrams and telephone calls. Each of these people needed a personal answer. It was much more than Bill and Ruth Hock could handle, and they called for volunteers. In 1941, A.A. membership went from 1,500 to 8,000, by 1944 there were 10,000 members in almost 400 groups, and by 1946 there were 30,000 members.

Chapter Twenty-eight:

Trabuco College

In many ways, by the beginning of 1942, it might have seemed that Bill Wilson's troubles were over. Five years of sober striving had been rewarded. A.A.'s future was assured, and groups were spreading to cities and towns all across the United States. At last the book *Alcoholics Anonymous* had healthy sales. The debts undertaken to pay the publisher had been retired. Shares in Works Publishing actually had some real worth. For the first time, Bill Wilson was glad that he and his colleagues had published the book themselves instead of selling it to Gene Exman at Harper & Brothers. Although Bill Wilson and Lois were still hard up financially, they had a wonderful place to live in Stepping Stones, and Bill Wilson was convinced that his Yankee know-how around the house could fix any of its problems.

On the train from Bedford Hills to New York City, where he put in two or three days a week at the 24th Street office, Bill Wilson read the morning paper. War was everywhere. He still disliked Roosevelt, but Pearl Harbor had changed the way he felt about war. The world was in disarray. At age forty-seven Bill Wilson decided to enlist in the Army. He remembered his days as an officer in France with longing; he came from a proud tradition of patriotic soldiers; he knew he could help.

His application for Army service is a strange document because it demonstrates some of the difficulties of anonymity and the near impossibility of explaining Alcoholics Anonymous to those who are not part of it. The application tells the story of a failed stock analyst and salesman who doesn't amount to much. There is Bill Wilson's old success from before the crash, followed by failed positions as a salesman for a wire rope company and as a boat salesman. At the very end of the application, Bill Wilson wrote a few lines about his involvement in the founding of Alcoholics Anonymous, but he couldn't begin to tell the story of his own importance or even enclose the Jack Alexander article in which he is mentioned by another name. When the Army turned him down, he was bitterly disappointed.

At the same time, some of the popular success that he was experiencing began to have a backlash. The jealous and disappointed Hank Parkhurst was spreading the rumor that Bill Wilson was getting rich on A.A., and the new Cleveland group demanded an accounting of the huge sums of money they imagined piling up in New York. Bill Wilson went to Akron, and he and Dr. Bob traveled to Cleveland to hear what the group had to say. It was more like an interrogation than a dinner among members of a fellowship. The Cleveland group, led by Clarence S., was convinced that Bill Wilson had pocketed $64,000 of A.A. money, and they had heard that he was a close friend of John D. Rockefeller's and had been seen coming out of the Rockefeller bank.

Bill Wilson and Dr. Bob had come with an accountant and a certified audit of all A.A. financial transactions since 1938. The audit showed that Dr. Bob received no salary or royalty from *Alcoholics Anonymous*. In fact, the only money he was paid for all his A.A. work was the $30 a week specified in the Rockefeller grant. Bill Wilson also received $30, as well as an additional $25 a week from the book company. Cleveland apologized, but Bill Wilson thought about what had happened for a long time. He wondered if this kind of public humiliation was the price of success. He began to think about ways to insulate A.A. from the intense emotional charge around money. Possibly, he even began to think about detaching himself from his own creation.

The Akron group was also a source of occasional envy. In many ways Bill Wilson and Dr. Bob had opposite styles, and this was what made them work so well together. Bill Wilson was attracted to wealth and power; Bob was not. Bill Wilson gave long speeches, Dr. Bob rarely talked more than a few minutes. Bill Wilson was young and magnetic, Bob was older and liked to stay in the background. Some people in Akron drew conclusions from this that weren't warranted. "Why are you spending so much valuable time in the present trying to make a name for yourself in the future," Henrietta Seiberling complained to Bill Wilson in an angry letter about the difficult relationship between the Akron groups and the New York groups. "It's futile and won't mean anything to anyone but yourself. It's all so sad and pathetic. Why don't you change?" Bill Wilson wrote back inviting Henrietta to come to a dinner and hear him speak, and she soon was back in the fold, cooing about "the old Bill." Often, however, it seemed as if the moment he stopped paying attention to anyone or any group, the envy trouble started.

The household improvements Bill made at Stepping Stones sometimes showed more imagination than engineering skill. The water in the house had to be pumped up the hill, so he built an attic reservoir to hold it and improve the flow. He created the new water tank by hoisting a cattle trough purchased from Sears, Roebuck up to the attic and rigging a pipe down to the bathroom. A float in the tank turned on a red light in the kitchen when the water was low; a bell rang when the pump had filled the tank.

The system worked, but the day came when no one was home to hear the bell and water went cascading down the stairs. Still, the attic reservoir was kept in place for years. The house was heated by a coal furnace with a door that was closed at night. In the morning when the door was opened, the heat from the furnace spread throughout the house through a register in the floor. Bill Wilson rigged up an alarm clock to trigger the furnace door, but the clock got clogged with coal dust. At the time, his half-sister, Helen, was staying in a downstairs bedroom. Bill Wilson drilled a hole through the floor and ran a string through it attached to the alarm clock. When the alarm went off, Helen pulled the string, which released a cement block that opened the furnace door. It worked well, except of course when Helen wasn't there.

In October of 1943, the Wilsons took the first cross-country trip to visit A.A. groups, beginning a tradition of travel for A.A. that would continue throughout their lives. They went from city to city and from group to group, landing in Chicago, Omaha, Denver, Portland, and Seattle, among others. Bill was always in demand. He would tell his story and soak up the different ways that each group had found to deal with the problems of money, leadership, anonymity, and service. In New Orleans the group leader spoke from behind a curtain. In Ohio some of the groups wore black costume masks when they talked with the press. Other groups used both first and last names and didn't seem to care about anonymity. The Wilsons stopped at the Grand Canyon. Because it was wartime, tours had been suspended. Bill and Lois rode down the side to the river on mules, and Bill "got the squeams," Lois wrote.

For three months they slept on trains or in strange beds. At each stop they were met by a welcoming group and then taken to a house or hotel. Then there would be a dinner and a meeting. After breakfast the next morning the couple would be taken back to the train station. Bill spoke at meetings while Lois began to meet with the families of alcoholics in gatherings that would one day lead to her own establishment of Al-Anon.

Bill Wilson was teaching on this trip, but he was also learning. He began to think about a set of guidelines for the program, rules that would enable the groups to handle many of the worst problems he saw. These guidelines would cover money, power, and prestige. This was the beginning of the idea which, ten years later, became the Twelve Traditions, bylaws that incorporate many early stories from Alcoholics Anonymous. Bill was a political conservative, but he was also a Vermont-bred freethinker. He saw that only the purest form of democracy would work to hold together people as opinionated, intelligent, and ego-driven as recovering alcoholics.

At last he was a famous person, a real number-one man. At each stop he was greeted by groups of enthusiastic fans. Men admired him and their wives adored him. He was getting the adulation and respect that he had dreamed of as a boy. Crowds of people applauded when he spoke. The awful thing was that he hated it. "Why any one wants to be a public character is more than we can fathom," he wrote his mother. For all his showmanship and flamboyance, Bill was horrified by people who waited for hours or traveled for miles just to be in his presence. He was abashed at becoming a celebrity and disappointed that he was unable to take advantage of the anonymous comfort and solace of meetings in his own program.

"I wish I could just go to an A.A. meeting," he would later say plaintively. He began dreaming of ways to escape his own fame, and over the years he developed a series of hideaways near Bedford Hills and in Vermont where he could avoid the throngs of people who wanted to hear him speak, or see him, or even just touch him.

Bill and Lois met his mother in San Diego for Christmas. Emily was living in pathetic circumstances in a hotel there, although she owned several apartment buildings. Her husband, Dr. Strobel, had died five years earlier, and Emily's miserliness seemed to have been released by his death. She had studied in Vienna with Freud's sometime colleague, Alfred Adler, and officially, as she reached seventy, she was practicing Adlerian analysis in San Diego. She didn't have many patients.

Emily didn't seem impressed by the crowds of admirers and students Bill attracted because of his role in founding Alcoholics Anonymous even in San Diego. She loved to tell the story of his birth and the way they had both almost been killed by it, seemingly failing to notice that this was a painful story for her son to hear. Bill was sober, though, and he treated his difficult mother with unfailing courtesy and generosity. He never told the story that might have been painful for *her* to hear: the story of how she had abandoned him when he was ten and left him and his sister to live with her parents; the story of how she had angrily divorced his father and taken off to live her own life and follow her own dreams; the story of how she had left her small children to breathe in the dust of her own ambitions.

In Palo Alto, Bill and Lois had been introduced to the philosopher Gerald Heard and the writer Aldous Huxley. Heard and Huxley were already close friends. Heard, who was five years older than Huxley, had won honors at Cambridge, done graduate work in the philosophy of religion, and left college without taking a degree in order to become a writer. Like Huxley, he was an inspired speaker and a brilliant scholar. A homosexual in a society that condemned any sexual deviance, he was also a committed pacifist and socialist who wanted to do service to humanity. "Cosmology must end in ethics," he wrote.

A strange, mesmerizing presence, Heard was also a student of Eastern religions who led Huxley to meditation, yoga, and the "kinesthesiology" of the body advocated by Australian therapist F. M. Alexander. The Alexander method, as it was called, was based on the idea that people develop bad habits in using their bodies and that these bad habits have a negative effect on their mental health as well. By realigning the body, a patient could realign his psyche. Thus the Alexander method—practiced by George Bernard Shaw and John Dewey, as well as Heard and Huxley—was a cure for depression as well as other age-related problems. Both Huxley and Heard came to believe the best cure for social ills would be the cure of each individual member of society. Heard, who had been studying mysticism for decades, introduced Huxley to Vedantism, the idea that although we may think of ourselves as individuals we are actually part of a changing field of energy and intelligence.

The Vedantists also believed that truth is ultimately experiential; that some kind of spiritual enlightenment was the goal of all proper human activity. At the same time, Huxley became friends with Jiddu Krishnamurti, an Indian holy man who had come from the Theosophist movement. The Theosophists, founded by Russian psychic Madame Blavatsky, moved to India, where Blavatsky was succeeded by Annie Besant, an Englishwoman.

By the time Bill Wilson met Aldous Huxley and Gerald Heard, it would seem as though they would have had to invent each other if they had not already existed. They were political opposites and spiritual brothers. Although Heard and Huxley were pacifists and Bill was an admirer of the military, and although Heard and Huxley were socialists, convinced that the betterment of society would come from some kind of experiment in community and community education, while Bill was a staunch conservative and lifelong Republican, the men had much more important things in common.

Wilson and his movement represented the practical application of the philosophy that Heard and Huxley devoutly believed. His program and its adherents had proved that change was possible, that the human soul existed, and that it was almost infinitely malleable. If change was possible, then change for the better was possible, and an enlightened society was only a matter of finding the right formula. Heard and Huxley were theorists in a way; Bill had actually proved that his theory, which grew out of experience, held true. Huxley, with his literary success—he had written *Brave New*

World and his novel *After Many a Summer Dies the Swan* had become the great movie *Citizen Kane*—legitimized the small-town boy in Bill. Huxley later said that he considered Bill a "modern saint," but the accomplishment that impressed him most was the wide-open democratic principles expressed in Bill's twelve traditions. These were written by "the greatest social architect of the twentieth century," Huxley wrote.

Huxley and Heard invited Bill, Lois, and Emily to spend a Vedantic New Year's week at Trabuco College in the desert behind Laguna Beach, near San Clemente in California's Orange County. In 1942, Heard had established Trabuco College with land bought by his wealthy patrons, David and Lucille Kahn, who were also followers of the psychic Edgar Cayce. After a meeting in their Central Park West apartment, they agreed to help establish a monastic branch of the Vedanta Society in California. And it was monastic. Huxley and Heard had imagined that at Trabuco they would accomplish the grandiose purpose of redefining the goals of life. "The desert's emptiness and the desert's silence reveal what we may call their spiritual meanings only to those who enjoy some measure of physiological security," Huxley wrote. "The enormous draughts of emptiness and silence prescribed by the eremites are safe medicine only for a few exceptional souls." Heard and his followers as well as Huxley and Wilson were among those exceptional souls.

The college itself, a kind of loony desert version of Walden Pond, consisted of a group of frame buildings in a desert canyon that was also home to quite a few rattlesnakes. Walking at night was not recommended. Many people carried heavy sticks with which they thumped the ground as they walked to flush out snakes. Groves of avocado and bougainvillea dotted the sandy hills. Everything at Trabuco would be simple. There was no electricity. They rose with the sun and went to bed when it got dark.

Although he now knew what worked for many alcoholics, Bill

never stopped searching for chemical cures for alcoholism. He and Huxley both believed that certain chemicals could change perceptions and alter addiction. Huxley wrote about this theory brilliantly in the essay that became the Bible of sorts for experimentation with mind-altering substances: *The Doors of Perception.* The essay, with its vivid descriptions of internal travel, remained inspirational for decades. Singer Jim Morrison named his band the Doors after the Huxley essay.

Huxley and his wife, Maria, along with Heard, were more interested in Eastern Indian mysticism than Bill would ever be. They also shared a fascination with the dead and a belief in psychic phenomena. "Our philosophy has no place for free will or for anything which might be described as the soul," Huxley wrote in a 1954 piece for *Life* magazine in which he promoted the possibility of paranormal experience and wrote admiringly of Dr. J. B. Rhine's laboratory of parapsychology at Duke University. Bill was also a fan of Rhine's.

Later, when Maria Huxley was diagnosed with breast cancer, both Huxleys acted on their belief in the friability of the line between the living and the dead. Huxley talked his wife "through" death, urging her toward the light as she gradually expired. It was a calm letting-go. In 1956, when Huxley was dying, he instructed his wife, Laura, to inject him intradermally with 100cc of LSD as he died and to talk him through it in the same way. She did, urging him on lovingly toward the light, hour after hour until his last breath.

Chapter Twenty-nine:

Depression

Bill's depression began almost as soon as Lois and Bill got back from their triumphant cross-country tour. Spring was coming to the Westchester woods, with violets poking out through the winter leaves, the grass getting greener, the wrens nesting in the eaves of the porch, the sticky green leaves unfolding on the maple and oak trees around the house. The brook at the bottom of the hill was overflowing, and piebald ducklings paddled in the lake on the other side of Cherry Street. After seven years of struggle, Bill Wilson could rest assured that Alcoholics Anonymous would survive—the trip had shown him that. Already thousands of people had been saved through the program that he and Dr. Bob had sketched out during those first months in Akron. Hundreds of groups were thriving, each with its own problems and solutions.

Bill had been hailed as a hero in towns he had never heard of; he had been thanked again and again by powerful men and beautiful women who looked at him as if he were some kind of god. He had received what he called "the deity treatment." With all this, Bill slowly sank into a depression worse than anything he had known as a sober man. Life seemed useless. Nothing seemed worth doing. Mortality was the only certainty. There were times when he felt barely able to control his own hysteria. Sometimes he was afraid he couldn't breathe. Nothing brought him any pleasure. There were many days when he could not even get out of bed.

Bill had always been physically fragile. He was often sick: his stomach hurt and perhaps it was an ulcer; his heart was palpitating and perhaps it was a heart attack. Lois called him "almost" a hypochondriac. Even as a healthy adult he spoke of his illnesses as if he were a little boy, and nursed them as if he were the mother he had lost long ago. Now he was hit with something worse. Smothered by hopelessness, Bill Wilson struggled to write a report on the successes of the trip. He had always loved walking, but now he rarely left the house. Lois made sure that he ate, but she was incapable of fully understanding what he was going through. "I didn't understand why he couldn't get up," she said. In *Lois Remembers*, her memoir of this time, mention of Bill Wilson's depression does not appear.

On those days when he made it to the train station, and went to the city to the new larger A.A. offices on Lexington Avenue near Grand Central Terminal, he often just sat for hours with his head on the desk or with his head in his hands. He couldn't respond to questions. When he raised his head, he was sometimes weeping. No one knew what to do. Some people in A.A. started wondering if their leader was drinking again.

This was the fourth time in his life that Bill Wilson had been ambushed by the disease he called "my ancient enemy, depression." It had happened first when he was a ten-year-old boy; his father went West and his mother called in a divorce lawyer and then went to Boston, leaving him with his grandparents in a town that mocked the family for their misfortune. After that he slowly rebuilt his life until he was a leader at Burr and Burton with Bertha Bamford at his side. The depression had come again, after Bertha's awful, sudden death. That time, it had been harder to restore his sense of well-being. He had lost everything.

Ultimately, it had been the young Lois Burnham who had saved him from that bout of panic and depression. The third time it had happened was during the depths of his alcoholic drinking in 1934, when his life seemed over and his alternatives limited to either confinement to an asylum or an early death. In the joyous years of early sobriety, followed by the distractions of the difficult struggle to launch A.A., Bill hoped that he had seen the last of these debilitating depressions. Perhaps they had something to do with drinking, he thought at the time, hoping that they were behind him forever.

There are many theories about why depression leveled Bill at this time. "Bill himself saw we didn't need him—all we needed was his book," said one of the men he had visited in Los Angeles. The facts are that his depression overwhelmed him at the exact moment when his dreams had come true. In his own language, on his own terms, he had hit a ten-strike. He was the number-one man. "Just now my problem is success," he wrote to old friend Mark Whalon. "I confess I do not find it any easier than the problem of defeat. In some ways it's more difficult. I find it a hopeless undertaking indeed to keep up with people's expectations of me."

Bill Wilson's levels of depression varied over an eleven-year period from 1944 to 1955. Despite this, he was astonishingly productive during these years, accomplishing what may have been his most important work. He outlined the Twelve Traditions and wrote the second seminal book for Alcoholics Anonymous, titled *Twelve Steps and Twelve Traditions*. Against a great deal of opposition, he insisted Alcoholics Anonymous should not have leaders like himself and Dr. Bob, but rather should be run by a General Service Office consisting of rotating trustees and a rotating board with regular General Service conferences where any and all A.A. members could be heard. Each meeting could send a representative to the conference. Everyone would be represented.

Finally, in 1955, his depression lifted after the first, hugely successful General Service Convention when he officially handed over the leadership of the program to its own representatives. At the moment that he was no longer in charge of his movement, he appeared once again to feel in charge of his life.

Depression is an ancient human problem written about by philosophers and psychologists from Aristotle to Freud. Each age has seen it in a different way, from the romantic depressions of the Victorian poets, to the more practical disease and pharmacology model we have today. Depression is also intimately connected to alcoholism. Many alcoholics start drinking to alleviate their anxiety and depression, little realizing that alcohol is itself a depressant. It will lift the spirits temporarily, but in the long run alcohol is the worst thing a depressed person can consume—almost the way scratching a mosquito bite feels wonderful but ultimately is painfully counterproductive. Sometimes when people get sober, they are left with the severe depression that caused them to drink in the first place. Bill Wilson may have been one of these people.

Even now, though, there are no simple answers about depression and what causes it. "Some people suffer mild depression and are totally disabled by it; others suffer severe depression and make something of their lives anyway," writes Andrew Solomon in his book *The Noonday Demon*. "There is an interaction between illness and personality; some people can tolerate symptoms that would destroy others; some people can tolerate hardly anything. . . . Since depression is highly demotivating, it takes a certain survivor impulse to keep going through the depression, not to cave into it. A sense of humor is the best indicator that you will recover." But when his mind went black, Bill lost even that sense of humor.

Depression is also a form of grief, and Bill was a man who had suffered tremendous and unexamined losses, from the departure of his father and mother to Lois's inability to have children. Then, in the year before his depression descended, he had been rejected by his own beloved U.S. Army at a time when he could see that they needed his help. His service in the last war had been a wonderful

1

2

3

East Dorset, Vermont, as it looks today, facing east,
with the red, dormered Wilson House (top) and the
white Griffith House (bottom, right).

Bill Wilson at about age four, before the family
moved to Rutland, Vermont.

The young Emily Griffith before her marriage
to Gilly Wilson.

Emily Griffith Wilson in graduation robes.

Fayette Griffith, Bill Wilson's maternal grandfather.

Bill Wilson's father, Gilman (Gilly) Barrows Wilson,
in the 1930s, twenty-five years after he left his family
behind in Vermont.

Bill's first love, Bertha Bamford, at Burr
and Burton Academy.

10

11

Second Lieutenant Wilson and the men of the
Coastal Artillery unit. Bill Wilson is in the bottom row,
the farthest right.

(facing, top) Second Lieutenant William G. Wilson,
on the dock at Emerald Lake.

(facing, bottom) Second Lieutenant William G. Wilson
of the 66th Coastal Artillery.

(top) Bill Wilson on a trip to investigate the Pennick
and Ford plant in 1929.

(bottom) Bill Wilson in Vermont, going fishing.

Bill Wilson the successful stockbroker.

Bill and Lois Wilson at Yosemite National Park
on their first cross-country tour
to visit Alcoholics Anonymous groups.

(facing, top) Lois and Bill in California in the winter
of 1943–44 on their cross-country trip.

(facing, bottom) Lois and Bill in Paris in 1950.

Lois and Bill in the garden at home in Bedford Hills.

Bill in June of 1958 at the first Founder's Day Services for Alcoholics Anonymous in Akron, Ohio, at Dr. Bob's grave.

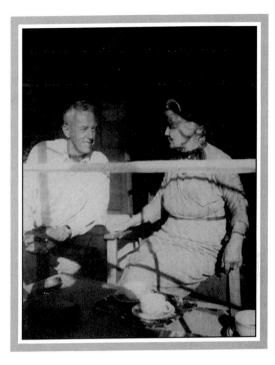

Bill and his mother, still deep in conversation in about 1960.

An AA picnic at Stepping Stones. Left to right: Bob Smith, Lois with Bill on the right in back.

Bill Wilson in April of 1970 at the General
Service Conference in New York City, less than a year
before his death.

time for him, marred only by the fact that he hadn't been able to do more. Now he never would have that chance. He didn't talk much about this—"It was hard," was all he said—but much of his identity was tied up in soldiering. His grandfather had even tried to cheer him out of an earlier depression by taking him to see the place where the brave Vermonters had charged up the hill during the Battle of Gettysburg.

There is a genetic component to depression. The Wilson family included many alcoholics, and Emily Griffith Wilson became increasingly unstable as she grew older. Her father, Fayette's, rectitude and sadness may also have masked depression, a depression exacerbated by the loss of his son Clarence the year before Bill and his sister went to live with him.

By the early 1940s Bill's heavy smoking had begun to be a problem; he couldn't seem to cut down on the number of cigarettes he smoked each day, and nicotine can also act as a depressant. Fortunately, by the grace of God, he had been able to stay sober. He never had a drink again after his experience at Towns Hospital in 1934—he kept that vow. His other promises to himself—promises about smoking or coffee drinking or financial responsibility or sexual behavior—turned out to be much harder to keep. This realization was depressing too.

By the time this latest depression hit, Bill was essentially a man under a microscope. Hundreds of people were watching his every move, circulating information, speculating on his frame of mind. His colleagues had other theories about what happened to throw him into a psychological abyss. Some thought he needed to be the center of attention, and when that faded, he faded. Advertising executive Tom Powers, who became a close friend and colleague and edited *Twelve Steps and Twelve Traditions*, believed that the depression came from spiritual exhaustion.

Bill Wilson loved the limelight, but being adored was clearly a very complicated thing for him. Everywhere he went, people wanted to talk with him, to get him to recognize their own specialness, to listen to their stories and problems. And he did. From city to city he listened and learned, and recognized other people's struggles, other people's stories, other people's uniqueness. At the end of three months of this, he was an empty man.

Bill himself often said that his depressions came from a weakness of faith. "We are apt to be swamped with guilt and self-loathing," he wrote in *Twelve Traditions*. "We wallow in this messy bog, often getting a misshapen and painful pleasure out of it. . . . This is pride in reverse." Yes, of course, that's true. At heart, though, it appears that his relationship with the people he helped, the people for whom he became a kind of father, was both satisfying and painful. After all, Bill had never really had a father of his own. Nevertheless, he became a man who had to take care of everyone. He sent checks to both his parents and took charge of his mother's financial affairs. He made sure that his friends from the early days were provided for. Ebby Thacher got a regular check from Bill until the end of his life. "Bill took care of everyone," said his secretary, Nell Wing. His friend Tom White speculates that Bill was good at struggle and not as good at pleasure, and in that context, he quotes the Confucian scholar Meng Tse: "Grief and trouble bring life, whereas prosperity and pleasure bring death."

In spite of his frailties, Bill was an eminently practical man. He continued to talk with and visit Dr. Bob for sustenance; he spoke often with Father Ed Dowling, who reminded him that even St. Francis found the spiritual life to be painful. In the face of his depression, he did something else that was startlingly unconventional for the time, and especially unorthodox for the man who had written that the program of A.A. would rocket its followers into another dimension. Twice a week he drove down from Bedford Hills to visit psychiatrist Dr. Harry Tiebout in his Greenwich, Connecticut, offices. Tiebout was a fan, the man who had brought Bill's friend Marty Mann into Alcoholics Anonymous, and he at least understood that the "new happiness" promised in the Twelve Steps of A.A. did not necessarily preclude other psychological problems.

Later in his depression Bill also regularly saw another psychiatrist, Dr. Frances Weekes. Weekes told him that she thought his position in A.A. was inconsistent with his needs as an individual. And Bill's understanding of God also began to shift. "I've certainly come to go along with the Catholic doctrine of pain," he wrote Mark Whalon, using words that would later be reflected in *Twelve Steps and Twelve Traditions:* "It is the key to all evolution, the touchstone of spiritual progress, and the springboard to all real joy." Bill had been raised in the Congregational Church and married in the Swedenborgian Church. Now he wanted to search for a church that would suit him personally.

CHAPTER THIRTY:

OUR COMMON WELFARE
SHOULD COME FIRST

On trips around the country and eventually to Europe to visit A.A. groups, Bill Wilson's presence at a meeting electrified the participants. He was always asked to speak, and he always obliged. His new celebrity quickly became a burden. Wherever he and Lois went, Bill was recognized. On a trip to the Laurentian Mountains, their cover was blown by a waiter who called in the cook, who ended up flying in a planeload of grateful A.A. members to meet Bill. The same thing happened in Bermuda. Because of his height, Bill was easy to spot, and there were thousands of people who felt that they knew him intimately and that he had saved their lives. Even when his purpose in traveling was to avoid A.A. groups, Bill's easy-to-recognize lanky form and long face made it likely that his personal anonymity would not be observed for long. Later, in the 1960s, Bill went to great lengths to go unnoticed. In Vermont he holed up at the Londonderry Inn, and no one but Lois and his secretary, Nell Wing, knew where to find him. He and Lois rented a small house in Pound Ridge, New York, as a refuge from Bedford Hills, and that address was a carefully guarded secret.

To help preserve some privacy in the meantime, Bill built a simple cinder-block studio with a tin roof on a hill above Stepping Stones. Lois called it, cutely, Wit's End, but Bill and his friends referred to it as "the shack." The building, without plumbing or electricity, had a fireplace, a kerosene stove, and huge windows looking out into the trees. A studio couch was pushed against one wall, and Bill worked at the desk and in chairs he had bought from Hank way back when they liquidated Honor Dealers and moved out of the Newark office.

During the summer months the studio was invisible, although Bill could look down through the leaves and see if visitors to the house were people he wanted to talk with. On those occasions Lois simply told everyone he wasn't at home, which was true. He was a few feet up the hill in the book-lined room of the shack. Two or three days a week Bill walked down the road, through the woods, and across the bridge over the new Saw Mill Parkway to the railroad station in the hamlet of Bedford Hills. The train into the city stopped at Pleasantville and White Plains and ran through pleasant woods. Sometimes Bill spent weekday nights in Manhattan at the Bedford Hotel.

His days were spent at the new offices at 415 Lexington, and later at larger offices around the corner on 44th Street, where he tried to deal with the hundreds of letters that poured in from groups and individuals. A.A. was coming of age. Dr. E. M. Jellinek established the Yale Summer School of Alcohol Studies at Yale University in 1943, and Bill Wilson was the keynote speaker on the final day of the six-week course.

Finally, the *Reader's Digest* ran an admiring story on A.A. in the October 1944 issue, and the mail increased exponentially. The harrowing movie version of Charles Jackson's novel *The Lost Weekend*, in which the power of alcoholism over an alcoholic was represented in its starkest reality, brought more mail. Secretary Ruth Hock had been replaced by Bobbie, and there were more paid staffers although not nearly enough to begin to answer the mail. Nell Wing came to work as Bill Wilson's secretary and assistant. Some of the staffers helped Bill; others published the organization's new newsletter, the *AA Grapevine,* whose first issue appeared in June of 1944. The *Grapevine,* which Bill called "a meeting in print," was to provide an outlet for his writing on the subject of A.A. for the rest of his life. Now, as he sorted through the letters, he began to see certain specific problems emerging.

Who was supposed to handle the dues and fees that came in? What happened when there was too much money or too little? Should there be rules for membership, or could anyone join A.A.? Should groups get involved in campaigning for other good causes? Should alcoholics who help other alcoholics ever get paid? What about public relations? Plenty of new members thought they could recruit others with a snappy advertising campaign—was this a good idea? Should members always be anonymous? What if they were asked to appear on radio and television shows and talk about alcoholism? And what about the wealthy members who were so thrilled with their sobriety that they wanted to build hospitals and start education centers to spread the word? Who could settle disagreements among members? Who decided how long a meeting should last or how it should be conducted?

On his cross-country trip Bill had noticed that many A.A. groups had the same set of problems but that there seemed to be dozens of different solutions. As he traveled, he began collecting lists of regulations developed by each group, and once back in New York, he asked the groups to send in their own rules. The results were terrifying. "If all these edicts had been in force everywhere at once," Bill said, "it would have been practically impossible for any alcoholic to ever have joined A.A." Some of the groups banned women while others either required "proof" of alcoholism, in the form of written testimonials, or "proof" of sobriety. Some had a minimum fee, and others discouraged latecomers. Some welcomed visitors while others were only for "real" alcoholics.

As these same questions came over his desk again and again, and

Bill typed out answer after answer, rephrasing the question and relating the experience of the New York groups, he saw that A.A. needed guidelines, some kind of codification of these answers that was gentle enough to be acceptable to defiant alcoholics, but direct enough to solve some of the problems that many of the groups seemed to be having. He began working on some form of bylaws, which he titled "suggested points," scribbling them down on a yellow pad at the office and then taking them back out to Westchester and refining them at his desk as he looked out at the trees.

Later he titled these guidelines "Twelve Points to assure our future," and described them as "a set of general principles, simply stated, which offer tested solutions to all of AA's problems of living and working together and of relating our society to the world outside." Eventually, they became the Twelve Traditions posted at the front of almost every meeting room, along with the Twelve Steps.

"Each member of Alcoholics Anonymous is but a small part of a great whole," he wrote. "A.A. must continue to live or most of us will surely die." These points appeared first in the *Grapevine* and were quickly edited down to a shorter form. "Our common welfare should come first," the shorter form says, showing the difference in Bill Wilson's prose after it had been worked on and edited—it was at once less dramatic but more concise. "Personal recovery depends on A.A. Unity." The only authority over a group, he explained, was a loving God, "as he may express himself in a group conscience." In other words, after discussions, the majority would rule. "The only requirement for membership," he decreed, wiping out scores of rules and regulations that had already sprung up across the country, "is a desire to stop drinking." The traditions explained that each group should support itself through contributions of the members and that no group should express any opinion on outside issues or be drawn into public controversy.

Drawing on his experience, using anecdotes from his own life and stories he had heard from groups across the country, Bill wrote a small essay illustrating each of the traditions. He drafted a section at a time and then sent it around for suggestions to Tom Powers; another editor, Betty Love; and Jack Alexander, who had become a friend. These essays comprise an extraordinary history of Alcoholics Anonymous as written by its cofounder. The principles of a leaderless democracy in which the problems of money, property, and prestige are brilliantly set aside, are all here. The social architecture of the traditions protects A.A. against the human egos of its members. A.A. members say that the Twelve Steps keep them from committing suicide, but the Twelve Traditions keep them from committing homicide. They prescribe poverty, an apolitical stance, a turning away from controversy and "outside issues," and a tremendous tolerance for anyone who seeks help.

All through this time, Bill's depression persisted. Sometimes as he dictated to Nell Wing, he would just slow down and stop, apparently unable to continue. Waylaid by his thoughts, he would put his head in his hands or down on the desk. When he looked up, Nell could see that he was weeping. She just sat there until he was ready to go on. As the traditions took shape, written and rewritten with the help of friends, and in the light of letters that came in after a point appeared in the *Grapevine,* it was clear that the first ten would be concerned with the mechanics of each group. Points eleven and twelve would deal with the connection of the group to the outside world.

Bill Wilson wrote that "our relations with the general public should be characterized by personal anonymity . . . our public relations should be guided by the principle of attraction rather than promotion," and, "we believe that the principle of anonymity has immense spiritual significance. It reminds us that we are to place principles before personalities; that we are actually to practice a genuine humility."

In his almost ten years of being a sober member of A.A., Bill Wilson had done more thinking about the principle of anonymity than anyone else on earth. He had watched as people went to great lengths to protect their anonymity because they were afraid of the stigma of being an alcoholic. He understood people who feared for their jobs if their "secret" affiliation to A.A. was discovered. He had also seen the opposite thing happen when a famous ballplayer had broken his anonymity in his eagerness to tell the world about his new sobriety, and then had gone out and started drinking again to the delight of the press and people who had doubts about A.A.

Bill's friend Marty Mann brought the anonymity issue to a head when she started fund-raising for her National Committee for Education on Alcoholism, now the National Council on Alcoholism and Drug Abuse. Marty was the first woman to come into Alcoholics Anonymous. Attractive, smart, and energetic, she supported Bill Wilson and Lois in their homeless days and stayed part of their lives. Her new committee made good copy, and as she toured the country promoting it, she freely told her own story, including the lifesaving fact of her membership in A.A. When she asked for Bill's approval, he gave it. In 1944, *Time* magazine did a piece on Marty and her committee, and her affiliation with A.A. was part of the story.

Soon the New York office was flooded with checks sent in response to what people assumed was a financial appeal from A.A. Along with them came letters of protest. Then there were the proposals from other members who wanted to use their membership in A.A. to promote their own projects. If Marty Mann could raise money for her own cause, however worthy, by talking about the benefits of A.A. and saying that money raised would benefit A.A., then why couldn't everyone else do the same? At first anonymity had come from the A.A. members' fear of being exposed as alcoholics; now it was clear to Bill that anonymity served a much deeper purpose. He began to understand the principle that would become one of the most controversial aspects of A.A., the principle that anonymity was not for the protection of the individual—although it also functioned that way—but rather it was a way of seeing the world.

"These experiences taught us that anonymity is real humility at work," Bill Wilson wrote; ". . . moved by the spirit of anonymity, we try to give up our natural desired-for personal distinction." Although both Bill and Marty realized that they would not be able to control what other A.A. members did, they chose to set an example. Bill apologized for his support of Marty's breach, and Marty stopped invoking A.A. in her fund-raising efforts. However, Bill's own humility was soon to get its ultimate test.

The story of Bill Wilson and the Yale degree shows the conflict that persisted in Bill and made him a great teacher, a man who struggled with desire as he searched for humility. In February of 1954, Bill got a letter and a visit from the secretary of Yale University offering him a Doctor of Laws degree. Yale would respect his anonymity, giving the degree to him as W.W. and not using his name. Bill wanted the degree, for many reasons. He saw how much the publicity might help A.A., reaching alcoholics who might find out about the program and be helped. He also wanted the degree and the recognition for himself. But by this time he was sufficiently sophisticated in his own principles to know that accepting it was somehow a bad idea.

Nevertheless, Bill decided not to make the decision alone, perhaps because he hoped he might be persuaded to act against his instincts. He brought the letter to the next meeting of the Alcoholic Foundation, the association that had been established by the Rockefeller men with a board consisting of alcoholic and nonalcoholic trustees. His spirits were buoyed to find that all but one of the trustees thought he should accept the degree. These were wise men!

The one exception was Archibald Roosevelt. According to Lois Wilson, Archie explained to Bill and the board that his father, Theodore Roosevelt, had been very worried about his own attraction to power. As a result of this, Theodore Roosevelt had decided he would never accept a personal honor. He made an exception only for the Nobel Peace Prize. Bill knew that he was hearing the right message. He was human, though. He decided to decline the degree, but then he couldn't quite do it. He wrote an eloquent letter explaining the principles of anonymity and asking if the fellowship could get the degree. "I'm wondering if the Yale Corporation would consider giving A.A. itself the entire citation, omitting the degree to me," he wrote.

This time, Yale declined, very respectfully. "After hearing your magnificent letter," the Yale secretary wrote, "[the committee members] wish more than ever they could award you the degree—though it probably in our opinion isn't half good enough for you. ... We understand completely your feelings and we only wish there were some way we could show you our deep sense of respect for you and A.A." By the time he wrote to Mark Whalon about turning down the Yale degree, Bill understood the principle of anonymity in a new way. Later he declined to be on the cover of *Time* magazine, even, as the editors suggested, with his back to the camera. He also turned down at least six other honorary degrees and a number of overtures from the Nobel Prize Committee.

Chapter Thirty-one:

Dr. Robert Holbrook Smith

I'm from the Oxford Group," Bill Wilson told Henrietta Seiberling on the telephone that afternoon of May 11, 1935, "and I'm a rum hound from New York." To Henrietta it sounded as if God were answering her prayers for her friend Dr. Bob Smith. In that case, He was also answering a prayer for Bill Wilson. Bill liked to rush ahead, and his emphasis was often on the technical rather than the spiritual aspects of a problem. Bob was the older, wiser man with a deep-seated belief in the power of God and the efficacy of Protestant teaching. Reading their history, it's clear that without everything each one of them thought and said, separately and to each other, the program of Alcoholics Anonymous would not have survived.

People in Ohio witnessed the extraordinary contributions of Robert Holbrook Smith in helping alcoholics, including the admission of more than 4,000 alcoholics to St. Thomas Hospital, where he worked with Sister Mary Ignatia Gavin, a clerk in the admissions office who ultimately helped thousands of alcoholics. These Akron and Cleveland A.A. members sometimes feel that Dr. Bob's contribution is not sufficiently recognized by the New York faction of A.A. Bill Wilson is not the founder of A.A., they are quick to remind anyone who speaks as if he were; Bill Wilson is the *cofounder* of A.A.

People in New York, especially those who watched Bill Wilson dedicate himself to creating guidelines for the program and struggling to find a way for it to survive its founders, sometimes feel that Bill's contribution is underrecognized by the Ohio groups. Friends of the Smiths and their children sometimes mention pointedly that the Smith children never inherited any money, while royalties from the book titled *Alcoholics Anonymous* made Lois Wilson a wealthy widow. Friends of Lois's point out that the book was written by Bill Wilson, after all, and that Lois gave most of her money to the Stepping Stones Foundation.

In fact it is A.A.'s good fortune to have grown up in two separate places with two separate traditions in a way that fostered a necessary tolerance, as well as a broad spectrum of acceptable behaviors.

The true forge of A.A. was in the long nights this failed salesman and a half-failed proctologist spent in Akron in the summer of 1935, and again in 1937, after two years of sober experience, discussing and rediscussing the principles that seemed to have led to their mutual and miraculous sobriety. One of the principles, it was clear to both of them, was the necessity of one drunk talking to another. With that realization, they started trying to get other men sober. They often failed; they learned from their mistakes.

Both men were also still thinking of their program in terms of the Oxford Group's four absolutes—honesty, unselfishness, purity, and love; its five C's—confidence, confession, conviction, conversion, and continuance; and its five procedures—giving in to God, listening to God's direction, checking guidance, making restitution, and sharing for witness. In addition to these tenets, they had the Bible, which Dr. Bob felt held the answers to most human questions; he called it "The Good Book" and especially loved to read and reread the Sermon on the Mount, the 13th Chapter of I Corinthians, and the book of James.

They agreed that once they settled on a prospect—a man with a drinking problem—they would approach his wife. This method would prepare the way and give them some background information. After all, that's what Bill and Henrietta had done with Anne and Bob. After that they would approach the drunk directly by going to his house or bringing him to the Smiths. If he was amenable, they would ask him to pray and make an official "surrender."

Often this surrender would take the three men upstairs to a bedroom, although sometimes it happened in a kitchen or a hospital room. The "surrender" was a confession of powerlessness, and a prayer saying that the man believed that a higher power could restore his sanity. With Dr. Bob kneeling at the edge of the bed on one side and Bill on the other, the prospect would be led to admit his problems. Before a man had officially surrendered, Bill and Bob believed, he wasn't ready to attend one of the meetings at the Smiths' or at the Williamses' house.

Once the prospect had surrendered and was ready to go to the next step, he was put on a strict diet of sauerkraut, tomatoes, and Karo corn syrup that both Bill Wilson and Bob Smith thought would help with alcohol withdrawal symptoms. Both men believed that this diet would also dampen a craving for alcohol. Then their prospect was hospitalized for five to seven days—usually in a private room at City Hospital with many visits from the three or four men who had already gotten sober through this arduous process.

No one was allowed in a meeting without being sponsored, and new recruits were visited by every recovered alcoholic in Akron, sometimes as often as twice a day—this could mean dozens of visits and dozens of prayers while kneeling at the edge of the bed, not to mention dozens of cups of coffee. Dr. Bob would regale the new man with the medical facts of alcoholism. He would explain that the body was allergic to alcohol, and that, under the circumstances, taking a drink was just like taking poison. "If you were allergic to strawberries, you wouldn't eat them, would you?" he would ask.

Reading about the methods of the two founders, it sometimes sounds as if their prospects quit drinking out of exhaustion. Surrounded by the tall, zealous founders, backed up by dozens of converts, sickened by Karo corn syrup and sauerkraut, men may have stopped drinking just to get away. The Smiths' house on Ardmore Avenue became a center of alcoholics who often just dropped in.

When Anne and Bob heard the coffee being made in the morning, they weren't sure if the job was being done by a drunk who happened to spend the night on their sofa or by a sober man who had come over to take Bob on a twelfth-step call. It took a long time for any of these prospects to get sober, and many of them started drinking again after a few weeks. Slowly, though, there were three truly sober men, and then six, and then twenty. By November of 1937, when Bill visited the Smiths in Akron, both men realized that they had started a chain reaction. Men were getting sober and staying that way. "We actually wept for joy," Bill remembered.

Bill had come to Akron that fall partly to look for business opportunities and mostly to meet with the members about the possibility of a book and his fund-raising ideas. Bill and Bob already had a sympathetic, mutually agreeable working relationship that would last until the end of their lives. "They moved toward rather than away from each other—a tendency that we take to be the AA way," writes the anonymous author of *Dr. Bob and the Good Oldtimers.* "Between these two men there was a willingness to agree and act together." They loved each other. They were a team. Bob called Bill "Willie," or "Prince William." By February 1938, when Rockefeller's man, Frank Amos, visited Akron for the purpose of assessing the program, the process of sobering up drunks had become a system, which he analyzed for the benefit of John D. Rockefeller, Jr.

1. An alcoholic must realize that he's an alcoholic.
2. He must surrender.

3. Not only must he want to stop drinking, he must remove his life from other sin.

4. He must have a quiet time of prayer every morning.

5. He must be willing to help other alcoholics.

6. He must meet frequently with other alcoholics.

7. It is important but not vital that he attend some religious service weekly.

T. Henry Williams, a devout Oxford Grouper, opened every meeting at his home with a prayer. With his penchant for brevity Dr. Bob never spoke for long. "No souls are saved after 15 minutes," he liked to say. But by 1939 the Akron A.A. members began to argue about the advisability of continuing with the Oxford Group and attending meetings at the Williamses'. Finally, in an early display of group conscience, they voted about what to do, and the group who wanted to sever their ties with the Williamses and the Oxford Group prevailed. The first meeting at the Smiths' house on Ardmore Avenue was held a few days after New Year's in 1940. Seventy-four alcoholics packed the room. One of them checked to see if there was a room that might be available to them at the nearby King School, and that's where the group began to meet every Wednesday night.

In his own way, Bob was a true Vermont character. He used graphic language—"Who slipped me that slobber," he asked when a friend kissed him—and he loved to tell stories. Most of his stories were as laconic as any Yankee joke. Robert Smith was in his fifties when he got sober, and he had the manners and courtliness of a man from an earlier century. One story has it that when he was a guest at an out-of-town meeting, he got up to speak. Everyone settled into their seats to hear the founder. Bob started by saying that the world's greatest speeches had been short ones like the Sermon on the Mount and the Gettysburg Address. "With this in mind," he said, "I propose to give a short talk. In fact I just did."

Bob began every morning with meditation and prayer and twenty minutes of Bible study. Like Bill, Bob believed in paranormal possibility and the two men spent time "spooking," invoking the spirits of the dead. Bob also had a reputation as a healer, and during the 1940s and '50s, even after the Wednesday night A.A. meetings had been moved to the King School, five to ten people a day dropped by the gabled frame house at 855 Ardmore Avenue to get help and counseling from Bob, or just to share the coffee that had become the communion of A.A. members in the East and the Midwest.

Often when they left, people would ask Bob to remember them in his prayers. "I was always glad to think I was included in those prayers," Bill Wilson said. "And I sort of depended on him to get me into heaven. Bob was far ahead of me in that sort of activity. I was always rushing around talking and organizing and 'teaching kindergarten'; I never grew up myself."

When Bill slowly concluded in the late 1940s that Alcoholics Anonymous should be administered by a group of rotating representatives from meetings all over the country—the General Service Organization—rather than by an appointed board of alcoholic and nonalcoholic trustees, he knew that he needed Dr. Bob's blessing if anyone in the fellowship was to take his idea seriously. He also knew that all his work on the traditions would be worthless unless Bob endorsed them. At first Dr. Bob did not agree. He had just been diagnosed with cancer and shut down his medical practice so that he and his beloved Anne could live out whatever time they had in peace. Unfortunately, there was no peace in A.A. business affairs. A stream of visitors representing both sides of the issue began to arrive at Ardmore Avenue.

In 1949, Bill wrote a long letter begging for Bob's support in his desire to transfer the management of the Board of Trustees, the General Service Office, and the *Grapevine* into the "direct custody" of regional representatives. Bob was reluctant to endorse the Twelve Traditions, bylaws that had been developed by Bill out of his experience in New York. Bill traveled to Akron to explain what he saw as the importance of the traditions and of turning all power over to the program's representatives. Bob still balked. But at the 1950 First International Convention, his last appearance was made in order to support the man who would carry on their legacy, the legacy of the program that was first hatched years earlier in the gatehouse parlor at Stan Hywet.

For a long time after Bob's death, no one sat in the seat on the right side of the aisle at the King School meeting place where Bob Smith had always sat, quietly smoking and listening, and occasionally speaking up and saying the kinds of things that people would remember for the rest of their lives. No one who knew him could bear to sit there. Finally, a newcomer came in one night, someone who had never known Dr. Bob Smith, and sat in that empty chair to listen to the meeting.

PART FOUR

Life After A.A.

Chapter Thirty-two:

The Spook Room

Bill Wilson was an enthusiast, a man who was fascinated by whatever was happening at the moment. He bent his lanky body eagerly toward whoever was speaking; he paid such close attention that the ash often fell off his forgotten but still-smoking cigarette. Once he got hold of an idea, he explored it from every angle until he let it go—*if* he let it go. Catholicism fascinated him. His spiritual adviser, Father Ed Dowling, was a devout Roman Catholic, and although Bill had stopped going to church in a formal way when he left the Congregational Church of his boyhood, he had become a Christian without a church.

Nevertheless, Bill Wilson insisted that belief in God was not a prerequisite for membership in A.A. He knew how important it was to the survival of the program that it be in no way religious or associated with any religion. He was proud of the way the program had avoided associating itself with a specific God, limiting itself in the steps to what was called *God as we understood him.* Even so, as soon as many drunks heard the word God, they headed for the door.

In the 1940s Bill met Monsignor Fulton Sheen, the popular Catholic radio host. Sheen, who later converted Clare Boothe Luce to Catholicism, was a man Bill Wilson could talk with. He began visiting Sheen for instruction every Saturday. Perhaps this—a different kind of religion—was the answer. In his darkest times he had found solace in a prayer of St. Francis of Assisi, a Catholic saint.

Bill wrote letters to Ed Dowling about the sweetness of Catholicism, and letters to Sheen laying out his questions. "I *feel* more like a Catholic," he wrote Sheen, "but I *think* more like a Protestant." Perhaps if this struggle had happened later in his life, it might have had a different result. But his wrestling with the possibility of conversion with its divine certainty was happening in the 1940s. He was still very much the leader and guide of his beloved A.A., and he knew that anything he did would be publicly allied with the program.

Bill Wilson was a man keenly aware of history, especially the history of other groups like his own. He studied the Washingtonians' story and wrote about the group himself. Under the title "Modesty One Plank for Good Public Relations," he wrote about the organization that had at one point enlisted almost 100,000 alcoholics who helped each other stay sober. In his article Bill listed four reasons for the complete dispersal of the Washingtonians: overdone self-advertising; competition with other organizations instead of cooperation; indulgence in controversy; refusal to stick to their original purpose of helping alcoholics.

Bill was also impressed by the story of Mary Baker Eddy, another New England teacher who had preached the connection of the soul and the body in an idea similar to those behind Alcoholics Anonymous. Eddy also believed, as did Bill, that the living could communicate with the dead. A powerful woman who had her epiphany after she fell on the ice of a New Hampshire lake and prayed herself back to health, Eddy's movement promoted the idea that all physical ailments were actually spiritual ailments and could be cured through prayer.

Although Eddy's Christian Science Church is still extant, Bill studied the way in which her movement had been damaged by both her refusal to step down as a leader and her willingness to take credit for the work of others. He was also struck by her trials with the membership of the religion she had founded.

Bill Wilson was also distressed by the absolutism of Roman Catholicism, even in the gentle interpretations of Monsignor Sheen. He hated the idea of the infallibility of the pope, and he found it hard to believe in transubstantiation—the literal rather than the metaphorical belief that the sacraments of the bread and wine became the body and blood of Christ. At heart, he was always suspicious of authority—that was part of his genius—and the authority wielded by the Roman Catholic Church and all churches was not attractive to him. "The thing that still irks me about all organized religion is their claim how confoundedly right all of them are," he wrote to Bob E., an Akron A.A. member. He also believed that a conversion to Catholicism on his part would profoundly hurt A.A. His longing for the one true church, whatever that might be, was part of his restlessness in his role as the man who represented Alcoholics Anonymous.

Bill's spiritual quest extended beyond organized religion. During the calm postwar years of the Truman presidency Bill and Lois, along with Anne and Bob Smith, continued to investigate psychic and spiritual phenomena. These days, psychic phenomena and the ways people use to understand them and identify them are completely out of favor. For Bill Wilson and Bob Smith, though, their investigations were part of a tradition of activity in rural New England at the end of the nineteenth and the beginning of the twentieth century. There was no television then and little electricity. When night fell on the small houses in New England towns, the people who lived there found other things to do. Theirs was a society intimate with death; the death rate for children was high, and even healthy men and women often died in their fifties. There were no funeral homes. The dead were laid out in their own homes and mourned before they were taken to the churchyard at the edge of town, where they were buried by those who had loved them the best.

Perhaps we are right to think that the dead are gone forever, locked away somewhere that makes communication with us impossible. Or perhaps that isn't what has happened. Perhaps what has happened is that our modern world distracts us and distances us so completely that we no longer hear the voices of the dead. Even when we are present at a deathbed, and this is a rare occurrence, the corpse is whisked away by men from the funeral home and reappears in a sanitized version, dressed and made up and laid in an expensive box.

Usually, though, the coffin is closed, and the grave prepared by strangers and then filled in by them after everyone has gone home. Today we are so removed from the process of dying and burying the dead that it's no wonder that the dead don't seem to be around. Both Bill Wilson and Bob Smith came from a different world, an old-fashioned world where the difference between the living and the dead was not as clear.

Sometimes the Wilsons used a Ouija board. A flat piece of wood marked with two lines of the alphabet and two lines of numbers, with the words "Yes" and "No" printed at the corners and the words "Goodbye" at the bottom, the board was operated by a triangular piece of plastic or light wood with a small window in its center. Lois and Bill, or two or three of the other participants, rested their fingers lightly on the board, closed their eyes, and allowed the unconscious pressure from their fingers to move the triangular marker across the smooth surface. Sometimes it stopped on Yes or No; at other times it spelled out what seemed to be words.

On evenings when they decided to use the table instead of the Ouija board, they gathered around it, each person with their fingers resting lightly on the table's sharp edge. They dimmed the lights. Bill's voice would often ask the questions. "Are there any spirits in the room?" he would ask. "Are there any spirits who have a message for us?" Breathing slowed. The spirits seemed to gather in the room's dark corners, above the shelf where Bill's violins and musical instruments were kept, or in the angle of the wall and ceiling near the window.

Then the people seated around the table would hear a soft, hesitant tap. Sometimes, if Bill had asked a direct question, the taps meant yes or no: one for yes and two for no. At other times the spirits had a longer message. If it tapped once, that meant the letter A, twice for the letter B and so on. In an evening the table might tap out a phrase or two. According to both Bill and Lois, on more than one occasion they succeeded in levitating the table a few inches off the floor.

At other times the Wilsons and their guests experimented with automatic writing. Bill Wilson was very good at this. He would set a pen down on a piece of paper, close his eyes and wait for the spirit to guide his hand. On some evenings Bill would relax his long frame out on the living room couch in front of the big stone fireplace and wait in a state of half-dreaming, half-consciousness, the smoke curling up from his cigarette. Lying there, he would receive messages, sometimes whole, as when he heard the Reverend Dwight Moody warning him against the past, and sometimes they would come to him letter by letter.

One evening the message spelled out appeared in Latin. Not knowing Latin, Bill took the message to John D. Rockefeller's associate Willard Richardson, who studied it and said it appeared to be an account of early Christianity in Italy. In Nell Wing's version of this story, Willard Richardson was in the room while Bill was receiving the message, and the Latin turned out to be a sermon written by St. Boniface. "They were working away at spiritualism," says a friend who was often a visitor there. "It wasn't just a hobby."

On a visit to Nantucket in 1947, Bill was making coffee in the dim, early morning light in the kitchen at the house of his A.A. host when he was accosted by the shade of a Norwegian sailor, complaining that he saw people dimly and that when he spoke no one listened. The sailor was soon joined by the spirit of a man who introduced himself as David Morrow. Morrow told Bill that he had been killed with Admiral Farragut during the Battle of Mobile Bay. Then, as morning came and the kitchen grew brighter, he was joined by two other spirits: former whaling captains named Pettingill and Quigley.

When Bill told this story at breakfast, he was met with friendly disbelief. People usually tried to humor Bill in order to avoid arguing with him. Later in the Wilsons' visit to Nantucket, they happened to be at the head of Main Street; there they saw a small Civil War memorial engraved with the name David Morrow. A subsequent visit to the Nantucket Whaling Museum confirmed that indeed Pettingill and Quigley had been the masters of whaling ships.

Some A.A. members were disturbed by these psychic activities and by Bill's interest in the paranormal. In the 1940s and '50s, before stepping down at the 1955 St. Louis Convention, Bill went along with the suggestions of the group and its other leaders, as if he did need to live his life in a way that would help A.A. and build the program and its precepts. But as the forties ended, Bill seemed to realize that he didn't want to spend the rest of his life as the founder and leader of Alcoholics Anonymous.

In fact, Bill Wilson's life can be seen as a struggle to achieve peaceful separations. His parents and his first girlfriend were torn away from him; Lois stayed with him even when she, perhaps, should have left. Male friends and colleagues like Hank Parkhurst and Tom Powers stormed off after working with him. It was in the task of separating from the program he had founded, built, and poured his life into expanding that he had the worst time. Was it fair that everything he did had a huge effect on A.A.? No. In his last years Bill stopped going to meetings. He was unable to be anonymous in any meeting, he complained, so he never got the benefit that meetings had for normal recovering alcoholics.

Just as some A.A. members concluded that his depressions might mean that A.A. didn't work, they now decided that Bill's search for voices beyond the grave somehow cast aspersions on the program. Closer to home, the men who worked with Bill almost every day—sophisticated men and women who had come from fields like advertising and publishing—were concerned about Bill's activities in the spook room and on the living room couch at Stepping Stones.

Some members thought the psychic activity Bill indulged in made him look crazy; others, who actually believed that he was able to summon spirits from another world, were afraid that he was speaking with evil spirits, or a hodgepodge of ghosts who would almost definitely give him bad advice or try to confuse him.

One of the members of the Chappaqua A.A. group, Tom P., remembers that he and a group of fellow recovering alcoholics got so upset about Bill's spooking that they decided to do something about it. To the men who counted themselves his followers, many of Bill's activities came to seem ones unbecoming to a great leader. Since Bill Wilson never wanted to be a leader, he was not inclined to listen.

The Chappaqua group, which met in the small, wealthy town of Chappaqua near Bedford Hills and had become the self-appointed guardian of local A.A. powers, was joined by another recovering alcoholic named Sumner Campbell and a few of the men who worked with Bill. Another one of the men, Tony Guggenheim, wrote to a man they all respected—C. S. Lewis at Cambridge, England—to describe Bill and Lois's activities and to ask what he, Lewis, thought of them. Tom P. remembers that Lewis wrote back with total disapproval. "This is necromancy," he wrote. "Have nothing to do with it." Apparently, Bill's colleagues thought that an indictment from a man like Lewis would influence Bill to change his private beliefs. Apparently, they didn't know him very well.

By this time Bill and Lois were drawing away from the many rules and regulations that the membership of Alcoholics Anonymous would have liked to impose on their lives. So despite the controversy, they continued to communicate with spirits. In the evening, with a few friends, they would watch the light fade through the big oak and maple trees and arrange themselves around a table in the room at the back of the house, or in the wooden and upholstered chairs in the double-height living room in front of the big fireplace. Sometimes they would be joined by believing neighbors, sometimes by A.A. visitors from out of town, sometimes by one or two people from the office or one of the local A.A. groups. Their séances were never a secret.

* * *

A quiet would come over them, almost as if they were conducting a group meditation. Lois would calm her beating heart and gaze out at her gardens. Up the hill, in the fading light, she could just make out the outline of Wit's End. Bill would take his place on the long sofa—one of the few pieces of furniture that could accommodate his entire length.

Outside, they could hear birdsong, the warblers and finches from the garden. Sometimes Bill would unfold his body from the sofa, take down one of his violins, and saw out some sweet country tune. Then he would lie down and there would be silence again in the room, now lit with a few candles.

There would be a slight, almost imperceptible stir in the silent air, as if someone had come invisibly to keep them company. The curtains rustled in the evening breeze. The smoke rising from the ashtray wavered. The smell of the outdoors, the new-mown grass in the summer or smoke from the piles of burning leaves in the autumn, would fade from their senses. Even the sounds from nature seemed to enter the trance. They could hear a silence beyond silence. Then there would be an almost inaudible tap, or Bill's quiet voice would begin to form a letter.

Bill and Lois had a rich past together, and on these evenings they were in the presence of the past, in the company of the Yankee householders clustered around their kitchen tables on cold nights before they had electricity. They were in the presence of all their own dead, of Bill's cousin Clarence whose sad violin had been Bill's first fiddle, and the stern Fayette and Ella Griffith, of Lois's beloved mother, and her handsome father who read Swedenborg's teachings to his children in their Clinton Street living room, of all those who had passed on before them.

Chapter Thirty-three:

St. Louis, Missouri

In 1955, Vladimir Nabokov published *Lolita,* and movie audiences watched Marilyn Monroe's white dress billow up around her as she stood on a New York subway grating in the film *The Seven Year Itch.* It was the year that Albert Einstein and Charlie Parker died, the year that a golfer named Jack Fleck beat Ben Hogan in the U.S. Open, and the year that the great horse Nashua won the Preakness and Belmont Stakes with Eddie Arcaro up. Dwight D. Eisenhower was president, teenagers were dancing to "Rock Around the Clock," and it was the year that Alcoholics Anonymous was officially turned over by its surviving founder, Bill Wilson, and its Board of Trustees to a group of elected representatives from the memberships of groups in the United States and Canada.

On the afternoon of July 3, the Kiel Auditorium in St. Louis, donated by the city fathers for the A.A. convention and the celebration of its twentieth anniversary, was packed with 5,000 of the hundreds of thousands of worldwide members. They faced a stage crowded with seventy-five delegates, the staff and secretaries from the A.A. offices in New York, Bill Wilson, his wife, Lois, and his eighty-five-year-old mother, Emily, all flanked by tripods of American flags that were echoed by the stars and stripes bunting along the balconies. A banner with the new A.A. symbol, a triangle within a circle, which represents the three legacies of Alcoholics Anonymous—recovery, unity, and service—hung above the stage where Bill stepped to the lectern for the final event of a convention that had featured three speeches by him alone as well as dozens of talks by other members and directors.

At first Bill's idea—that he and Dr. Bob and the Board of Trustees of the Alcoholic Foundation should turn Alcoholics Anonymous over to its own membership—had been met with furious opposition. How would the representatives be elected? Wouldn't that create great personal friction? Could alcoholics really run this thing? Before his death, Dr. Bob argued that the existing Board of Trustees worked too well to change. Bill had won Dr. Bob's and the foundation's permission to try and form a General Service Conference for an earlier convention in New York in 1951.

He changed the name of this new group from Foundation to Conference because alcoholics didn't like the paternal, charity sound of the word "foundation." With foundation trustee Bernard Smith, Bill suggested a system of voting that would avoid the frictions caused by personal nominations. Each group would form a conference of volunteers, and written ballots would be submitted until someone had a two-thirds vote of the members of the group. If a two-thirds majority could not be reached, Bill suggested what he remembered from the old town meetings in East Dorset: each candidate put their name in a hat and a name was impartially drawn.

Now he stood before the crowded auditorium. The child he and Dr. Bob had nurtured through thick and thin was an adult, he explained. If a seventeen-year-old boy got the family cook in trouble, he said in a parable in his speech, his father would help sort out the situation. But if a twenty-one-year-old got the cook in trouble, his father would lovingly explain that the situation was something the boy—now a man—had to handle on his own. From now on, Bill Wilson said, A.A. would handle things on its own.

By the end of three days the audience was exhausted and hushed. They had read the congratulatory telegram from President Eisenhower—"your society's record of growth and service is an inspiration"—they had heard dozens of stories and met hundreds of fellow alcoholics from all over the world. They had toasted their French counterparts, who had at first fought to keep wine as part of a nutritional diet rather than an alcoholic drink. They had met their British counterparts, who took anonymity so seriously that it was often difficult to locate a meeting.

Just before four o'clock on the afternoon of Sunday, July 3, Bill Wilson got up to speak. After a short introduction he read the resolution that he had worked so hard to produce. He wanted it to reflect his hopes of a true democracy, a democracy so fair and so without hierarchy that even alcoholics could respect it.

BE IT THEREFORE RESOLVED: That the General Service Conference of Alcoholics Anonymous should become, as of this date July 3, 1955, the guardian of the Traditions of Alcoholics Anonymous, the perpetuator of the world services of our society, the voice of the group conscience of our entire fellowship, and the sole successor to its cofounders, Dr. Bob and Bill.

When Bernard Smith asked for the vote, a roar of approval went up from the audience. People cheered and cried as Bill emotionally let go and then physically stepped down from the lectern and sat in his chair on stage. An era had ended after twenty years, during which Wilson had been obsessed with helping other alcoholics, and with establishing a program that would help them to help each other. In pursuit of this goal, he had bankrupted himself and his family, filled the precious Burnham family house in Brooklyn with drunks and crazy people and then lost the house, inflicted two years of homelessness on his wife and himself, and devoted twenty-four hours a day to thinking, writing, and producing a document which he hoped would provide the program with a structure that would allow it to survive. "Clearly my job henceforth was to Let Go and Let God," he wrote after the 1955 convention. "Alcoholics Anonymous was safe—even from me."

The 1955 convention was also a symbolic triumph for Bill Wilson. His mother, Emily, was there, now a wealthy octogenarian with a comfortable life in San Diego. Bill had bought his mother a few shares of Giant Portland Cement back in the 1920s, and while he drank his luck away, she had become an astute investor. Nell Wing, Bill's New York secretary, who would become so close to Bill and Lois that she practically lived at Stepping Stones in Bedford Hills during Bill's last years, was there. Father Ed Dowling was there, the Jesuit priest who had appeared in the rain at the old 24th Street office one night when Bill was filled with despair. The Jesuit priest had become the most important man in Bill's spiritual life—a man Bill could really talk with, a man he considered his "spiritual sponsor." "Father Ed is made of the stuff of saints," Bill explained when he introduced Dowling as a speaker during the convention.

Willard Richardson and Frank Amos from the Rockefeller Foundation were at the convention, and Bill remembered his desperation when John D. Rockefeller nixed Amos's recommendation that he give A.A. a $50,000 start. Dr. Harry Tiebout, the first psychiatrist to recognize the work of A.A., and a man Bill had consulted about his depressions, had come to St. Louis from Greenwich, Connecticut, to speak at the convention, along with Bill's friend and adviser Dr. Jack Norris, associate medical director of Eastman Kodak in Rochester, New York, who was an admirer of A.A. and a member of the Foundation Board, which he chaired for seventeen years.

Bill's longtime friend the great preacher Sam Shoemaker was there. Shoemaker had introduced Bill to the Oxford Group and then been part of the group's breakup with Bill Wilson's bunch of drunks. Also there as Bill's special guest was Ebby Thacher, his old friend from Manchester Village and his partner in drunken escapades.

Bill Wilson's connections to people and their ideas were always passionate and sometimes problematical. He wrote again and again that it was important to place "principles before personalities." This was hard for him. Personalities were sparked by Bill's outsized ego and intelligence, and he often sparked back. In reading, however, Bill Wilson was able to receive ideas without any of the static caused by the people who propounded those ideas. Reading allowed him to understand principles without having to deal with personalities. His own work, especially the St. Louis resolution, is an amalgam of the principles that were the underpinning of his own thinking.

The St. Louis convention was a time for Bill to think about and honor everyone who had helped him, whether they were there in the audience or merely responsible for the seething mass of ideas and stories that he had in his head. "At the convention it was widely appreciated for the first time that nobody had invented Alcoholics Anonymous," he wrote in his account of the convention titled *Alcoholics Anonymous Comes of Age,* "that many streams of influence and many people, some of them nonalcoholics, had helped by the grace of God to achieve A.A.'s purpose."

The convention also showed the continuing importance of two books: the second edition of *Alcoholics Anonymous,* in which the case history section—the personal stories that make up the second half—had been expanded, and A.A.'s *Twelve Steps and Twelve Traditions,* which Bill Wilson had been working on for four years in the shack at Stepping Stones with some editorial assistance from Tom Powers and Betty Love. Published in 1953, the "Twelve and Twelve," as it came to be known, had sold almost 50,000 copies by 1957.

"For Lois and me the autumn of life has now rolled around," Bill told the conventioneers. "For your sake and for ours we think that we should no longer pursue the strenuous activities of other days. We feel that we are facing a season of reflection on all that has happened."

In July of 1955, Bill Wilson was a handsome fifty-nine-year-old with an electrifying way of telling a good story and a penchant for public speaking. For the first time in his life he had a home and enough income to live comfortably, thanks to steady sales of the book *Alcoholics Anonymous*, which had topped 300,000. Twenty-one years had passed since he had had a drink, twenty-one years since his epiphany on the upper floors of Towns Hospital on Central Park West. Thirty-three years stood between Bill on the stage of the Kiel Auditorium and that awkward lieutenant in a new Army uniform, mingling uneasily at an elegant cocktail party.

During the fifteen years before the convention, Bill Wilson had suffered from another bout of crippling depression. He was often sick. "Those terrible colds," he wrote to his mother. Sometimes, if he made it up to the shack to work, he suddenly would be so overwhelmed that he put his head down on the desk and the day's work was over. After the convention Bill's depression lifted. For the last sixteen years of his life, the sixteen years after he turned A.A. over to its members, he embarked on a series of adventures and conducted a series of experiments in a search to find help for other alcoholics as well as for himself. He involved himself with activities and interests that might not have been appropriate for an official founder and head of Alcoholics Anonymous, but which were fascinating and informative for plain old Bill Wilson. Bill Wilson was not the stuff of saints.

Chapter Thirty-four:

Marty Mann

Bill Wilson was incapable of a dispassionate connection to anything. He had great appetites for almost everything he liked. When he drank, he drank to oblivion. When he decided to be in love with Lois Burnham that day at the Emerald Lake railway stop, they were engaged within a few hours. He was as stubborn as he was passionate. He didn't just smoke; he sucked in cigarettes, not wanting to miss a puff. He didn't just have friends; he had close friends who loved him or hated him. A psychoanalyst might say that Bill Wilson's history with men, with a jolly father who abandoned him and a taciturn, Yankee grandfather who could hardly bear to love him, made it hard for him to have a calm, day-to-day friendship with anyone he really cared about.

Tom Powers, who was hired as the official A.A. writer in 1948 and traveled with Bill and worked with him on *Twelve Steps and Twelve Traditions,* has feelings that are typical of the way loyalty to Bill Wilson sometimes turned to anger. Powers is ninety-one, and lives in East Ridge, the commune in upstate New York he founded after breaking with Bill over Bill's behavior in 1958. If Bill Wilson's fiery connections to some of his male friends made trouble, his connections to women made even more trouble. Bill's relationships with women were sometimes professional and loving, and sometimes passionate and sexual. Bill's first relationship with a woman was with his mother. "Neither Dorothy nor I have ever stood in quite the right relation to mother in spite of our efforts to do so," he wrote Emily's California doctor, Dr. Fred Breithut, in 1946, ten years after the death of Emily's second husband, Charles Strobel.

Although Bill spent time and energy taking care of his mother as she aged, putting her on stage at the St. Louis convention and finally bringing her to live at Bedford Hills, he continued to turn to her as if he were the little boy he never got to be. The need was mutual. When he hurt his foot on a walk in the woods during one of his dozens of stays at the Londonderry Inn, the eighty-three-year-old Emily wrote to her fifty-seven-year-old son, "If I had been with you in Londonderry I would have kept just as quiet as a little mouse. I could have taken care of you when you were hurt."

Bill's relationship with his stepmother, Christine, who had married his father in Vancouver, was also strange and unsatisfying. Gilman and Christine lived in a shack in the Canadian wilderness at the north end of Kootenay Lake, so far from civilization that it took Bill days to visit them when passage was even possible. He sent them money to install plumbing. Christine wrote back saying they preferred to leave things the way they were. He invited them to Bedford Hills. Christine wrote back saying no thank you, no thank you very much.

When Gilman was finally old and sick enough to have Christine agree, Wilson arranged for them to live in the house of an A.A. family in Vancouver. There they were both cared for by a nurse that he paid for. That wasn't good enough either, according to Christine. The house where they were staying was too noisy, Christine wrote her supportive stepson. In one typical letter she let out her worst fears. In order to sleep she had to take out her hearing aid, she wrote. She had awakened one morning to find herself tied to the bed. Gilman had used his belt to fasten her hands and torso while she slept. He did it, he explained, so that she couldn't leave him. "I have spared you sacrifice by sacrificing myself," Christine wrote.

In addition to these complicated relationships with women in his family, Bill lost his first girlfriend—the woman in whom he had rested all his new hopes as a young man—to a tragic sudden death. And Bill grew up in a different time, in a world in which people believed that men liked sex and women didn't, a world in which a man got as much sexual satisfaction as he could before he settled down for the tamer satisfactions of procreation, a world in which birth control was a sometime thing. One of the great female influences in Bill Wilson's life was Marty Mann, who came to the Clinton Street meeting one night in 1939, after being enticed to a fancy dinner on Sutton Place given by a wealthy A.A. couple who then lured her to Brooklyn. In 1939 there were only two A.A. meetings anywhere— at Clinton Street and in Akron—and many of the men who had gotten sober in A.A. did not believe that a woman could be an alcoholic.

Mann had become despairing and desperate after her alcoholism had led to a long stay at the Blythewood Sanitarium, which in turn had led to confinement at Bellevue Hospital in Manhattan. Soon after being welcomed by the Wilsons to their Brooklyn living room, she found herself being piled into a car with another couple for the drive to Cleveland, where a few men were trying to start a new meeting.

Marty and Bill became great friends and colleagues. For the first few months after surviving the Cleveland trip, Marty would get sober and relapse, get sober and relapse. On one of her last relapses, when she had escaped from Bellevue and was on her way to the liquor store, she spotted a skinny derelict outside her own apartment building, a man dressed in a frayed peacoat with too-short sleeves. Bill had come to help her get sober again. He was trying to help a fellow alcoholic, but from an outsider's point of view, he looked worse than the people he was trying to help. In his zeal to teach what he knew, he had let his appearance and his finances slide. Marty later said that she took him in and invited him upstairs, because she felt sorry for him. She got sober again.

In many ways Marty Mann was a perfect teacher for Bill Wilson, who quickly became her sponsor, the person delegated to guide a newcomer through the twelve steps, and into life as a sober person. Marty Mann was educated and glamorous. She had lived in Italy and spent years in London, where she hung out with the Bloomsbury group and made friends with Vita Sackville-West and Nancy Cunard. Marty's drinking had taken her to the proprietorship of a small hotel in the Cotswolds, home on the *Queen Mary*, and to long stays in Doctors' Hospital, a facility established so that wealthy patients would have the comforts of home when they were sick. Finally, she ended up in Bellevue Hospital and at Blythewood. Because Marty was a lesbian, her friendship with Bill was never complicated by his erotic hunger, or by the adulation, sometimes expressed physically and erotically, that many women came to feel toward him. Wilson heard Marty Mann's fifth step—the reading of the fearless moral inventory that A.A. members write in the fourth step—"Made a searching and fearless moral inventory of ourselves." Hearing a fifth step, in which the person reading or speaking talks about everything they have ever done that has caused them shame, anger, guilt, fear, or resentment, creates an unusual and intense kind of intimacy.

Marty's journey to the depths of alcoholism had gone on for years; she was often attended by loving friends and brilliant doctors, but no one knew what was wrong with her. To read her story is to revisit the sad ignorance that the medical establishment had about alcoholism as recently as the 1930s. When *Alcoholics Anonymous* was first published, and called the Big Book because Bill Wilson feared it was too short and had it printed on the thickest paper the association could afford, the American Medical Association panned it. "This book is a curious combination of organizing propaganda and religious exhortation," read the AMA review. Not that they had a better idea. Most alcoholics, if they were ever even diagnosed, were given a hopeless prognosis. They could try expensive drug and rest cures like those at Towns Hospital or at the Austen Riggs Center in Stockbridge, Massachusetts, but everyone knew that these cures only worked as long as the alcoholic was incarcerated. This kind of ignorance was especially apparent when it came to women. Neurological wards were crowded with women suffering from alcoholic neuropathy, and asylums were filled with women whose problem was nothing more than an addiction to alcohol.

Chance and determination had saved Marty Mann. In England, on one of the days she had promised to quit drinking, she came upon William Seabrook's account of stopping drinking titled *Asylum*. Seabrook, who later relapsed, had found sobriety at the Westchester Psychiatric Hospital. Mann headed for New York and ended up in Bellevue under the care of the famous Dr. Foster Kennedy. His best idea was to put her in a neurological ward for another six months. At Bellevue she met Dr. Harry Tiebout, a Greenwich, Connecticut, psychiatrist, who sometimes visited Bellevue looking for patients for Blythewood, his new mental hospital in Connecticut.

Mann and her alcoholism confused and frustrated Tiebout just as other patients' alcoholism had been confusing and frustrating doctors for years. Then one day in 1939 an early galley of the book *Alcoholics Anonymous* found its way into his hands through a friend of a friend who needed a doctor to read it because its authors—Bill Wilson and his A.A. editors—wanted to be sure that there was nothing medically objectionable in the book. Tiebout called Marty Mann before he had even finished reading. She devoured the book but was reluctant to meet the men responsible. Tiebout arranged to have her taken to Brooklyn after the dinner in Sutton Place.

Those were the early days of A.A., the lean times before the group really even had a name. After Marty had relapsed and been sobered up and relapsed again, Bill and Lois took her to the summer camp where they were living on Green Pond in the Poconos—an uninsulated shack that had been lent to them by an A.A. member. There Marty got sick, was nursed back to health by Lois, and shivered through the winter with Bill. The house was heated by an ancient woodstove. To pass the time on nights when it was too cold to sleep, or when rain was dripping in through the leaky frame roof, Marty and Bill stayed up talking. She brought a new balance to his thinking, as well as a new sophistication.

Marty Mann was a writer, and a practical thinker like Bill. Her friendship shifted his view of women, but it also broadened his views dramatically on the subject of homosexuality, especially when Marty fell in love with and lived with *Vogue* editor Priscilla Peck, a beautiful young New Yorker who also got sober through A.A. This broadening led to his writing of the third tradition, provoked by a letter from an Ohio group about a member whom they considered a sexual deviant.

Marty also became a kind of literary alter ego for her friend Bill. In the 1950s and '60s homosexuals were openly demonized. In many states homosexual activity was illegal. At Smith College the brilliant teacher and critic Newton Arvin had federal agents barge in and arrest him for nothing more than having sexual pictures of men in his possession. The Army-McCarthy hearings featured Senator Joe McCarthy ranting about the evils of homosexuality. Although Marty kept her sexual orientation a secret, knowing how much the scandal over it might hurt her cause, her friends knew that she was a lesbian. She set a precedent for the importance of

keeping sexual secrets from the public and even from the membership of A.A.

As a glamorous, smart gay woman in the 1940s in the United
States, Marty Mann became a figure in a certain kind of literary set.
She had long affairs with Carson McCullers and Paul Bowles's wife,
Jane, neither of whom was ready to change her ways and stop drink-
ing. McCullers, who fell hard for Marty, continued to hang around,
trying to get sober, long after their affair was over.

*   *   *

Lois Wilson was a complicated woman with complicated reactions
to her husband's moods and behavior. Their relationship began
when Bill was psychically so fragile that he had dropped out of
school and quit work and had become, for the moment, an unsuccessful salesman with time on his hands. Lois knew what she was
taking on, but for reasons of her own she patiently persevered.

While Bill was still drinking, Lois's tolerance seemed to consti-
tute a disease of its own. A normal woman would have kicked such
a man out—that's how it seems to many people, as they hear or read
the stories of Bill's broken promises, followed by more desperate
promises, all of them desperately broken. Lois seemed to have an in-
exhaustible tolerance for Bill's bad behavior.

In 1954, the year after Wilson's father Gilman died in the house
in Vancouver, Lois had a heart attack that brought them all up
short. Lois had never been sick, and indeed she lived long after her
husband to be an active nonagenarian. She had spent the day before
shoveling snow out of the Bedford Hills driveway and then gone
into New York to celebrate her wedding anniversary on January 24
with Bill. He was staying at the Bedford Hotel, as he often did during the week. While she was shopping, Lois began to have chest
pains as well as severe pains in both arms. She went to the movies,

and for a while the pain went away, but then it came back. She called the Bedford, she called the A.A. office, but she couldn't find Bill. Eventually, she dragged herself to his room at the Bedford and called her brother-in-law, Leonard Strong, who called an ambulance. The doctors prescribed a year of rest for her ailing heart.

Chapter Thirty-five:

526 Bedford Road

Almost twenty-five years after Bill Wilson's death, years in which many aspects of his work and his experience have been studied and restudied, some parts of his life, including his sex life, are still officially secret. Many people know a few facts about Bill Wilson's life. Well-informed people who have read the two authorized biographies that Lois read and approved— *"Pass It On,"* published anonymously in 1984, and Robert Thomsen's *Bill W.* published in 1975—know that Bill Wilson palled around with Robert Oppenheimer and thought about moving to the Institute for Advanced Study in Princeton, New Jersey, and that he took LSD, as well as niacin and vitamin B. People know that he flirted with the idea of converting to Roman Catholicism and had regular sessions with the Reverend Fulton Sheen, and that he was friends with Aldous Huxley and Gerald Heard.

It's also no secret that Bill Wilson believed in life after death and that he received visits from spirits and ghosts, and in one case a group of men who had been long dead. Visitors smile indulgently when they are shown the spook room on the first floor of Stepping Stones. But Bill's sex life is still a secret, something A.A. members buzz about over coffee after meetings, but something which has been excised from the official literature and—for the most part— from the official A.A. archives.

During the fifteen years after the St. Louis convention, Bill tried many experiments, some wise and some not so wise. All of them are subjects that have found their way into what is called "conference-approved literature," with one exception: sex. Because Bill's sexual behavior is shrouded in secrecy, discussions about it evoke passion. Some people believe that none of it is true; others claim that Bill was a sexual compulsive whose need for sex compromised every-thing else he believed in. One person believes that after Lois's heart attack, Bill was plotting with a mistress to move to Ireland after Lois died, and the sooner the better. Another says that Bill had to have sex two or three times a day, that he organized his A.A. travels around this need, and that this compulsion and the resulting ex-haustion were the true reason for his depressions.

Certainly, some of Bill's problems with the men he worked with had to do with his sexual attraction to and for the women he worked with—whether or not he acted on it. Most of those who knew and worked with Bill say that he certainly had a sex life outside of his marriage to Lois. He "stepped off the reservation," they say, still using one of the old-fashioned euphemisms of the time when it hap-pened.

"He was torn, he was really torn," says a man who worked with Bill in those years, reflecting the opinions of many of Bill's col-leagues. Many people in A.A. worried that Bill Wilson's sexual be-havior would be discovered and reflect badly on the movement. Whether or not they were necessary, self-appointed "Bill watchers" usually stayed close to him at meetings and conferences to prevent him from interacting with attractive newcomers in a way that might appear unseemly. These men also served the purpose of warning away members who might take up too much of Bill's time. Bill's well-meaning friends kept him from interacting with newcomers, male or female, although Bill himself was the man who discovered the efficacy of a drunk talking with another drunk. His program's success had become Bill's worst enemy.

Members tell a story about Bill running a red light in Brooklyn when he happened to have his woman of the moment in the car. The policeman pulled the car over and began writing out a ticket. Knowing that being stopped in these circumstances would raise hell with the trustees—and with the public if word got out—Bill, by then a celebrity, engaged the policeman in conversation and revealed who he was: Bill Wilson, the founder of Alcoholics Anonymous. By coincidence the cop had two brothers who had gotten sober through the program, and he was thrilled to meet Bill, and pretty soon there were smiles and autographs all around. For those who had devoted their lives to protecting Bill Wilson's image, it was a scary story.

Lois made enough of a peace with her husband's behavior to keep it under wraps. In the last fifteen years of his life, Bill spent many nights in New York City, after nonchalantly walking down from Stepping Stones to the Bedford Hills train station with that loping, easy gait of his. Although Bill and Lois had a passionate physical relationship at the beginning, his years of drinking certainly damaged that. In *Alcoholics Anonymous,* Bill frankly discussed the impotence that afflicts many alcoholic men after they get sober. A photograph of Bill and Lois in 1957 shows a raffish man who might be in his thirties with his long arm around a kindly looking white-haired woman with her blouse buttoned up to the chin. He was sixty-three, and she was sixty-seven. They look like mother and son.

Lois lived almost seventeen years after Bill died. Seventeen years during which she read and organized the voluminous papers that had moved with the two of them from place to place and which were finally stored in the basement of a house in Bedford Hills that she built for her secretary. Although the papers hadn't been indexed or properly archived until recently, Lois seemed to have read them all. Many of the letters are annotated in her handwriting; others have notes on them from her to direct the reader's attention. "First drink," says a note clipped to the letter Bill wrote her about having a beer at the rarebit dinner in Newport. However, nothing in the archives directly documents Bill's life with other women. In his book about Bill Wilson, *Bill W.,* Francis Hartigan, who served as Lois's secretary for a while after Bill's death, paints him as an unreliable womanizer. Nan Robertson in her 1988 book, *Getting Better,* also briefly discusses Bill's sex life.

The archives contain photographs of Bill playfully embracing visitors in skimpy bathing-suit tops, and Bill leaning toward women in low-cut dresses in restaurants. As the power and fame of A.A. grew, Bill was beloved by many people, some of them very attractive women. He loved them back. Bill was human, extraordinarily human. In many ways, with sex, with smoking, with depression, his life was a constant struggle—and that struggle is what made him a great teacher. Many of the suggestions in the Twelve Steps of Alcoholics Anonymous, both in the book by the same name and in *Twelve Steps and Twelve Traditions,* are about sex and sexual needs. In the book *Alcoholics Anonymous* the most egregious example of a wrong that can be done but which ultimately must be forgiven has to do with betrayal and philandering. In his discussion of Step Four, Bill used a hypothetical situation in which an alcoholic might be resentful because a friend told his wife about the alcoholic's mistress.

In all his writings, Bill identified the sex drive, along with the drive for security and status, as a natural human trait that could at times rage out of control, often causing an alcoholic to drink. The Twelve Steps, with their admission of powerlessness, categorizing of past sins, confession, and restitution and call to prayer, meditation, and service, are meant as a behavioral goal, not as an A.A. admissions test. Progress, not perfection, Bill Wilson wrote. We are not saints. Bill Wilson's humanness does not diminish him, it makes him a writer, guide, and teacher who understands what it is to be human.

In trying to find a way to accommodate his sexual desires while also maintaining his ability to help other alcoholics by being a representative of A.A., Bill Wilson ran straight up against a kind of weird American duality. We are the most puritanical country on earth, and the most profligate. We like our vices simple and our virtues even simpler. It seems impossible, or at least unacceptable, that a man whose brilliant spiritual development caused him to turn down honors and refuse gifts of money was also flawed by sexual compulsion. Sexual compulsion itself is still a confusing secret in our world, even today. On the one hand, we chuckle at a sexually compulsive athlete, and even encourage the circumstances of their compulsion, but on the other hand we decry it. Our girls must be virgins, but they must also be sophisticated. Our boys must be man enough to score, but also gentleman enough to provide emotional and permanent financial support for any child they father.

In the world in which Bill Wilson matured, men were assumed to be sexually driven creatures whose bestial desires could only be tamed by the love of a gentle woman, if they were lucky enough to find that gentle woman. In the meantime, bundling boards—low walls clapped into place across the bed—and homemade chastity belts were used to keep the beast at bay. In a world without birth control, the general result was men trying to express themselves sexually and women, terrified of pregnancy, failing to respond. In a world where infant mortality was a fact of life and most people didn't live beyond the age of fifty, sex had a different role to play. It was business rather than pleasure, and it was business that men craved and women loathed. As Bill Wilson became more famous, and the 1960s unfolded into a full-blown sexual revolution, whatever inhibitions he may have had were swept away.

"In the religion of the once-born the world is a sort of rectilinear or one-storied affair whose accounts are kept in one denomination, whose parts have just the values which naturally they appear to have, and of which a simple algebraic sum of pluses and minuses will give the total worth," writes William James in *Varieties of Religious Experience*, a book that Bill read and reread. "In the religion of the twice-born on the other hand, the world is a double-storied mystery. Peace cannot be reached by the simple addition of pluses and elimination of minuses from life." James then cites Alphonse Daudet's complaint that he is "homo duplex," forever a being split between the good Alphonse and the "terrible second me." Bill Wilson was clearly a homo duplex, a man with a terrible second me.

James himself had no patience for the reductionism that would diminish great teachers because of their humanity. In a furious argument against those who say that the real reason behind Martin Luther's Reformation was that Luther was gay, he points out that there is often a complicated cause for a positive, spiritual result.

Bill Wilson's sexual life didn't interfere with his work life, although it certainly gave another dimension to his spiritual life. He and Lois spent every Thanksgiving together at the Londonderry Inn in South Londonderry, Vermont. Whenever he needed time to think or write, or just to walk out his depressions, Bill also returned to South Londonderry for peace and quiet, and for access to the comforts and memories of East Dorset over the mountain. He is remembered there as a quiet guy. He and Lois traveled together all over the world, year after year. Every Sunday afternoon they hosted a kind of A.A. open house at Bedford Hills. It was Lois in the end who nursed Bill through the final months before his death from emphysema.

Of all the women Bill was close to outside his marriage, none had as much of an impact as Helen Wynn, an actress whom he met at a meeting in the 1950s, and who shortly after their meeting went to work at the offices in New York on the staff of the organization's newsletter the *AA Grapevine*. Lois and Helen knew each other; Lois certainly knew what was happening. Helen worked diligently and became the editor of the *Grapevine,* and helped shape it into a bulletin that carried news as well as Bill's writing and essays from members all over the country.

Helen was born in Utah and by the age of seventeen was managing a bookstore in Duluth, Minnesota. Interested in psychology, she traveled with two friends to Vienna to study with the psychiatrist Alfred Adler—the founder of the Adlerian therapy practiced by Emily Wilson in San Diego. When the money was gone, Helen left a series of postdated letters with her friends to be mailed to her parents and took off for New York, where she got a job at Macy's. She began acting in summer stock, founded the Surry Arts Players, and married fellow player Shepperd Strudwick in 1936. They had a son, and divorced in 1946. Helen and her son eventually moved to a house near Stepping Stones on Bedford Road in Pleasantville. Some of the time Bill Wilson lived there too.

Helen was younger than Bill, apparently very attractive, but with a positive spirit that made people forget her good looks. She came into A.A. with a great deal of gratitude and willingness to help. When a close associate of Bill's needed help, Helen would often be delegated. One old-timer remembers that when his wife needed medical care, Helen dressed up in her best suit and went off to find it for them. Helen and Bill became a couple in many ways, both in the New York office, where people remember them together, and in Helen's house at 526 Bedford Road in Pleasantville. Although there is no direct evidence of Bill's relationship with Helen except the stories of those who remember them, there are many letters from Helen to A.A. members referring to Bill in a way that made it clear he was staying with her.

Helen was always broke, though, a condition that Bill could relate to. To alleviate her financial problems, Bill decided that she would inherit a percentage of his royalties from the book *Alcoholics Anonymous,* which by this time was a solid moneymaker. Some oldtimers remember that Bill had larger financial dreams for Helen. They worked together on the experiments and distribution of LSD and niacin, which became one of Bill's late-life enthusiasms. Some A.A. old-timers say that Lucille and David Kahn, the couple who financed much of the LSD research, were poised to give a lump sum for a research headquarters to be run by Helen. Ultimately, that didn't happen.

Then the A.A. trustees—the new truly democratic government of A.A.—refused to allow Helen the percentage of the *Alcoholics Anonymous* royalties that Bill had earmarked for her. Eventually, they gave in and helped Bill execute a new royalty agreement that gave Helen 10 percent of his book royalties after his death and Lois 90 percent. For the most part, though, all three players in this odd drama seem to have kept their heads. Helen bought a house in Ireland, perhaps for herself and Bill, but he never lived there.

Bill Wilson's sexual behavior didn't go unchallenged even by those closest to him. Tom Powers remembers going to Stepping Stones and meeting Bill for a day of writing. Sometimes Bill would write at one desk while Tom edited and wrote at another. Other times, exhausted from his own internal struggles, Bill would just put his head down on the desk and weep. "Bill was crashingly and murderously depressed all the time," Powers remembers. Powers, whose wife had divorced him, would scold Bill about his sex life. "This sex thing ran through the whole business," Powers says. "It wasn't just an episode."

Powers believes that if Lois had refused to accept what was happening, she might have had a greater effect on her husband's behavior than she did. "If Lois had thrown Bill out of the house," Powers believes, "he might have straightened out." Everyone agrees that no matter what happened, Bill continued to love his loyal, feisty wife of more than fifty years. Bill's penchant for pretty women seemed to wane once he took up with Helen Wynn. Suddenly, it was too late for Lois to kick him out. He had a place to go (Helen's house) and he often went there. If Lois wouldn't nurse him when he had a cold or felt depressed, Helen would.

According to Tom Powers, Bill's inability to change was the reason Powers ultimately left A.A. and started his own recovery program in Hankins, New York. Powers believed that, as he remembers, "Bill had to get this sex thing straightened out in program terms so he wasn't lying about it all the time." Bill would agree, and then relapse, Powers says. But by this time Bill was a special kind of celebrity, a man who had no trouble finding people who agreed with him. And in fact, Bill wasn't lying to anyone about his behavior either. Lois knew, and somehow accepted what was happening, at least enough to enable their life together to continue. The men and women who worked with him knew. As for everyone else, now that he was a private man and A.A. was administered by its own members, his private life wasn't really anyone else's business.

Chapter Thirty-six:

The Family Afterward

In many ways Bill Wilson's reflections on his sexual behavior and the conflicts it provoked both within himself and within the membership of Alcoholics Anonymous are a subtext of *Twelve Steps and Twelve Traditions,* the book he wrote in the shack above Stepping Stones in the early 1950s. "When and how, and in just what instances did my selfish pursuit of the sex relation damage other people and me?" Bill wrote in Step Four. "Just how did I react to these situations at the time? Did I burn with a guilt that nothing can extinguish? Or did I insist that I was the pursued and not the pursuer and thus absolve myself? How have I reacted to frustration in sexual matters? When denied did I become vengeful or depressed? Did I take it out on other people? If there was rejection or coldness at home, did I use this as a reason for promiscuity?"

In Step Six, he notes that "since most of us are born with an abundance of natural desires, it isn't strange that we often let these far exceed their intended purpose." And in Step Nine, where the alcoholic is urged to make restitution, Bill notes that "we cannot for example unload a detailed account of extramarital adventuring upon the shoulders of the unsuspecting wife or husband. And even in those cases where such a matter must be discussed, let's try to avoid harming third parties whoever they may be."

By being sexually less than perfect, Bill seems to have given his own trustees a weapon against him. He had a weakness; they knew his weakness. Another colleague tells about being in New York City's Roosevelt Hotel during a three-day A.A. convention when Bill and everyone else was working twenty-four hours to provide the thousands of visitors with all the information and inspiration they could possibly want. Wandering the halls late at night, Bill stepped into a room where two men were writing a summary of the events, working against an early morning deadline. He sat down and talked and wept for hours, one of the men there said, adding, "He just spilled his guts out. We turned off the tape recorder."

Apparently, there were days and nights when both Helen and Bill thought that they might end up together. Lois could die; Bill could leave her. One story has another friend staying up all night to talk Bill out of leaving his wife. Whatever Bill did or didn't do, and in these last fifteen years of his life he seemed to pack in many of the things he may have been putting off for decades, it's clear that he would never have done anything to damage the foundation of A.A. For the good of A.A., he declined the degree from Yale he wanted so much; for the good of A.A. he did many things—and it may have been for the good of A.A. that he refused to leave his wife, the woman who had been in many ways a cofounder of and contributor to the program.

Bill Wilson's nature sometimes seemed to have been designed for the task at hand—the job of synthesizing six or seven different streams of philosophical thought, some from books, some from other teachers, and some from the very air he breathed while growing up in a small Vermont town. He had the understanding to see what worked and what didn't work for himself as well as for other drunks, and the stubbornness to persist in trying to help his tiny program spread, even when doctors said he was crazy, when Frank Buchman said he was "not maximum," and when he had so little money that he often didn't know where he and his wife would sleep. His experiences—as a child growing up in a temperance state, as an

Army officer, as a Vermonter—all added up to a background that helped him understand the way power and political opinions could corrupt even the best intentions of the most intelligent people. He was not a perfect man, but he was the perfect man for the job.

*   *   *

One of the secrets of the endurance of Alcoholics Anonymous as Bill Wilson laid it out in his writing is the way it revels in its own paradox. It does not avoid contradiction; in fact, it embraces contradiction. Even as it maintains the tension between the two strains in American religious thought—the evangelical strain and the self-realization and self-help strain—it also contains a powerful energy source in its ability to hold two contrasting ideas on any one subject at the same time. "Consistency is the hobgoblin of small minds," Ralph Waldo Emerson noted, and in this regard, Bill Wilson had one of the larger minds of his century.

One of the principal tensions built into the A.A. literature as early as the 1930s concerns the role of the alcoholic's family both when the alcoholic is still drinking and after he or she has entered A.A. and, perhaps, has stopped drinking. Of course, this was an area in which Lois Wilson felt she was an expert, but when she asked her husband to let her write a chapter in the book *Alcoholics Anonymous,* he declined, giving the excuse that the book should be written in one style. Perhaps he understood that it took a particular kind of mind to present both sides of so many problems at the same time. In the chapter entitled "To Wives," Wilson urges women to separate themselves, lovingly, from their husbands' behavior. If the alcoholic wants to stop drinking, he teaches, the best help he or she can get is from other alcoholics. He warns families not to try to shield their alcoholic spouses from temptation. "If he gets drunk, don't blame yourself," he writes. "God has either removed your husband's liquor problem or he has not." This is the attitude which Lois, Anne

Smith, and the other wives of early recovering alcoholics used to create a basis for Al-Anon.

However, the very next chapter in the book, "The Family Afterward," sounds a different note. In this chapter Bill tells the story of a man who gave up drinking but continued to smoke and drink coffee. His wife thought that these activities were almost as bad as drinking. She nagged him so much that he went back to drinking. The man in Chapter 8, in other words, will drink or not, depending on his own readiness, the help he gets from other people like him, and whether or not God has removed his drinking problems. The man in Chapter 9, however, can easily be driven to drink by a little marital nagging. Of course, both of these things are true. The balance that creates a successful family around an alcoholic is trickier than the balance of a tightrope artist on a bicycle. Families of alcoholics must both separate themselves from the alcoholic and involve themselves intimately with the alcoholic, and they must do this at the same time. The difficulty of striking this balance in a way that benefits all concerned has helped build Al-Anon into a program with millions of members. In writing, Bill Wilson was able to present and embrace both points of view, creating a tension between the two poles like the tension that keeps a high wire suspended.

Another place in *Alcoholics Anonymous* in which two contradictory ideas are advocated by Bill Wilson is the area of addictive problems left to be solved after an alcoholic stops drinking: problems like smoking, coffee drinking, food addictions, gambling, irresponsibility with money, and sexual compulsiveness. In one way, an alcoholic who stops drinking is a walking miracle, a man or woman whose life has been so changed that the addiction that twined through all of his or her behavior has been removed. But what if this miraculously recovered alcoholic is a chain-smoking gambler who continues to snarl up the family finances and endanger his or her own health and the health of the family? There are no answers to these questions, of course, only paradoxes, balances, daily readjustments. In embracing the two sides of each of these questions in his writing, Bill Wilson left room for each alcoholic to find his or her own accommodation with recovery.

Even the principle of anonymity, which is the subject of Step Twelve and Tradition Twelve, had two sides to be argued. If a famous person publicly said that Alcoholics Anonymous had saved his or her life, that might help hundreds of other alcoholics by causing them to seek help. If this person drank again, the efficacy of A.A. could be compromised. In averring that Alcoholics Anonymous should recruit by "attraction not promotion," and cramping the style of the evangelical element of his fellowship, Bill Wilson seemed to be inviting sober men and women to break their anonymity. How can people be attracted to something unless they know it exists? What is more attractive than to have someone who is admired leading the way?

Marty Mann chafed at this restriction of anonymity. Bill himself was often tempted to push the anonymity question aside. His fellowship is based on a brotherhood of equals, at the same time he knew how much people needed leadership.

When it came to secrets, Bill again faced both sides of a difficult issue. "Nothing pays off like restraint of pen and tongue," he wrote. At the same time, he stated early in the book *Alcoholics Anonymous* that the one requirement for sobriety was "rigorous honesty." But what would happen when restraint of pen and tongue led to withholding of information, which in turn conflicted with rigorous honesty? Marty Mann, for instance, kept her sexual preferences a secret for years. She called herself "Mrs. Marty Mann," although she wasn't married, in order to protect her secret.

Yet when Bill wanted to keep his sexual behavior secret, he was met with controversy. It seemed to some men in A.A. that Wilson should try to keep this aspect of his life under wraps. Others thought he should divorce Lois. After all, once he had stepped down from being the official leader of A.A. in 1955, wasn't his private life once again private? This question was furiously argued within the group of men and women who were close to Bill. Some of them saw a clear solution; Bill should stop behaving that way; he of all people should be flawless.

When Bill said and wrote, as he often did, that no one person had founded Alcoholics Anonymous, and that its ideas were a synthesis of many components, from William James to Swedenborgian thought to Vermont democracy to the lessons of dozens of mistakes made in the early years of the fellowship, he was right. Yet out of his personal genius came this ability to present both sides of many, many issues, thus leaving plenty of space for the struggles that characterize the lives of individuals and families.

CHAPTER THIRTY-SEVEN:

CARL JUNG

After 1955, Bill Wilson seemed to be looking for teachers because he was weary of being the teacher himself. Unfortunately, many of his students weren't ready for the idea that he could be just another student. He gracefully stepped off the pedestal in St. Louis, but in the minds of many people who had put him there, he would always be there. Through Gerald Heard, Aldous Huxley and his brother Julian, Bill had heard about the work of two doctors, Abram Hoffer and Humphry Osmond. Hoffer and Osmond, the founders of what they called orthomolecular psychiatry, were experimenting with the possibility of helping schizophrenics and alcoholics with a substance called lysergic acid diethylamide, manufactured in Switzerland by a company called Sandoz.

Huxley, on the rebound from an unsatisfactory stint as a Hollywood writer; the charismatic Heard; Drs. Hoffer and Osmond; and a Dr. Sidney Cohen were all doing experiments at Trabuco College, including the administration of lysergic acid diethylamide, or LSD, as it is commonly known. In the early 1960s the substance called LSD was still mysterious as well as being completely legal. Furthermore, it was used as a part of a series of experiments being conducted by great minds, men deeply committed to creating a society better than the one that was responsible for two world wars and a host of other horrors.

Trabuco appealed to the older Bill Wilson on many levels. His spiritually unorthodox side, inherited directly from the New England traditions of psychics like Annie Besant, Madame Blavatsky, and even Mary Baker Eddy, was always looking for breakthroughs. Just because he had turned over Alcoholics Anonymous to its own membership didn't mean that he was any less concerned about helping alcoholics than he had ever been. He also wanted to help himself.

More specifically, he may have been looking for a way to stop smoking. Although his emphysema didn't slow him down until the 1960s when he first started carrying an L-shaped inhaler on his walks, he could already feel constriction in his lungs. Most of all, Bill was a believer, a zealot, a man who thought there were answers to all problems—after all, hadn't he found one for the worst problem that medicine ever knew? At heart what drew him to Trabuco was the promise of a new cure.

At first, Hoffer and Osmond had thought that LSD might induce an experience like delirium tremens which could—if experienced—frighten alcoholics so badly that they might be ready to stop drinking. When they administered the drug to alcoholics, though, the subjects weren't frightened at all. They became happy rather than sad. Sometimes they were ecstatic. They reported something that sounded like an epiphany, a new clarity of vision, a new vividness of experience. When he heard about this from Huxley, Bill thought a sudden spiritual experience like the one he had had at Towns Hospital might be induced by the drug. If LSD could produce an artificial hot flash, the results would be anything but artificial.

Bill had visited Trabuco in the 1940s, but in the late 1950s and early 1960s he went back with a new freedom provided by the fact that he was no longer the head of Alcoholics Anonymous. He was just Bill Wilson from New York. Under the supervision of Dr. Cohen, with Huxley and Tom Powers standing by, he took his own dose of LSD on August 29, 1956, just after lunch. Gerald Heard took notes. At 1:00 P.M. Bill reported a feeling of peace. At 2:31 he was even happier. "Tobacco is not necessary to me anymore," he reported. At 3:15 P.M. he said he felt "an enormous enlargement" of everything around him. At 3:22 he asked for a cigarette. At 3:40 he said he thought people shouldn't take themselves so damn seriously.

Bill loved LSD. He urged everyone he knew to try it, including Lois, his secretary, Nell Wing, his friend Dr. Jack Norris, the Reverend Sam Shoemaker, and Father Ed Dowling. He even thought his mother might benefit. Lois obliged and reported that she didn't feel very changed by it; she just saw things a little more clearly. Nell Wing was also underwhelmed by the new miracle drug. When word of the doings at Trabuco College got back to the membership of A.A.—and Bill Wilson was never good at keeping secrets, especially when the secret was something as important as a new substance that might help alcoholics—there was grumbling.

Bill took the position that he had stepped down as the leader of Alcoholics Anonymous and that he should have the freedom to live his life the way a normal person would. As usual, the membership of A.A. and quite a few of his contemporaries did not agree. "St. Louis was a major step toward my own withdrawal," he wrote to Sam Shoemaker. "I understand that the father symbol will always be hitched to me." Bill argued, "I feel that complete withdrawal on my part should be tried." Wilson had given thirty years of his life to service. He wasn't planning to stop doing service, but he didn't see why he should continue to be held responsible for the feelings and spirit of an organization for which he, specifically, had decided to lay aside responsibility. Still, by the end of 1959, he had stopped exhorting friends to take LSD, and ended his own experiments.

Around the same time, Timothy Leary and Richard Alpert experimented with LSD at Harvard with disastrous results. Initially, Leary had approached Bill, asking to be included in his experiments, but by that time Wilson had withdrawn from experimenting with LSD. Soon after, LSD was outlawed. In the next decade, during a period of extreme cultural upheaval, it became a popular, notorious street drug that was illegally produced in basement laboratories.

Emily Wilson died in May of 1961 in a nursing home in Dobbs Ferry, New York, some twenty miles south of Bedford Hills. Bill had finally persuaded her to move east, and then put her in a nursing home in Hastings-on-Hudson. She hated it, so he found another one. "It seems that conditions in this life have prevented our spending much time together, in somewhat ironical disregard of the physical ties that should have bound us in much closer companionship," she wrote him near the end of her life. She was ninety-one when she died, and her son arranged to have her buried in the Griffith family plot in the cemetery on the side of the hill in East Dorset where it all started.

The 1960s were a time when the whole world seemed to come unmoored. Suddenly, the old bastions fell, authority was first wrong and then evil, and everything that had been a no-no became a yes-yes. This was also true in Bill Wilson's life. Dr. Bob was dead, and now his mother and real father were gone as well. In his own mind he was free of the constraints he had had as the leader of Alcoholics Anonymous. There were fewer and fewer people he had to please.

Bill had always said that the program of Alcoholics Anonymous owed a great debt to the thinking and writing of psychoanalyst Carl Jung, who had treated Bill's friend Rowland back in the 1930s. Now he had the time to write Jung and thank him. To Wilson's delight, Jung responded in 1961 with a long letter, remembering his difficulties with Rowland, the problems he and others had with treating alcoholics, and the "misleading platitudes" that were usually the diagnosis of those treating alcoholics. Jung agreed with Bill that the only answer for an alcoholic was some kind of change of heart, and congratulated him on his discovery and his recovery. "Alcohol in Latin is spiritus," Jung wrote, "and you use the same word for the highest religious experience as well as for the most depraving poison. The helpful formula, therefore, is *spiritus contra spiritum*."

Then in the early sixties, Dr. Hoffer and Dr. Osmond reported that they were having some success treating detoxing alcoholics and schizophrenics with a substance called niacin, or vitamin B3. Bill Wilson was elated. He read the literature, reviewed the experiments, and looked at the doctors' statistics. After speaking with them and seeing their results, he felt that they had discovered the exact nature of the allergy that Dr. William Silkworth had described when he said that an alcoholic is someone who is allergic to alcohol. Silkworth's allergy, Bill thought, was the result of some kind of shift in blood chemistry that made an alcoholic crave a drink and then become unable to stop drinking. Experience had shown that the craving seemed to be related to low blood sugar; people getting sober could sometimes eliminate their drink cravings with a brownie or a candy bar. Hoffer and Osmond thought that niacin could prevent drops in blood sugar, and therefore prevent the cravings that alcoholics experienced.

Bill started taking niacin. It wasn't a drug, it was a vitamin. What got him in trouble was his enthusiasm for it. He extolled the virtues of niacin to anyone who would listen, as well as a great many people who were not quite willing to listen. He also believed that niacin was good for depressions, and here Helen Wynn, who also suffered from depression, totally agreed with him. When Bill Wilson was excited about something, whether it was a good thing like Alcoholics Anonymous or a questionable thing like niacin, or a thing that was soon to become illegal like LSD, he told everyone and urged everyone to try it. He was no longer the great white leader of Alcoholics

Anonymous, but he often found himself talking with people who happened to be members of Alcoholics Anonymous, people who seemed to forget that he was, in his own words, just another drunk.

Bill's problems with the men he was closest to became more severe. These were usually sober men whose lives had been a nightmare sliding toward death when they met Bill or when they encountered his program for the first time. As they recovered, they felt enormous gratitude toward the program that had saved their lives, and the men—Bill Wilson and Bob Smith—who had developed and nurtured the program. Often these men were exceptionally talented, and they wanted to give back to A.A. by using their recovered talents. If they were writers or editors, they were put to work on writing pamphlets or working on the *Grapevine*. If they were accountants, they helped keep the General Service Conference books in order. If they were public relations people or ad men, they tried to find ways to sharpen the communication between A.A. and its members.

These men close to Bill made a god of A.A.—after all, it had saved their lives and often their families—and they sometimes made a god of Bill Wilson. After a while, because Bill was not a god, or even a saint, but a human being with his own struggles, these men became disappointed. Then they became furious. Beginning with Hank Parkhurst's defection, and continuing with Clarence Snyder of the Cleveland, Ohio, group, who had angrily asked for a financial accounting, Bill Wilson's career is characterized by the fury and sense of betrayal of many of the men who worked with him. "It's an almost insane anger," said one of them. "Maybe it's jealousy, I don't know, but it felt stronger than that." The anger of these men who turned on Bill often fueled a group anger both among those in the program and among the trustees.

Now once again Bill Wilson was in trouble with the fellowship he had established. People said that in talking about niacin Bill was violating his own traditions against affiliating A.A. with any outside issues, and specifically was violating Tradition Six: *A.A. ought never endorse, finance or lend the A.A. name to any facility or outside enterprise.* Bill didn't want to represent A.A., but A.A. continued to want to be represented by him. The problem got big enough to be addressed at the 1967 conference, where it was decreed that "all inquiries pertaining to B_3 and niacin are referred directly to an office in Pleasantville. In order that Bill's personal interest in these items not involve the fellowship," the board requested that Bill's stationery carry an address other than the General Service Office. The address in Pleasantville became niacin headquarters, where mail was answered by another person who thought that B_3 was an answer to many things, Helen Wynn.

The 1960s were also Bill Wilson's last decade, and his life was repeatedly slowed by the emphysema caused by his smoking. He relied more and more on the inhaler and added occasional hits from an oxygen tank. He struggled with cigarettes, repeatedly giving them up and then becoming such a pest borrowing from others that he took them up again. Bill's smoking seemed as much a part of him as his coffee cup or his long face or his lanky body that never quite seemed to fit his clothes. He always had a cigarette going, and ashes dropped onto his papers and his clothes, making tiny burn holes. The edges of desks and tables reflected the long burns of cigarettes he left there, and ashtrays were everywhere at Stepping Stones and in the A.A. offices, which moved again, in the 1960s, to Park Avenue. When he sat still over a book, or scanning something he had written, a plume of smoke rose from him as if the ignition of ideas was actually a fire. Meanwhile, his breathing got worse.

Chapter Thirty-eight:

Miami

By the time Bill Wilson almost quit smoking in 1969, it was too late. The tiny capillaries in his lungs were coated with tar, with years and years of darkness. His long, angular body was often racked with coughs, his nasal passages clogged, his lungs not quite working well enough to make breathing easy. The connection became clearer and clearer; many of Bill Wilson's illnesses, his bouts with bronchitis and pneumonia especially, were a direct result of the cigarette that was always burning in his hand. He still couldn't stop.

By the late 1960s Bill was dependent on an oxygen tank to get through the day. He and Lois and Helen all continued to take niacin, but that didn't help either. There are stories about his trying to decide if he needed another cigarette or more oxygen, and deciding on a cigarette. Bill was an addict; like most addicts, he was addicted to many different things. Although he officially quit smoking in 1969, he apparently still kept cigarettes in his car for secret puffs. He would turn the car left down the hill out of the new Stepping Stones driveway and head south on Cherry Street toward the station or toward the little hamlet of shops and restaurants, where everyone knew everyone. As long as he was well enough to drive, he was well enough to smoke.

As he lived into his seventies, this hale, vigorous man who in many ways looked much younger than his age, was dying. He put up a good front. Only Lois, Nell Wing, and Harriet, the Wilsons' housekeeper, knew how bad his nights could be, but in 1970, when he began his speech at the opening dinner of the General Service Conference in New York, he was forced to stop because of breathlessness. No one had ever seen Bill Wilson stop talking before. He was seventy-five, and suddenly he looked old. Disease had changed him into an almost unrecognizable version of his former self. His hair was thinning, he needed heavy glasses, and the effort of breathing had developed strong cords in his neck.

Fourteen thousand people gathered in Miami, Florida, that year for the International Convention. In Miami, Bill was ferried by ambulance from his hotel to the Miami Heart Institute, where a Dr. Ed McBain had hoped to help him. Although he was unable to appear at a series of press conferences, on Sunday morning he arrived at the back entrance of Convention Hall by ambulance. A hoist lifted him up in his wheelchair and deposited him backstage. He had a nasal tube and was taking oxygen from a tank. Once on stage, he was held up by people on either side of him, and he spoke for only four minutes. Bill and Lois stayed on in Miami so that Bill could be treated at the heart institute, and in August they returned to Bedford Hills, where Bill promptly came down with pneumonia.

Through that summer and fall of 1970, the pneumonia persisted. He would spend a few days at Northern Westchester Hospital in Mount Kisco and then come home for a while. Sometimes he was well enough to walk, but he was losing his grip on the world. By September he had gone upstairs to bed permanently. The room where Bill spent his final six weeks, nursed by Lois, and then finally cared for by two round-the-clock nurses who took turns being with him every minute, faces east onto the lawns, trees, and gardens of Stepping Stones. It's a room that runs the width of the house and has space for a few tables and chairs.

The last six weeks at Stepping Stones were his time to say goodbye. People who had loved Bill came to pay their respects, as did some of those who hated him. Tom White drove Tom Powers down from Calicoon, New York, and waited outside while Powers went upstairs to say goodbye. Two male nurses, James Dannenberg and Mike O'Loughlin, watched Bill day and night, keeping hourly logs on a wide green-lined pad, with a page for each shift. They noted when Bill was up all night, as he was on November 20. They noted when he had dry skin, when and how much of the "Bennett" breathing machine, which administered oxygen, was used. They made note of everything he said and did.

On James Dannenberg's log for December 25—Bill Wilson's last Christmas Day—at six-ten in the morning, after a long night, the patient "asked for three shots of whiskey," Dannenberg noted. He also noted that Wilson was quite upset when he couldn't have what he asked for. There was no whiskey at Stepping Stones. A few days later he became belligerent and tried to punch the nurse.

On the second of January, Bill asked Nurse O'Loughlin for a shot of whiskey. He didn't get one. The next day he was more cheerful. He told Dannenberg that he was determined to be ready for walks in Vermont in February. On January 4, Bill and the nurses listened to President Nixon's State of the Union speech on the radio. The country was in turmoil. Student demonstrations against the Vietnam War had torn neighborhoods and families apart. The previous spring, when Bill could still come downstairs for an occasional walk, four students were killed by the National Guard at Kent State. President Nixon defended the war and announced that the United States was bombing Vietcong supply routes in Cambodia and conducting a large-scale bombing mission against North Vietnam.

On the seventh of January, Nurse Dannenberg noted that Bill had been visited by some family members and that after the visit he and Lois had an angry argument. The next morning Bill again asked him for whiskey. Instead of complying, Dannenberg sat down and asked Bill if he wanted to talk. Bill described his marital difficulties and complained about Lois. Dannenberg sympathized. Bill wept.

By the fourteenth of January, Bill Wilson, a man who hadn't had a drink in almost thirty-seven years, a man who had discovered what is still the only successful way to treat alcoholism, was asking for whiskey again. He was an alcoholic. Alcoholics drink, they love to drink, and for a long time drinking works for them. Some discover, as Bill had, that it is almost impossible for them to stop drinking. Many never stop wanting to drink. It's a measure of the power of alcohol that even in his last days alive, Bill Wilson still wanted a whiskey.

Bill Wilson was an alcoholic, a chain smoker, a man who for all his struggles was never able to be the man his followers wanted him to be, or that his wife wanted him to be—or even, on most days, the man *he* wanted to be. He knew this and tried to discourage the idea that he was a leader, or any kind of model for human behavior. He had a lot of help, and he always acknowledged that. He fought the idea of himself as a hero; he knew better. The brilliance of his guidelines for the operation of A.A., the Twelve Traditions, reflects his understanding of his humanness and his desire to be judged as a man, not as a leader.

Bill Wilson never held himself up as a model; he only hoped to help other people by sharing his own experience, strength, and hope. He insisted again and again that he was just an ordinary man who, because of his bitter experience, discovered, slowly and through a conversion experience, a system of behavior and a series of actions that works for alcoholics who want to stop drinking. Alcoholics drink, but, as Bill wrote, with the intervention of Alcoholics Anonymous they may stop drinking a day at a time depending on their level of "spiritual fitness." Now, as he lay dying, he was living his own prophecy.

In late January, at the urging of Dr. Ed McBain from Miami and with the loan of a small plane from some wealthy friends, Bill, Lois, and Nell flew back to Miami to readmit Bill to the Miami Heart Institute. Dr. McBain had a new machine, somewhat like the oxygen delivery machines used for underwater diving, that he thought might help Bill. The flight south, with Lois and Nell for company, was grueling. The plane seat was too short for Bill's long body. They got to the hospital by ambulance in the evening. It was Sunday, January 24, 1971. During the night, while Lois and Nell were asleep, Bill Wilson stopped breathing.

Bill's body was flown home, the newspapers ran their obituaries, and there was a private service at Stepping Stones with a reading of the St. Francis prayer. Memorial services were held across the country and beyond—at St. John the Divine in New York, the National Cathedral in Washington, D.C., Notre-Dame Basilica in Montreal, and St. Martin-in-the-Fields in London—during which hundreds of thousands of people paid their respects. On May 8, when the stony Vermont ground had thawed enough for an interment, his body was buried with a simple headstone in the Griffith plot next to his Uncle Clarence, the dead boy whose life shadowed Bill's childhood.

Even now, on a winter day at Stepping Stones, when the sun disappears behind the ridge early in the afternoon, it's easy to imagine Bill starting off for one of his February walks in the woods. He heads past the big oak tree and the edge of the garden toward the road to town, passing the back window where he first broke into the house more than thirty years before, when he was a young man and when it seemed as if living there was an impossible dream. Bill was in the business of the possible. He's wearing a scarf, a sweater, and a frayed tweed jacket that looks a little small for him as he walks between clumps of snow and skeletal trees, and in the distance he can see a row of evergreens and the shimmer of a frozen pond. A squirrel rustles in the tree above him, his long strides quicken, and the air feels just warm enough—it is February after all—for Bill to unwind his scarf and head on down the hill.

Afterword

In the thirty-three years since Bill Wilson's death, his influence has grown much more than anyone—even he—could have guessed. Although his name is not famous, his ideas are among the most influential of the twentieth century. His writing has changed the way we think about addiction and, in turn, the way we think about human nature. Before Alcoholics Anonymous, addiction was treated as a mental illness or a failure of willpower. Alcoholics were treated with barbarous drug and fasting protocols, even with electric shock treatment. Everyone knew these were hopeless cases; everyone knew it was somehow the alcoholic's own fault. In the end, the lucky ones died, and the less fortunate were permanently hospitalized or lived out their lives in institutions. Alcoholics Anonymous and its literature, written primarily by Bill, have provided a way for many, many alcoholics to get sober and lead useful lives. Alcoholics Anonymous has spawned a dozen parallel programs, all of which depend on the book *Alcoholics Anonymous* and most of which also use the book *Twelve Steps and Twelve Traditions*.

Twelve-step programs for gamblers, debtors, people with eating disorders, drug addicts, and sexual compulsives have changed the lives of millions more people and their families. (These programs are separate from Al-Anon, the program for people whose problem is their relationship with alcoholics—recovering or otherwise.) As a result of these burgeoning programs, each adding members every year, Bill Wilson's ideas have entered the common consciousness and changed how we define being human in a way certainly as powerful as the ideas of Sigmund Freud or Thomas Jefferson.

Alcoholics Anonymous is often misunderstood by outsiders who draw conclusions about it without reading its basic literature, the book *Alcoholics Anonymous*. Bill Wilson took great pains to explain that A.A. is not a religion, and that A.A. does not require any beliefs from its members. Although the word "God" is mentioned in the Twelve Steps of Alcoholics Anonymous, it is a qualified God: *God as we understood him*. Although Harvard psychologist B. F. Skinner, a fan of Bill Wilson's, went so far as to create a new version of the Twelve Steps for nonbelievers, it was unnecessary. Many atheists and agnostics have been able to use Alcoholics Anonymous to get sober.

In fact, Bill wrote that none of the "rules" of A.A. are rules. They are, he explained, merely suggestions. In establishing the purest possible democracy, Bill founded a unique organization. There are no leaders in A.A. There is no accumulation of money and power. It is a growing organization still run, as it was when he died, by representatives and trustees who are elected by the membership or by each other. The General Service Organization, based in New York City, has a rotating membership. They do not govern A.A. Their job is to make decisions based on the wishes of the majority of A.A. members everywhere.

A.A. does not forbid drinking. A.A. meetings often welcome people who are still under the influence of alcohol. In some meetings these drinkers are asked not to speak. In others they are welcome to talk for as long as they like. Bill Wilson understood that if an alcoholic is ordered not to do something, he or she will most probably end up doing it. The only requirement for membership in A.A. is a desire to stop drinking, he wrote. This desire can be momentary; it can be engendered by a hangover; it can be felt by someone who has just stumbled out of a bar. The steps of Alcoholics

Anonymous, which are suggested for members, follow the pattern of many ancient and modern religious and self-help organizations: confession, restitution, a new life. But by combining them with an absolute lack of mandate, and by setting up an organization without hierarchy, Wilson founded a way of recovery that has worked for sixty-seven years and is still working well for many alcoholics.

The nature of addiction and the addictive personality has become clearer through Bill Wilson's teaching than it was when he was alive. Many alcoholics who get sober, and many drug addicts who get clean, find themselves turning to another addiction to compensate. They smoke, or they overeat. Some even become "addicted" to going to A.A. meetings. Alcoholics Anonymous does not promise human perfectibility; it holds out the hope of not drinking, and this, for most alcoholics, is a huge, unprecedented step forward. Even as Bill himself was unable to stop smoking, some sober alcoholics find themselves involved in gambling, smoking, or sexual compulsiveness.

A.A. meetings are more loosely organized today than they were at the beginning, when a few drunks recruited from the Oxford Group and the Calvary Mission met in the Burnham house on Clinton Street. They are held in all sorts of public spaces, in churches and schools and hospitals. Meetings usually start on time with a reader, or the introduction of a topic by the chairperson—a job that usually rotates frequently. Many people come late; others leave early. Many members of Alcoholics Anonymous never speak at meetings. They come to listen. Others speak at length—there are no time limits on speaking. Some members announce day counts or anniversaries—how many days or years they have gone without a drink; others don't. A.A.'s almost anarchic nature seems to encourage its members' good will.

Although certain meetings of Alcoholics Anonymous are "open" to the public and others "closed," in practice almost all meetings are open to everyone, whether or not they have a drinking problem or a desire to stop drinking. Recovering alcoholics in meetings welcome almost anyone who wanders in no matter what their circumstances. The only time people are asked to leave is if they are disruptive. If meeting practices do not please members of the meeting, they can start another meeting. Two alcoholics can have a meeting anywhere in the world just by saying they are having a meeting.

As an alcoholic, Bill Wilson had an intimate understanding of what alcoholism is; he had knowledge of spiritual movements and of the temperance movement—of history—which made him understand how politics could be a force for both good and evil. He was a brilliant writer and a great, charismatic teacher. His life was complicated; his mission was simple.

* * *

It's a few days before Christmas at the Wilson House in East Dorset. The candles are in the windows and the wreaths on the doors. The windows are decorated with pine garlands and ribbons, and a decorated tree blinks in the corner. Outside the windowpanes it's snowing, and I can see across the green past the Congregational Church to the Griffith house. There's often a gathering in this corner of the living room, the corner where Bill Wilson was born, as Bonnie and Ozzie Lepper, who bought the Wilson House in 1987 and run it as a hotel with a special interest in recovering alcoholics, play host to strangers and visitors.

This morning Bonnie is talking about Bill and his problems with Henrietta Seiberling. The dogs, Barley and Laddie, bound around the living room threatening to upend the Victorian furniture. Ozzie tells the story of how the ten-year-old Bill, after his parents' divorce, climbed the oak tree at the top of Mad Tom Road and wouldn't come down. "He felt that it would hold him," he said. "Nothing else was holding him then." We have a wide-ranging conversation about Bill Wilson and the things that have been said and written about him in the thirty years since his death. He's alive for us, as alive as if he just happened to be down in Manchester for the day Christmas shopping. "He never got that peace he wanted," Ozzie says. "But we did," someone else responds.

From the kitchen the smells of dinner cooking waft down the narrow hallway past the windows Emily Griffith Wilson looked out as she prepared Thanksgiving dinner and tried to suppress her labor pains. The aroma reaches us in the living room where we sit more than a hundred years later. The snow outside is heavier now, faintly falling on the green and the railroad tracks that cut through the little town, and on the old stacks of marble blocks on the mountain and up further on the summit of Mount Aeolus, and falling faintly on the headstones of the cemetery on the side of the hill where Bill Wilson and his family and the Griffith and Wilson families are buried.

ACKNOWLEDGMENTS

More than most books, a biography is a collaboration, first between subject and writer, then between writer and the people who knew the subject, and finally between the writer and—in the case of Bill Wilson—the dozens of people who have written about him before. Bill Wilson's own autobiography as well as Lois Wilson's memoir, *Lois Remembers,* and biographies by Robert Thomsen, Nan Robertson, Francis Hartigan, Tom White, Bill Pittman, and the anonymous writers of *Pass It On* have been of inestimable help to me in understanding both the facts and the meanings of Bill Wilson's life. Other writers who have written about Alcoholics Anonymous and Bill Wilson less directly but just as importantly are Ernest Kurtz, who wrote an early and important book about Alcoholics Anonymous; Mel Barger, who has devoted much of his writing life to understanding Alcoholics Anonymous and its founder; and Nell Wing, who served as a secretary to Bill and Lois Wilson. Many of the men and women who have written about Bill Wilson also reached out to help me through the maze of material and opinion surrounding his life. Without them this book would not have been possible.

The idea for this book began in a number of ways, including conversations with my friend and literary agent Kim Witherspoon, Nelson Aldrich, Reba White Williams and Dave Williams, and Walter Isaacson, as well as other good friends and family, many of them also writers and editors, including Michael Wollaeger, Miriam Around, Frank and Phoebe Griswold, Hannah Griswold, Eliza Griswold,

Barbara Goldsmith, Jane Hitchcock and James Hoagland, Mary Beth Hughes and Duke Beeson, Jeanette Watson Sanger and Alex Sanger, Lenny Golay and Ray Sherman, Randy Lehrer, Paige Petersen, Laura Palmer, Ned Rorem, Don Rice, Maggie and Herb Scarf, Judy Collins and Louis Nelson, Erica Jong and Ken Burrows, Molly Jong-Fast and Matthew Greenfield, Carl Bernstein, Tina Brown and Harry Evans, Marcelle Clements, Jane Hirschfield, John and Janet Irving, Katherine Russell Rich, Susan and William Kinsolving, Muriel Lloyd, Malachi McCourt, Ron Gallen, Shelley Harwayne, Glen Horowitz, Ken Lauber, Gordon Miller, Rick Moody, Suzanne Oaks, Oren King, Patti O'Toole, Jeanette Mason, Ralph Bugli, and Marjorie Wolff.

Simon & Schuster is the publisher of the book, but the men and women there have also brought editorial genius and consummate skill to bear on the writing, editing, and publishing process. They are friends and colleagues as well as teachers. I have been very lucky to have the guidance of the astonishing Michael Korda, the brilliant Chuck Adams, and the amazing Gypsy da Silva, as well as invaluable help from Cheryl Weinstein, Carol Bowie, Victoria Meyer, Elizabeth Hayes, Anthony Newfield, and Fred Wiemer.

Biography requires a special balance of enthusiasm and endurance, and biographers who were generous to me in person and whose work inspired me include Gerald Clarke, Judith Thurman, Jackie Weld, Janet Malcolm, Jay Parini, and especially Lyndall Gordon, whose encouragement and guidance in conversations and in her extraordinary lectures at Bennington have redefined my idea of biography. I also want to thank Liam Rector and everyone at Bennington College, where I have given readings of sections of this book; my wonderful colleagues and my amazing students—I have learned a great deal from many of you and something from each one of you.

Elaina Richardson, Candace Wait, Lynn Faranell, Cathy Clark, and everyone at Yaddo, where I wrote most of this book, have been as sympathethic and supportive as any writer could dream, as well as providing a place that is the center of the writing life for many of us who have the privilege of working there.

At the Stepping Stones Archive and in the house where Bill Wilson lived with his wife, Lois, for the last thirty years of his life, I have been welcomed, and Darlene Smith at the Alcoholics Anonymous Archive in NewYork City has also taken extra time to get me the documents and permissions I needed. David Lewis and his colleagues at Brown University and the John Hay Library helped me through their wonderful archives. Bonnie and Ozzie Lepper have made the Wilson House a refuge for anyone interested in Bill Wilson and his program and have kept many of the Wilson family memories alive in East Dorset. They were unstintingly generous with me.

Ginger Rothe and Pat Weidenkeller and everyone at *Newsday* have been understanding and supportive; talking to Ginger always clarifies my ideas about anything and everything. Mark Piel and the New York Society Library are my secret literary weapons. My mother helped in general by carrying on the family literary tradition and in particular with the hilarious story of her visit to meet Lois Wilson. My brother, Ben, and his wife, Janet, are irreplaceable friends and colleagues—I reportedly wasn't pleased by the birth of a younger brother, but now I thank God for his help and support. My daughter, Sarah Tomkins, and my son, Quad Hinckle, are always my reason for writing—they are the center of my life and they are the heart of the next generation of readers and writers.

Most of all it's impossible to sum up the help I got from dozens and dozens of anonymous men and women who knew Bill Wilson, or who live by and carry on the work of Wilson and Dr. Bob Smith.

I got hundreds of letters and dozens of offers for help; almost everyone I contacted went out of his or her way to lend a hand or tell a story. These are the men and women who have helped me understand the immensity of Bill Wilson's accomplishment and the resonance of his discoveries in their lives and in my own. I am grateful. Thank you.

Chronology

son and begins work at U.S. Fidelity & Guarantee as a debt collector.

1920   January. Prohibition, the Eighteenth Amendment to the Constitution, becomes law. Bill Wilson's drinking continues.

1922   Lois suffers first ectopic pregnancy. Her second, with complications, will make it impossible for her to have children, ending both the Wilsons' fantasy of building a family.

1925–29 Bill becomes a securities analyst on Wall Street; his drinking gets worse.

1925   Bill Wilson and Lois Wilson go to Schenectady, N.Y., by motorcycle to investigate General Electric. This is the first stop on their year-long motorcycle journey up and down the East Coast investigating businesses for Wall Street.

1926   June. Bill Wilson and Lois Wilson return from their motorcycle journey. Lois's sister Kitty marries.

1927   Summer. Bill Wilson and Lois Wilson travel to Cuba to investigate the sugar industry. Bill's boss Frank Shaw worries about Bill's drinking. Bill assures him that he has stopped. He hasn't stopped.

1929   October. The stock market crashes. Bill Wilson is broke. In spite of many opportunities, his drinking prevents him from making more than a temporary financial comeback.

1930   December 24. Lois Wilson's mother dies of bone cancer in Brooklyn.

1933   May. Lois Wilson's father, Dr. Clark Burnham, remarries and deeds the heavily mortgaged house at 182 Clinton Street in Brooklyn to Bill Wilson and Lois Wilson. Because of the Depression, the bank begins to accept a token monthly payment.

1933   Autumn. Bill Wilson goes to Charles B. Towns Hospital on Central Park West for the first of three visits. He meets Dr. Duncan Silkworth, who tells him that he has a disease.

1933   December 5. Prohibition is repealed. Bill Wilson continues to drink, to promise to stop, and to drink again.

1934   Midsummer. Bill Wilson returns to Towns Hospital, unable to stay sober.

1934   November. Ebby Thacher visits Bill Wilson to tell him about his newfound sobriety and to recruit him into the Oxford Group. Bill scoffs. Later he finds his way to the Calvary Church Mission. He is drunk, but finds himself at the altar giving himself to God. Afterward, he continues to drink.

1934   December 11. Bill Wilson takes his last drink, from one of several cans of beer he has bought for the trip from Brooklyn to Towns Hospital. This time it's different. Bill Wilson experiences the epiphany he later calls a "hot flash." He never drinks again. On December 18 he leaves Towns Hospital for the last time. He and Lois begin attending Oxford Group meetings and gathering with other alcoholics who can't get sober. Bill stays sober.

1935   May. Bill Wilson goes to Akron to get involved in a takeover of the National Rubber Machinery Company. He hopes for another comeback. It doesn't work. He reaches out to other alcoholics and is introduced to Dr. Bob Smith at the gatehouse of Stan Hywet, the Seiberling estate.

1935   June 10. After a relapse Dr. Bob Smith takes his last drink. This is the official date of the founding of Alcoholics Anonymous, although it would be years before the two men gave their fellowship a name.

1935   Fall. Bill Wilson and Lois Wilson begin to hold special Oxford Group meetings for alcoholics on Tuesday nights at their house on Clinton Street.

1936   September. Dr. Clark Burnham dies.

1936   The Oxford Group leaders at Calvary Church forbid members from going to meetings at the Wilson house in Brooklyn. The Wilsons are "not maximum," they say.

1937   Bill Wilson and the New York alcoholics leave the Oxford Group.

1938   Oxford Group leader Father Frank Buchman tries to recruit Adolf Hitler. The Oxford Group is renamed Moral Rearmament.

1938   John D. Rockefeller, Jr., pays off Dr. Bob's mortgage and gives Bob Smith and Bill Wilson a $30-a-week stipend, but he declines to make the larger donations they had hoped for. He helps set up the Alcoholic Foundation with a five-member board—three non-alcoholics and two recovering alcoholics.

1939   April. The Big Book, written by Bill Wilson and edited by almost everyone in the fellowship, is published as *Alcoholics Anonymous*, which also becomes the name of the fellowship.

1939   April 26. Bill Wilson and Lois Wilson are forced out of the Burnham house on Clinton Street where Lois has lived all her life. They can barely pay for storage. They begin two years of homelessness, visiting friends and relatives.

1940 February 8. John D. Rockefeller, Jr., gives an A.A. dinner at the Union Club in Manhattan.

1941 March 1. A *Saturday Evening Post* article by Jack Alexander based on months of traveling with Bill Wilson appears. It is accurate and favorable and depicts Alcoholics Anonymous as a program that works. The Big Book begins to sell. Mail pours into the Manhattan office.

1941 The Wilsons buy Bil-Lo's Break, which they rename Stepping Stones.

1943 Bill Wilson and Lois Wilson make their first triumphal cross-country tour of A.A. groups. Bill Wilson tries to enlist in the U.S. Army and is turned down.

1944 Onset of Bill Wilson's third long depression.

1950 First International A.A. Convention meets. Bill Wilson explains plan to turn the fellowship over to its members and starts working on a charter that will ensure a pure democracy with no accumulation of money or power. The Twelve Traditions, which spell out guidelines for A.A. governance, are accepted. Dr. Bob makes his final appearance.

1950 November 16. Dr. Robert Holbrook Smith dies in Akron.

1951 April. The first General Service Conference meets.

1954 *Twelve Steps and Twelve Traditions* is published. Bill Wilson declines to accept a degree from Yale University.

1955 July. At the St. Louis convention, Bill Wilson gives A.A. its "formal release into maturity." The charter is met with a roar of approval.

1966 Ebby Thacher dies. He has had a series of relapses. Bill Wilson has supported him.

1967 Ratio of alcoholic to nonalcoholic trustees on the board is changed at Bill Wilson's urging.

1970 Bill Wilson makes his last appearance at the Miami convention. He is dying of emphysema caused by smoking.

1971 January 24. Bill Wilson dies in Miami after a long illness in Bedford Hills.

1988 October 5. Lois Wilson dies at Bedford Hills.

Appendix: The Twelve Steps and The Twelve Traditions

These two lists of Twelve Steps and Twelve Traditions are posted on the front wall at almost every meeting of Alcoholics Anonymous. The steps were drafted by Bill Wilson and edited by a committee of A.A. members in Akron, Ohio, and New York City before their publication in the book *Alcoholics Anonymous* in 1939. The traditions, which are the bylaws of A.A., first appeared in the late 1940s and early 1950s in a variety of forms in the A.A. newsletter, the *Grapevine*. Both steps and traditions were rewritten by Bill Wilson in this short form and in a longer chapter form in the study he built for himself on a knoll above Stepping Stones in Bedford Hills in 1945. The expanded form was published in 1954 as the book *Twelve Steps and Twelve Traditions*.

The Twelve Steps

1. We admitted we were powerless over alcohol—that our lives had become unmanageable.
2. Came to believe that a Power greater than ourselves could restore us to sanity.
3. Made a decision to turn our will and our lives over to the care of God *as we understood Him.*
4. Made a searching and fearless moral inventory of ourselves.
5. Admitted to God, to ourselves, and to another human being the exact nature of our wrongs.
6. Were entirely ready to have God remove all these defects of character.
7. Humbly asked Him to remove our shortcomings.
8. Made a list of all persons we had harmed, and became willing to make amends to them all.
9. Made direct amends to such people wherever possible, except when to do so would injure them or others.

10. Continued to take personal inventory and when we were wrong promptly admitted it.

11. Sought through prayer and meditation to improve our conscious contact with God, *as we understood Him,* praying only for knowledge of His will for us and the power to carry that out.

12. Having had a spiritual awakening as the result of these Steps, we tried to carry this message to alcoholics, and to practice these principles in all our affairs.

The Twelve Traditions

1. Our common welfare should come first; personal recovery depends on A.A. unity.

2. For our group purpose there is but one ultimate authority—a loving God as He may express Himself in our group conscience. Our leaders are but trusted servants; they do not govern.

3. The only requirement for A.A. membership is a desire to stop drinking.

4. Each group should be autonomous except in matters affecting other groups or A.A. as a whole.

5. Each group has but one primary purpose—to carry its message to the alcoholic who still suffers.

6. An A.A. group ought never endorse, finance or lend the A.A. name to any related facility or outside enterprise, lest problems of money, property and prestige divert us from our primary purpose.

7. Every A.A. group ought to be fully self-supporting, declining outside contributions.

8. Alcoholics Anonymous should remain forever nonprofessional, but our service centers may employ special workers.

9. A.A., as such, ought never be organized; but we may create service boards or committees directly responsible to those they serve.

10. Alcoholics Anonymous has no opinion on outside issues; hence the A.A. name ought never be drawn into public controversy.

11. Our public relations policy is based on attraction rather than promotion; we need always maintain personal anonymity at the level of press, radio and films.

12. Anonymity is the spiritual foundation of all our traditions, ever reminding us to place principles before personalities.

NOTES

Most of the material in this book came from the works cited in the Bibliography and from the two principal Wilson archives in New York City and at Stepping Stones in Bedford Hills, New York. I also visited the archive at East Dorset, Vermont. Many stories about Bill Wilson's life are told in different versions in a variety of places. I have chosen the sources closest to the time when the events occurred and narrated by the people involved wherever possible.

ABBREVIATIONS

SSA   Stepping Stones Archive, Bedford Hills, New York

AANYC   Alcoholics Anonymous Archive at General Service Offices in New York City

VV   *Vermont Voices, 1609 through the 1900s: A Documentary History of the Green Mountain State*

WGW   William Griffith Wilson

LBW   Lois Burnham Wilson

EGW   Emily Griffith Wilson

ONE: THE WILSON HOUSE

page

3   *very confused:* Letter from EGW to WGW on his birthday, 1938, AANYC.

3   *a few pumpkins still lazed against the cold earth:* DeGraaf and Yamasaki, *New England Wildlife.*

4   *Slow-moving oxen pulled the great blocks of marble:* Resch, *Dorset.*

5   *fought for the Union Army during the Civil War:* Coffin, *Full Duty,* 187. Interview with Gettysburg Civil War archivist Scott Hartwig in Gettysburg, Pa.

6   *"a little young barbecued pig"*: EGW to WGW, June 1945, AANYC.
      Clarence: Anonymous, *"Pass It On,"* 28.
7   *named for its windy summit*: Resch, *Dorset,* 9.
8   *wrote Rudyard Kipling, who was living nearby*: Murray, *Kipling in Vermont.*

Two: East Dorset

page
9   *Bill Wilson started smoking as a teenager*: WGW to LBW, SSA.
9   *Ethan Allen, from a Dorset family*: Botkin, *New England Folklore,* 296.
10   *Bell and his assistant*: Cheever, *Treetops.*
11   *Emerson lent him on Walden Pond*: Richardson, *Emerson.*
11   *The flowering of the age of temperance*: Lender and Martin, *Drinking in America,* 84.
12   *The Washingtonians were very successful*: Ibid., 77.
14   *Quarry work was dangerous*: Resch, *Dorset.*
14   *gangs of Canadian laborers who swarmed*: George Ellsworth Hooker, "Labor and Life at the Barre Granite Quarries." *VV,* 232.

Three: The Wilson Family and the Griffith Family

page
16   *she beat him with a hairbrush*: Wilson, *Bill W.*
17   *In the eight years William Wilson lived*: Wilson, *Bill W.,* 4, and Thomsen, *Bill W.*
17   *Emily's father was a strong, silent type*: Anonymous, *"Pass It On,"* 15.
17   *"On my grandfather's side"*: Wilson, *Bill W.,* 4.
18   *There was no anesthetic*: EGW to WGW, AANYC.
18   *Mark Whalon, remembered a crowd of local boys*: Wilson, *Bill W.,* 3.
18   *"When they brought you to me you were cold"*: EGW to WGW.
19   *Emily Wilson's neighbor, Annette Parmalee*: Vermont League of Women Voters Papers. *VV,* 261–67.
19   *Bill was transferred*: Anonymous, *"Pass It On,"* 22.
20   *Buffalo Bill shoot the aces*: Wilson, *Bill W.,* 11, and Thomsen, *Bill W.*
20   *breathing through a paper tube to get fresh air*: Wilson, *Bill W.,* 7.

FOUR: DORSET POND

page

22   *The pond, dyed a mysterious green by runoff:* Brown, *The History of Emerald Lake State Park.*

22   *Bill could tell that something was wrong:* Wilson, *Bill W.,* 8.

23   *blue bachelor's-buttons scattered in the grass:* Brown, *The History of Emerald Lake State Park,* and Harritt, *Emerald Lake State Park Nature Trail Guide.*

23   *A red hawk:* DeGraaf and Yamasaki, *New England Wildlife.*

24   *"Somehow I learned that the divorce was complete":* Wilson, *Bill W.,* 9.

24   *"You and I were always extremists":* WGW to EGW, AANYC.

25   *learned the Morse code:* Wilson, *Bill W.,* 12.

25   *quarrying was hard and dangerous work:* Resch, *Dorset,* chap. 8.

25   *The building of the New York Public Library:* Ibid., 230, and Lois Wilson, *Lois Remembers.*

FIVE: THE GRIFFITH HOUSE

page

27   *"the spot where I first saw that mountain":* Wilson, *Bill W.*

28   *Thanksgiving at the nearby Londonderry Inn:* Letters from WGW to all, AANYC.

28   *the blizzard of 1888 closing the roads:* Resch, *Dorset,* 17.

28   *nitroglycerin in the woodshed:* Wilson, *Bill W.*

28   *"It is eventime at the parsonage":* WGW to EGW, AANYC.

29   *Vermont had lost relatively more troops than any other state:* Coffin, *Full Duty,* 356.

30   *When the boy threw his homemade boomerang:* Wilson, *Bill W.,* 13.

31   *he played jigs and he played waltzes:* Letters from WGW to LBW, 1917, SSA.

SIX: THE STATE OF VERMONT

page

32   *"green mountain":* Resch, *Dorset,* chap. 24.

32   *The town's earliest settlers:* Resch, *Dorset,* 22.

33   *The Wilson family were among the first:* Ibid., 220.

33   *the fact that he was a* Mayflower *descendant:* family charts at SSA.

34   *"To be a Vermonter still means":* Bryan, *Yankee Politics.*

35   *to check that his heart had not stopped beating:* Mark Whalon to WGW, AANYC.

35   *People in Alcoholics Anonymous sometimes say:* Interviews.

35   *Lois Burnham and her family:* Lois Wilson, *Lois Remembers,* 2.

36   *"Ebby," Thacher and his large Manchester Village family:* Kurtz, *Not-God,* 16.

Seven: Mark Whalon

page

37   *towns just gave up the ghost:* Coffin, *Full Duty,* 356–57.

37   *It was Mark's friendship:* Lois Wilson, *Lois Remembers,* 32.

38   *"Among all my childhood friends there is":* Wilson, *Bill W.,* 7.

38   *They talked about the books they read:* Kurtz, *Not-God,* 11, and Pittman, *A.A.: The Way It Began,* 141.

39   *a tall glass of cider in front of him on the worn wooden table:* Kurtz, *Not-God,* 12, and Thomsen, *Bill W.*

39   *a kind of everyman's Robert Frost:* "Alfred Eisenstadt in Vermont," *Life* magazine, October 1943.

40   *"summer people" who used these grand houses:* Lois Wilson, *Lois Remembers,* 14.

41   *"In Vermont too we are fortunate":* Governor John McCullough, Inaugural Address (1902), *Journal of the Senate,* October 3, 484–489.

41   *The Burnhams and the Thachers:* Lois Wilson, *Lois Remembers,* 9.

42   *"The secretary of Yale University":* WGW to Mark Whalon, 1954, AANYC.

43   *"I simply couldn't face it—even to talk to you":* WGW to EGW, September 1956, AANYC.

Eight: Mount Aeolus

page

44   *One weekend the County Temperance Institute:* Thomsen, *Bill W.*

45   *taught himself to play Clarence's beat-up old fiddle:* Wilson, *Bill W.*

45   *tin maple-sugaring buckets:* Thomsen, *Bill W.*

46 *All around him the rivulets poured down:* This view is based on the author's climb of Mount Aeolus in March 2000.
47 *the big Griffith Dictionary:* Lois Wilson, *Lois Remembers,* 13.

NINE: BURR AND BURTON

page
48 *Bill became a reading addict:* Wilson, *Bill W.,* 12.
49 *Burr and Burton boys wore tweed trousers:* Interview with Burr and Burton historian Frederica Templeton, May 2000.
49 *applied to Burr and Burton:* Anonymous, *"Pass It On,"* 33.
50 *he was a promising student:* Wilson, *A.A. Comes of Age,* 54.
51 *the daughter of Manchester Village's Episcopal minister:* Anonymous, *"Pass It On,"* 35.
51 *The Equinox Hotel is a vast structure:* Lewis, *The Equinox,* 59.
52 *Manchester Village is built for pleasure:* Photographs from archives of the Skinner Library. Author's visits to Manchester Village.
52 *the head of Main Street in Manchester Village:* Thomsen, *Bill W.*
52 *the same vein of limestone in Canada:* Interview with Frederica Templeton, May 2000.
52 *one of the happiest periods of Bill Wilson's life:* Anonymous, *"Pass It On,"* 35.
53 *"I am deliriously happy and am a success":* Wilson, *Bill W.,* 18.

TEN: BERTHA BAMFORD

page
54 *to have a small tumor removed:* Regarding Flower Hospital; Anonymous, *"Pass It On,"* quotes the *Manchester Journal* of September 21, but Kurtz, *Not-God,* places Bertha at Fifth Avenue Hospital. Thomsen, *Bill W.,* also gives a version of this story.
54 *the headmaster, Mr. James Brooks, stood up:* Anonymous, *"Pass It On,"* 36.
54 *a yellow piece of paper out of his pocket:* Kurtz, *Not-God,* 12.
55 *he didn't want to talk about the pain:* Wilson, *Bill W.,* 18.
55 *a trip to the battlefield at Gettysburg:* Anonymous, *"Pass It On,"* 38.
56 *The whole thing made Emily Griffith Wilson angry:* Thomsen, *Bill W.*
56 *"Success, success, success!":* Letter from EGW to WGW, AANYC.

56   *In the grip of a nervous breakdown:* Wilson, *Bill W.,* 18, and Wilson, *A.A. Comes of Age,* 54.

56   *arranged for her son to visit his father:* Anonymous, *"Pass It On,"* 42.

57   *"Everything is ragged and angular":* WGW to his Grandmother Wilson, August 1914.

ELEVEN: LOIS BURNHAM

page

58   *One summer they were horrified to find:* Lois Wilson, *Lois Remembers,* 9.

58   *The New Church:* Ibid., 2.

59   *Jerry and Bess:* Lois Wilson, *Lois Remembers,* 9.

59   *a visit to the Rockefeller mansion:* Ibid., 3.

60   *attachable mast and sail:* Ibid., 13.

60   *Her brother Rogers knew Bill Wilson:* Ibid.

61   *knew the name of every part of the boat:* Ibid.

61   *"laid down in the vestibule":* Wilson, *Bill W.,* 21.

62   *chattering through palpitations:* Ibid.

62   *"Some days I can eat nothing":* WGW to EGW, 1914.

62   *Bill cared about more than cars:* Anonymous, *"Pass It On,"* 46.

TWELVE: NEW YORK CITY

page

64   *Norman Schneider:* Anonymous, *"Pass It On,"* 48.

64   *one of them was Bill Wilson:* WGW to LBW after their engagement, in September and October of 1915, SSA.

64   *and they found themselves talking:* Lois Wilson, *Lois Remembers,* 14.

65   *tell her that he was no good:* Wilson, *Bill W.,* 22.

65   *"Lois came along and picked me up":* Ibid., 19.

65   *a tea arbor for travelers:* Lois Wilson, *Lois Remembers,* 14.

65   *peddling burners for kerosene lamps:* Ibid., 15.

66   *"I was longing every minute to be with Bill":* Ibid., 16.

67   *"It was as if all summer he had been standing in the sunlight":* Thomsen, *Bill W.*

67   *"She loves you because you are Bill Wilson":* WGW to LBW, September 1915, SSA.

67   *This earned him a failing grade:* Anonymous, *"Pass It On,"* 50, and Wilson, *Bill W.,* 22.
68   *tried to explain away his flirtation:* WGW to LBW, September and October 1915, SSA.
69   *shopping for their engagement ring:* Lois Wilson, *Lois Remembers,* 17–18.
69   *They were driving home from Montreal:* Letters from LBW at SSA.
70   *Tiffany made a new one:* Correspondence from friends of Lois Wilson and sales receipt from Tiffany, SSA.
71   *barely holding on:* Wilson, *Bill W.,* 24.
71   *he's a dashing young sailor:* Lois Wilson, *Lois Remembers,* 21.
71   *Bill and Lois didn't have the same story:* Phyllis Rose, *Parallel Lives* (New York: Vintage Books, 1983), 6.

THIRTEEN: NEW BEDFORD AND THE FIRST DRINK

page
72   *came to Bill Wilson's rescue:* Wilson, *Bill W.,* 23.
72   *all classes were canceled:* Lois Wilson, *Lois Remembers,* 21.
72   *the feelings of failure:* Wilson, *Bill W.,* 25.
73   *invited to many elegant dinner parties:* Anonymous, *"Pass It On,"* 55.
74   *Bill Wilson had never seen a butler:* Wilson, *Alcoholics Anonymous Comes of Age,* 54.
74   *"I'd been told how many of my ancestors":* Wilson, *Bill W.,* 26.
75   *"That strange barrier":* Ibid., 26–27.
75   *the elixir of life:* Wilson, *Alcoholics Anonymous Comes of Age,* 54.
75   *He felt a new kind of freedom:* Thomsen, *Bill W.*

FOURTEEN: FRANCE

page
79   *"I try to be a good boy":* WGW to EGW, AANYC.
80   *"Should we be teetotalers?":* WGW to LBW, 1918, SSA.
80   *"Where did she get that one?"* Anonymous, *"Pass It On,"* 58.
80   *"They don't like it here":* EGW to WGW, AANYC.
80   *There was a rumor that Bill's unit:* Anonymous, *"Pass It On,"* 58.
81   *The newlyweds took an upstairs apartment:* Lois Wilson, *Lois Remembers,* 22.

81   *They entertained often:* Wilson, *Bill W.,* 27.

82   *"A tremendous pall of gloom":* Ibid., 28.

82   *still wrapped in this odd sense of calm:* Ibid., 28, and Lois Wilson, *Lois Remembers,* 24.

83   *there had been real courage:* Wilson, *Bill W.,* 290.

83   *suffused with a feeling of peace:* Ibid., 31, and Wilson, *Alcoholics Anonymous,* 1. WGW letters to LBW (in the SSA) at this time suggest Bill missed this visit to Winchester Cathedral but visited it in 1950.

85   *a bottle of rum on a shelf:* Wilson, *Bill W.,* 33.

FIFTEEN: THE EDISON TEST

page

86   *failed to salute him:* Wilson, *Bill W.,* 34.

87   *They caught a huge eel:* Lois Wilson, *Lois Remembers,* 28.

87   *Brooklyn Law School:* Wilson, *Bill W.,* 36.

88   *"Young men capable of close observation":* Ibid., 36.

88   *flying into a temper:* Ibid., 37.

89   *the scar that Bill remembered:* When I inquired, the Edison archivist didn't remember this scar. Neither did it appear in Neil Baldwin's excellent biography published in 1995. Further investigation unearthed the story of the accident that caused the nitric acid scar in Dyer and Martin's two-volume biography of Edison published in 1910—the biography Bill Wilson would have read as a child.

89   *At each chair was a set of papers:* Ibid., 37.

89   *Edison's ad had also attracted:* Edison Archives in Edison, New Jersey. "Mr. Edison's Brain Meter," *Literary Digest,* May 28, 1921, and John Warren's unpublished essay "Amazingly Ignorant: Edison's Mental Fitness Test as a Dialogue on Education."

90   *They were delighted by the apartment:* Lois Wilson, *Lois Remembers,* 34.

90   *as far away as Los Angeles:* Wilson, *Bill W.,* 39, and Lois Wilson, *Lois Remembers,* 35.

90   *a job in acoustics:* Wilson, *Bill W.*

91   *never got around to picking up his law degree:* Wilson, *Bill W.* Letter from Dan Demarest at SSA.

SIXTEEN: BROOKLYN

page

92   *Lois arranged camping trips:* Lois Wilson, *Lois Remembers,* 31.

93   *the first of three heartbreaking ectopic pregnancies:* Ibid., 34.

94   *none of Lois's four brothers and sisters ever had children:* SSA.

94   *"For your Christmas I make you this present":* WGW to LBW, December 1922, SSA.

95   *"The remonstrances of my friends":* Wilson, *Alcoholics Anonymous,* 3.

95   *Harley-Davidson three-wheeler motor bicycle:* Lois Wilson, *Lois Remembers,* 36.

95   *If he were a farmer, he would never buy a horse or cow:* Wilson, *Bill W.,* 39.

SEVENTEEN: MOTORCYCLE HOBOS

page

96   *The neighborhood, streets of brick houses:* Interviews with residents of Clinton Street, and visits to the neighborhood.

98   *They would start with General Electric:* Wilson, *Bill W.,* 40.

98   *packed the sidecar with a tent:* Lois Wilson, *Diary of Two Motorcycle Hobos.* This is an illegal edition of Lois Wilson's diaries of their trip of 1925–27 found at Stepping Stones after her death. Most of the information in it is repeated in *Lois Remembers.*

98   *a field beside a brook near Poughkeepsie:* Lois Wilson, *Lois Remembers,* 39.

99   *"Well, of course everybody thought we were utterly out of our minds":* Wilson, *Bill W.,* 41.

99   *set the pattern for much of Bill's future research:* Ibid., 41–43.

100   *he started at the bottom:* Ibid., 44.

100   *came back to New York for good:* Lois Wilson, *Lois Remembers,* 60–61.

101   *slide under the turnstile:* Wilson, *Bill W.,* 45.

EIGHTEEN: MANCHESTER AIRPORT

page

102   *named Penick & Ford:* Wilson, *Bill W.,* 47.

102   *She left him and moved back to Clinton Street:* Lois Wilson, *Lois Remembers,* 72.

104   *rented the apartment next door:* Wilson, *Bill W.,* 46. This apartment in a

building called the Colonial is still there, around the corner from 182 Clinton Street, as is the building on Amity Street where Bill and Lois lived.

104 *"evidence to my pledge"*: WGW to LGW, SSA.

104 *stopped off in Albany:* Anonymous, *"Pass It On,"* 84, and Wilson, *Bill W.,* 77–78.

105 *Manchester would be his salvation:* Wilson, *Bill W.,* 47.

NINETEEN: MONTREAL

page

106 *even persuading his mother, Emily:* Anonymous, *"Pass It On,"* 85.

106 *old brokerage friend, Dick Johnson:* Wilson, *Bill W.,* 49.

106 *They rented another grand apartment:* Lois Wilson, *Lois Remembers,* 81.

107 *Lois lost the amethyst wedding ring:* SSA.

107 *Lois's mother was dying of bone cancer:* Lois Wilson, *Lois Remembers,* 81.

107 *Stanley Statistics:* Wilson, *Bill W.,* 52.

108 *Lois got a job at R. H. Macy's:* Ibid., 53.

108 *Before joining the syndicate, they made him sign a contract:* Anonymous, *"Pass It On,"* 90.

109 *it was something called Jersey lightning:* Wilson, *Bill W.,* 57.

109 *and called for the bellboy to get some more:* Ibid., 59.

110 *he and Lois headed for Vermont:* Lois Wilson, *Lois Remembers,* 84.

110 *furious letters to Franklin Delano Roosevelt:* These letters are in the archives at Stepping Stones.

110 *stole from Lois's purse to buy drinks:* Wilson, *Bill W.,* 66.

111 *Leonard Strong said he would pay the bill:* Ibid.

111 *Bill invited Ebby over to Brooklyn:* Anonymous, *"Pass It On,"* 111, and Kurtz, *Not-God,* 7.

112 *rescued his bottle of gin:* Kurtz, *Not-God,* 7.

112 *Oxford Group house party:* Pittman, *A.A.: The Way It Began,* 113.

112 *life-changing conversion experience:* Ibid., 8.

TWENTY: TOWNS HOSPITAL

page

114 *Towns Hospital at 293 Central Park West:* Anonymous, *"Pass It On,"* 100.

114 *Towns-Lambert treatment:* Pittman, *A.A.: The Way It Began,* 83.

114   *"phenomenon of craving"*: Anonymous, *"Pass It On,"* 102.
115   *On Armistice Day of 1934, Bill decided:* Ibid., 110.
116   *decided to wander down to the Calvary Mission:* Wilson, *Bill W.,* 87.
117   *managed to buy four beers on credit:* Ibid., 89.
118   *"If there be a God, let him show himself!":* Ibid., 93.
118   *Dr. Silkworth thought that Bill had had a genuine conversion:* Ibid., 94.
118   *she knew he had changed:* Lois Wilson, *Lois Remembers,* 89.
121   *"So this is the God of the preachers":* Wilson, *Bill W.,* 93.
121   *careful to distinguish between religion and spirituality:* Kurtz, *Not-God,* chap. 8, "The Context of the History of Religious Ideas."

Twenty-one: The Oxford Group

page
127   *Others credit William James:* Wilson, *Bill W.,* 96.
127   *"This Harvard professor, long in his grave":* Ibid.
128   *"The sway of alcohol over mankind":* James, *Varieties of Religious Experience.*
128   *"At this point my excitement became boundless":* Wilson, *Bill W.,* 99.
128   *regularly taking the subway across the river to meetings:* Anonymous, *"Pass It On,"* 127.
129   *They had made the mistake of offering:* Wilson, *Alcoholics Anonymous Comes of Age,* 64.
130   *so high on his own discovery:* Anonymous, *"Pass It On,"* 131.
131   *Dr. Silkworth gently suggested:* Ibid., 133.
131   *checked into Akron's Mayflower Hotel:* Wilson, *Alcoholics Anonymous Comes of Age,* 65.
132   *The bar of the Mayflower:* Ibid.

Twenty-two: Akron, Ohio

page
133   *the local newsstand where all the headlines:* From photos of the lobby in May of 1935.
134   *A huge rally featuring Frank Buchman himself:* From local news clippings in *"Pass It On."*
134   *Bill Wilson didn't want to call Henrietta Seiberling:* Wilson, *Alcoholics Anonymous Comes of Age,* 66.

135 *was also from Vermont:* Ibid., 68.
135 *he started getting into trouble:* Ibid., 68.
136 *What happened that night?:* Ibid., 70.
137 *left for Atlantic City brimming with confidence:* Ibid.
137 *he handed him a bottle of beer:* Ibid., 71.

Twenty-three: 182 Clinton Street

page
138 *finally moving into the shingled:* Wilson, *Alcoholics Anonymous Comes of Age,* 144.
138 *house of T. Henry Williams:* Ibid., 145.
140 *she too was enchanted by the prairie landscape:* Lois Wilson, *Lois Remembers,* 96.
140 *Fitz Mayo and Hank Parkhurst:* Anonymous, *"Pass It On,"* 152.
140 *He rented an office and hired a secretary:* Lois Wilson, *Lois Remembers,* 101.
141 *On Tuesday nights Bill Wilson held meetings:* Anonymous, *"Pass It On,"* 152, and Lois Wilson, *Lois Remembers,* 102.
141 *The Wilsons' dress clothes:* Lois Wilson, *Lois Remembers,* 105, and Anonymous, *"Pass It On,"* 155.
141 *"Booze was never this good":* Thomsen, *Bill W.*
142 *Charles Towns saw a way to end Bill Wilson's financial problems:* Wilson, *Twelve Steps and Twelve Traditions.*
142 *If he became a professional:* Ibid.
142 *"group conscience":* Ibid.

Twenty-four: Not Maximum

page
144 *the Oxford Group's dinner jackets:* Pittman, *A.A.: The Way It Began,* chap. 6.
144 *not allowed to attend:* Kurtz, *Not-God,* 45.
145 *owed a great deal to the Oxford Group:* Wilson, *Alcoholics Anonymous Comes of Age,* 74.
146 *longer to make the break:* Kurtz, *Not-God,* 47.
147 *When they compared notes in person:* Wilson, *Alcoholics Anonymous Comes of Age,* 76.

148   *eighteen Akron recovering alcoholics:* Anonymous, *"Pass It On,"* 180.

148   *They had said he could start writing a book:* Lois Wilson, *Lois Remembers,* 108.

TWENTY-FIVE: JOHN D. ROCKEFELLER, JR.

page

149   *He called Frank Shaw and Leonard Strong:* Lois Wilson, *Lois Remembers,* 108.

149   *his mother came to visit Clinton Street:* WGW to EGW, AANYC.

150   *once again came to the rescue:* Lois Wilson, *Lois Remembers,* 108.

150   *called Mr. Junior:* Chernow, *Titan.*

150   *Even when he was an Ohio stock clerk:* Ibid., 50.

151   *interested in meeting Bill Wilson:* Lois Wilson, *Lois Remembers,* 109.

151   *The meeting went well:* Anonymous, *"Pass It On,"* 184.

151   *He thought that a grant of that size would hurt:* Lois Wilson, *Lois Remembers,* 109.

151   *proposing to define alcoholic?:* Anonymous, *"Pass It On,"* 188.

152   *he sat down in the Newark offices of Honor Dealers:* Lois Wilson, *Lois Remembers,* 111.

152   *Ruth Hock:* Anonymous, *"Pass It On,"* 192.

152   *Eugene Exman:* Correspondence between Exman and Wilson at SSA; Wilson, *Alcoholics Anonymous Comes of Age,* 153.

153   *with a pencil and a scratch pad:* Lois Wilson, *Lois Remembers,* 113, and Anonymous, *"Pass It On,"* 197.

153   *there was still no title:* Ibid., 203.

153   *April of 1939:* Ibid., 206.

TWENTY-SIX: STEPPING STONES

page

154   *The day Bill Wilson stood on the sidewalk:* Lois Wilson, *Lois Remembers,* 125, and Thomsen, *Bill W.*

155   *On a sunny March day, with patches of snow on the ground:* Lois Wilson, *Lois Remembers,* 133, and Anonymous, *"Pass It On,"* 259. There is some controversy about the circumstances of Bill and Lois's first visit to the house that would be called Stepping Stones. Some people say that it was

inhabited when they visited; others say that Bill broke in. Lois has them
going into an empty house through an unlocked window.

156   *Mrs. Griffith offered to sell them the house:* Anonymous, *"Pass It On,"* 260.

156   *secondhand Stutz:* Lois Wilson, *Lois Remembers,* 134.

156   *Bookshelves line the walls:* In the small bookcase next to Lois's desk,
I found a copy of my own memoir about my father, *Home Before
Dark.*

158   *at home in the woods:* Wilson, *Bill W.,* 12, and Thomsen, *Bill W.*

159   *the secret of living deliberately:* Thoreau, *Walden.*

TWENTY-SEVEN: 334 ½ WEST 24TH STREET

page

160   *partly on the basis of* Reader's Digest: Anonymous, *"Pass It On,"* 195, and
Wilson, *Alcoholics Anonymous Comes of Age,* 158.

161   *Heatter was a prominent radio personality:* Anonymous, *"Pass It On,"* 209.

161   *attacked by a group of doctors:* Kurtz, *Not-God.*

162   *at New York City's Union Club:* Wilson, *Alcoholics Anonymous Comes of
Age,* 183, and Kurtz, *Not-God,* 98. "Squab on toast. For a bunch of ex-
drunks we were doing remarkably well," wrote Bill Wilson in *Alcoholics
Anonymous Comes of Age.*

163   *moved into two tiny rooms on the second floor:* Lois Wilson, *Lois Remembers,* 131.

164   *He began to rail against Bill:* Ibid., 129.

164   *There was a knock at the downstairs door:* Anonymous, *"Pass It On,"*
241.

165   *Curtis Bok, publisher of the* Saturday Evening Post: Wilson, *Alcoholics
Anonymous Comes of Age,* 190.

165   *Jack Alexander to check out the story:* Lois Wilson, *Lois Remembers,*
131.

165   *he give the reporter a tour of the groups:* Wilson, *Alcoholics Anonymous
Comes of Age,* 191.

166   *His* Saturday Evening Post *article:* Saturday Evening Post, March 1, 1941.

166   *finally get national attention:* Wilson, *Alcoholics Anonymous Comes of Age,*
191, and Anonymous, *"Pass It On,"* 248.

167   *membership went from 1,500 to 8,000:* Kurtz, *Not-God,* 101.

Twenty-eight: Trabuco College

page
168   *His application for Army service:* SSA.
169   *pocketed $64,000 of A.A. money:* Wilson, *Alcoholics Anonymous Comes of Age*, 193.
170   *wrote back inviting Henrietta to:* Correspondence between WGW and Henrietta Seiberling, AANYC.
170   *water went cascading down the stairs:* Lois Wilson, *Lois Remembers*, 137.
171   *When the alarm went off, Helen pulled the string:* Anonymous, *"Pass It On,"* 263.
171   *first cross-country trip to visit:* Lois Wilson, *Lois Remembers*, 143; Kurtz, *Not-God*, 117; and Anonymous, *"Pass It On,"* chap. 17.
173   *Heard and Huxley:* Lois Wilson, *Lois Remembers*, 143.
173   *A strange, mesmerizing presence:* Biographical information on Huxley, Heard, and their beliefs came from Sawyer, *Aldous Huxley*, and Bedford, *Aldous Huxley.*
175   *"The desert's emptiness and the desert's silence":* Huxley, *Complete Essays.*
175   *a kind of loony desert version of Walden Pond:* From many papers and manifestos about Trabuco College and its purposes at SSA.
176   *Huxley talked his wife "through" death:* Sawyer, *Aldous Huxley*, 162.

Twenty-nine: Depression

page
177   *Life seemed useless:* Anonymous, *"Pass It On,"* 292, and interviews with men and women who worked with Bill during those years.
179   *"Just now my problem is success":* WGW to Mark Whalon, AANYC.
180   *an ancient human problem:* Solomon, *The Noonday Demon.*
181   *a man under a microscope:* Anonymous, *"Pass It On,"* 294.
181   *spiritual exhaustion:* Interview with Tom Powers at East Ridge, 2001.
182   *"We are apt to be swamped":* Wilson, *Twelve Steps and Twelve Traditions.*
182   *"Grief and trouble bring life":* White, *A Different Kind of Hero.*
182   *Twice a week he drove down from Bedford Hills:* Anonymous, *"Pass It On,"* 295.
183   *Weekes told him that she thought his position:* Ibid., 335.

Thirty: Our Common Welfare Should Come First

page

184   *a planeload of grateful A.A. members:* Wing, *Grateful to Have Been There.*

184   *he holed up at the Londonderry Inn:* Ibid.

184   *built a simple cinder-block studio:* Anonymous, *"Pass It On,"* 304.

185   *Nell Wing came to work as Bill Wilson's secretary:* Ibid., 293.

186   *"If all these edicts had been in force":* Ibid., 305.

187   *some kind of codification:* "The basic ideas . . . came directly out of this vast correspondence," from Wilson, *Alcoholics Anonymous Comes of Age,* 203.

187   *"Each member of Alcoholics Anonymous":* Wilson, *Twelve Steps and Twelve Traditions.*

188   *Waylaid by his thoughts, he would put his head:* Wing, *Grateful to Have Been There.*

189   *Marty Mann brought the anonymity issue to a head:* Anonymous, *"Pass It On,"* 310, and Brown and Brown, *Mrs. Marty Mann,* 179.

190   *The story of Bill Wilson:* Anonymous, *"Pass It On,"* 311.

191   *The one exception was Archibald Roosevelt:* Lois Wilson, *Lois Remembers,* 157.

191   *"After hearing your magnificent letter":* Anonymous, *"Pass It On,"* 314.

Thirty-one: Dr. Robert Holbrook Smith

NOTE: I owe many of the stories and perceptions in this chapter to the biography of Dr. Bob commissioned by the General Service Conference, written anonymously and published in 1980: *Dr. Bob and the Good Old Timers.* Its companion volume, *"Pass It On,"* was published in 1984.

page

193   *after two years of sober experience:* Lois Wilson, *Lois Remembers,* 108.

194   *Often this surrender would take:* Anonymous, *Dr. Bob and the Good Old Timers,* 101.

194   *a strict diet of sauerkraut, tomatoes, and Karo corn syrup:* Ibid., 105.

196   *"With this in mind":* Ibid., 224.

197   *moved to the King School:* Ibid., 219.

198   *Bob still balked:* Ibid., 319.

198   *a newcomer came in one night:* Ibid., 336.

THIRTY-TWO: THE SPOOK ROOM

page
201 *Monsignor Fulton Sheen:* Anonymous, *"Pass It On,"* 282.
202 *"I feel more like a Catholic":* WGW to Msgr. Sheen, AANYC.
202 *almost 100,000 alcoholics who helped each other:* Wilson, *Alcoholics Anonymous Comes of Age,* 125, and Kurtz, *Not-God,* 116.
202 *also impressed by the story of Mary Baker Eddy:* Barger, *New Wine,* 104.
203 *investigate psychic and spiritual phenomena:* Wing, *Grateful to Have Been There,* and Anonymous, *"Pass It On,"* 275.
204 *Sometimes the Wilsons used a Ouija board:* Ibid., 278.
204 *they gathered around it, each person with their fingers:* Ibid., 279.
205 *the Reverend Dwight Moody:* Automatic writing in the archives at Stepping Stones.
205 *an account of early Christianity in Italy:* Anonymous, *"Pass It On,"* 278.
205 *and the Latin turned out to be a sermon:* Wing, *Grateful to Have Been There.*
206 *The sailor was soon joined by the spirit of a man:* Anonymous, *"Pass It On,"* 276.
207 *One of the members of the Chappaqua A.A. group:* Interview with Tom Powers, 2001.
208 *There would be a slight, almost imperceptible stir:* Anonymous, *"Pass It On,"* 278.

THIRTY-THREE: ST. LOUIS, MISSOURI

page
210 *and Charlie Parker died:* Bernhard Grun, *The Timetables of History* (New York: Simon & Schuster, 1975).
210 *all flanked by tripods of American flags:* Wilson, *Alcoholics Anonymous Comes of Age,* 46, and photo in the book.
211 *How would the representatives be elected?:* Wilson, *Alcoholics Anonymous Comes of Age,* 216.
212 *Just before four o'clock:* Ibid., 226.
213 *"the stuff of saints":* Ibid., 254.
213 *special guest was Ebby Thacher:* Ibid., 46.
214 *amalgam of the principles:* Barger, *New Wine,* chaps. 7–10. (This extraordinary book traces more than a dozen sources for the precepts of A.A.)

214   *"For Lois and me the autumn of life":* Wilson, *Alcoholics Anonymous Comes of Age,* 220.

215   *Bill's depression lifted:* Anonymous, *"Pass It On,"* 359.

215   *a series of adventures:* Kurtz, *Not-God,* 136.

Thirty-four: Marty Mann

page

216   *"Neither Dorothy nor I have ever stood":* WGW to Dr. Fred Breithut, AANYC.

217   *"If I had been with you in Londonderry":* EGW to WGW, SSA.

217   *Christine wrote back saying they preferred to leave things:* Christine Wilson to WGW, SSA.

217   *Gilman had used his belt to fasten her hands:* Christine Wilson to WGW, AANYC.

218   *an attractive, charismatic woman:* Brown and Brown, *Mrs. Marty Mann.*

218   *a skinny derelict:* Ibid., 132.

219   *she hung out with the Bloomsbury group:* Ibid., 72.

219   *Wilson heard Marty Mann's fifth step:* Ibid., 119.

220   *"This book is a curious combination of organizing propaganda":* Kurtz, *Not-God,* 92. In his note on unsympathetic reviews of the book *Alcoholics Anonymous,* Kurtz also quotes the slam from the September 1940 *Journal of Nervous and Mental Diseases,* which concludes "we think the methods of Forel and Bleuler infinitely superior."

220   *William Seabrook's account:* Brown and Brown, *Mrs. Marty Mann,* 82.

220   *Dr. Harry Tiebout:* Ibid., 94.

220   *a friend of a friend who needed a doctor:* Ibid., 102.

221   *especially when Marty fell in love:* Ibid., chap. 15.

222   *Carson McCullers:* Ibid., 222.

222   *Lois had a heart attack that brought them all up short:* Lois Wilson, *Lois Remembers,* 156.

Thirty-five: 526 Bedford Road

page

224   *palled around with Robert Oppenheimer:* Anonymous, *"Pass It On,"* 381.

225   *some wise and some not so wise:* Kurtz, *Not-God,* 136.

225   One person believes that after Lois's heart attack: Author's interviews.

225   "He was torn": Interview with Ralph B.

225   worried that Bill Wilson's sexual behavior: Various interviews.

226   a story about Bill running a red light: Ibid.

226   frankly discussed the impotence that afflicts: Wilson, *Alcoholics Anonymous*, 134.

226   Although the papers hadn't been indexed: In 2001 and 2002, the holdings of the Stepping Stones Archives were brilliantly indexed and archived by Lynn Hoke.

227   Francis Hartigan: Hartigan's book, *Bill W.*, has no endnotes or footnotes. His sources are not named.

227   Nan Robertson: Robertson, *Getting Better*, 84. Robertson does not cite specific sources.

228   "In the religion of the once-born": James, *Varieties of Religious Experience*, 166.

230   She began acting in summer stock: Hartigan, *Bill W.*, 190, and various interviews.

230   there are many letters from Helen: Helen Wynn to various people, SSA.

231   that didn't happen: This is part of Tom Powers's story about why he stopped working with Bill. "Helen went crooked," he said. Powers says he went to the Board and kept them from allowing Helen to get the money for an LSD research headquarters.

231   "he might have straightened out": Interview with Tom Powers.

THIRTY-SIX: THE FAMILY AFTERWARD

page

233   "When and how, and in just what instances": Wilson, *Twelve Steps and Twelve Traditions*, 50.

233   "since most of us are born with an abundance": Ibid., 65.

234   "He just spilled his guts out": Interview with Ralph B.

235   the evangelical strain and the self-realization and self-help strain: Kurtz, *Not-God*, chap. 8.

235   when she asked her husband to let her: Lois Wilson, *Lois Remembers*, 114.

237   Marty Mann chafed at this restriction: Brown and Brown, *Mrs. Marty Mann*, 178.

237   She called herself "Mrs. Marty Mann": Ibid., 218.

THIRTY-SEVEN: CARL JUNG

page

239   *Abram Hoffer and Humphry Osmond:* Anonymous, *"Pass It On,"* 369.

239   *on the rebound from an unsatisfactory stint:* Sawyer, *Aldous Huxley,* 146.

240   *Under the supervision of Dr. Cohen:* From a transcript of Cohen's notes on Bill's experience, SSA.

241   *"I understand that the father symbol will always be hitched to me":* WGW to Rev. Sam Shoemaker, SSA.

242   *Bill had finally persuaded her to move east:* Correspondence between WGW and EGW, 1960–61, SSA.

242   *Jung responded in 1961:* Anonymous, *"Pass It On,"* 383. Carl Jung's letter hangs on the wall at Stepping Stones and is displayed on the Stepping Stones Foundation Web site.

243   *What got him in trouble was his enthusiasm:* Kurtz, *Not-God,* 137.

THIRTY-EIGHT: MIAMI

page

246   *his lungs not quite working:* Interviews.

247   *he was forced to stop because of breathlessness:* Anonymous, *"Pass It On,"* 393.

247   *A hoist lifted him up:* Ibid., 400.

248   *keeping hourly logs on a wide green-lined pad:* Log entries are taken from nursing logs kept by Nurses O'Loughlin, Clazio, and Dannenberg for the final six weeks of Bill Wilson's life, SSA.

250   *The flight south, with Lois and Nell:* Lois Wilson, *Lois Remembers,* 160.

250   *On May 8, when the stony Vermont ground:* Anonymous, *"Pass It On,"* 406.

BIBLIOGRAPHY

Anonymous. *Dr. Bob and the Good Old Timers: A Biography with Recollections of Early A.A. in the Midwest.* New York: Alcoholics Anonymous World Services, 1980.

Anonymous. *Living Sober.* New York: Alcoholics Anonymous World Services, 1975.

Anonymous. *"Pass It On": The Story of Bill Wilson and How the A.A. Message Reached the World.* New York: Alcoholics Anonymous World Services, 1984.

Baldwin, Neil. *Edison: Inventing the Century.* New York: Hyperion, 1995.

B., Mel. *Ebby: The Man Who Sponsored Bill W.* Center City, Minn.: Hazelden-Pittman Archives Press, 1998.

Barger, Mel. *New Wine: The Spiritual Roots of the Twelve Step Miracle.* Center City, Minn.: Hazelden Foundation, 1991.

————. *My Search for Bill Wilson.* Center City, Minn.: Hazelden-Pittman Archives Press, 2000.

Barr, Andrew. *Drink: A Social History of America.* New York: Carroll & Graf, 1999.

Bateson, Gregory. *Steps to an Ecology of Mind.* New York: Ballantine Books, 1972.

Bedford, Sybille. *Aldous Huxley: A Biography.* Chicago: Ivan R. Dee, 2002.

Berryman, John. *Recovery.* New York: Farrar, Straus & Giroux, 1971.

Botkin, B. A. *A Treasury of New England Folklore.* New York: Bonanza Books, Crown Publishers, 1965.

Brown, Bruce, with interviews from Mrs. Fred Harwood. *The History of Emerald Lake State Park.* Vermont Agency of Natural Resources, Department of Forests, Parks, and Recreation, 1992.

Brown, Sally, and David R. Brown. *A Biography of Mrs. Marty Mann.* Center City, Minn.: Hazelden-Pittman Archives Press, 2002.

Bryan, Frank M. *Yankee Politics in Rural Vermont.* Hanover, N.H.: University Press of New England, 1974.

Burns, John, et al. *The Answer to Addiction.* Fremont Center, N.Y.: East Ridge Press, 2000.

Cheever, Susan. *Treetops.* New York: Bantam Books, 1991.

Chernow, Ron. *Titan: The Life of John D. Rockefeller, Sr.* New York: Random House, 1998.

Coffin, Howard. *Full Duty: Vermonters in the Civil War.* Woodstock, Vt.: Countryman Press, 1993.

DeGraaf, Richard M., and Mariko Yamasaki. *New England Wildlife: Habitat, Natural History, and Distribution.* Hanover, N.H.: University Press of New England, 2001.

Dyer, Frank Lewis, and Thomas Commerford Martin. *Edison: His Life and Inventions.* New York: Harper & Brothers, 1910.

Farren, Suzy. *A Call to Care: The Women Who Built Catholic Healthcare in America.* St. Louis: Catholic Health Association of the United States, 1996.

Fitzgerald, Kathleen. *Alcoholism: The Genetic Inheritance.* Lake Forest, Ill.: Whale's Tale Press, 1993.

Fitzgerald, Robert, ed. *The Soul of Sponsorship: The Friendship of Father Ed Dowling S.S. and Bill Wilson in Letters.* Center City, Minn.: Hazelden Press, 1995.

Ford, Betty. *A Glad Awakening.* Garden City, N.Y.: Doubleday & Co., 1987.

Graffagnino, J. Kevin; Samuel B. Hand; and Gene Sessions, eds. *Vermont Voices, 1609 through the 1990s: A Documentary History of the Green Mountain State.* Montpelier: Vermont Historical Society, 1999.

Hamill, Pete. *A Drinking Life.* Boston: Little, Brown & Co., 1994.

Hard, Walter. *Walter Hard's Vermont.* Brattleboro, Vt.: Stephen Daye Press, c. 1941.

Harritt, Ira. *Emerald Lake State Park Nature Trail Guide.* State of Vermont Agency of Natural Resources, Department of Forests, Parks, and Recreation, 1992.

Hartigan, Francis, *Bill W.* New York: Thomas Dunne Books, St. Martin's Press, 2000.

Hunter, Charlotte; Billye Jones; and Joan Zeiger. *Women Pioneers in 12 Step Recovery.* Center City, Minn.: Hazelden-Pittman Archives Press, 1999.

Huxley, Aldous. *Complete Essays, Volume V: 1939–1956.* Edited by Robert S. Baker and James Sexton. Chicago: Ivan R. Dee, 2002.

James, Henry. *Hawthorne.* Ithaca, NY: Cornell University Press, 1997.

James, William. *The Varieties of Religious Experience*. New Hyde Park, N.Y.: University Books, c. 1902.

Jeffrey, William H. *Vermont, Its Government: 1904 and 05 and 1912 and 13*. East Burke, Vt.: Vermont State Historical Society, Historical Publishing Co.

Jersild, Devon. *Happy Hours: Alcohol in a Woman's Life*. New York: Cliff Street Books, 2001.

Johnson, Charles W. *The Nature of Vermont*. Hanover, N.H.: University Press of New England, 1998.

Johnson, Vernon E. *I'll Quit Tomorrow: A Practical Guide to Alcoholism Treatment*. New York: Harper & Row, 1980.

Josephson, Matthew. *Edison: A Biography*. New York: McGraw-Hill, 1959.

Kurtz, Ernest. *Not-God: A History of Alcoholics Anonymous*. Center City, Minn.: Hazelden Press, 1991.

Lender, Mark Edward, and James Kirby Martin. *Drinking in America*. New York: Free Press, 1987.

Lewis, Phebe Ann. *The Equinox: Historic Home of Hospitality*. Manchester, Vt.: Johnny Appleseed Bookshop, 1996.

Mann, Marty. *Marty Mann Answers Your Questions About Drinking and Alcoholism*. New York: Holt, Rinehart & Winston, 1981.

———. *Marty Mann's New Primer on Alcoholism*. New York: Holt, Rinehart & Winston, 1981.

Mariani, Paul. *Dream Song: The Life of John Berryman*. New York: William Morrow & Co., 1990.

Maxwell, Ruth. *The Booze Battle*. New York: Ballantine Books, 1989.

Mendelson, Jack H., and Nancy Mello. *Alcohol Use and Abuse in America*. Little, Brown & Co., 1985.

Milam, Dr. James R., and Katherine Ketcham. *Under the Influence: A Guide to the Myths and Realities of Alcoholism*. New York: Bantam Books, 1983.

Murray, Stuart. *Rudyard Kipling in Vermont: Birthplace of the Jungle Books*. Bennington, Vt.: Images from the Past, 1997.

Newlove, Donald. *Those Drinking Days: Myself and Other Writers*. New York: Horizon Press, 1980.

Pittman, Bill. *A.A.: The Way It Began*. Seattle: Glen Abbey Books, 1988.

Proceedings of the Vermont Historical Society for the Years 1911–1912. St. Albans, Vt.: Vermont Historical Society.

Raphael, Matthew. *Bill W. and Mr. Wilson.* Amherst: University of Massachusetts Press, 2000.

Resch, Tyler. *Dorset: In the Shadow of the Marble Mountain.* West Kennebunk, Me.: Dorset Historical Society, Phoenix Publishers, 1989.

Richardson, Robert D. *Emerson: The Mind on Fire.* Berkeley: University of California Press, 1995.

Robertson, Nan. *Getting Better: Inside Alcoholics Anonymous.* New York: William Morrow & Co., 1988.

Roueché, Berton. *The Neutral Spirit: A Portrait of Alcohol.* Boston: Little, Brown & Co., 1960.

Rorabaugh, W. J. *The Alcoholic Republic: An American Tradition.* New York: Oxford University Press, 1979.

Roth, Lillian, with Mike Connolly and Gerold Frank. *I'll Cry Tomorrow.* New York: F. Fell, 1954.

Rucker, R. D. *Drugs, Drug Addiction, and Drug Dealing.* New York: Vantage Press, 1991.

Sawyer, Dana. *Aldous Huxley.* New York: Crossroad Publishing Co., 2002.

Seabrook, William. *Asylum.* New York: Harcourt, Brace & Co., 1935.

Shannonhouse, Rebecca, ed. *Under the Influence.* New York: Random House, 2002.

Solomon, Andrew. *The Noonday Demon.* New York: Scribner, 2001.

Thomsen, Robert. *Bill W.* Center City, Minn.: Hazelden-Pittman Archives Press, 1975.

Thoreau, Henry David. *Walden and Other Writings.* New York: Barnes & Noble Classics, 1993.

Time in New England. Photos by Paul Strand; text selected and edited by Nancy Newhall. Millerton, N.Y.: Aperture, 1977.

Vaillant, George E. *The Natural History of Alcoholism.* Cambridge, Mass.: Harvard University Press, 1995.

White, Tom. *Bill W.: A Different Kind of Hero.* Honesdale, Pa.: Boyds Mills Press, 2003.

Wholey, Dennis. *The Courage to Change: Hope and Help for Alcoholics and Their Families: Personal Conversations with Dennis Wholey.* Boston: Houghton Mifflin Co., 1984.

W., Bill. *Alcoholics Anonymous.* 3rd and 4th eds. New York: Alcoholics Anonymous World Services, 1976, 2001.

Wilson, Bill. *Alcoholics Anonymous Comes of Age.* New York: Alcoholics Anonymous Publishing, 1957.

———. *Bill W.: An Autobiography.* Center City, Minn.: Hazelden-Pittman Archives Press, 2000.

———. *The Language of the Heart: Bill W.'s* Grapevine *Writings.* New York: AA Grapevine, 1988.

———. *Twelve Steps and Twelve Traditions.* Alcoholics Anonymous World Services, 1953.

[Wilson, Bill; Bob Smith; et al.] *Living Sober.* New York: Alcoholics Anonymous World Services, 1975.

Wilson, Lois. *Diary of Two Motorcycle Hobos.* Edited by Ellie van V. Ottawa: Gratitude Press Canada, 1998.

———. *Lois Remembers.* Virginia Beach, Va.: Al-Anon Group Headquarters, 1991.

Wing, Nell. *Grateful to Have Been There.* Center City, Minn.: Hazelden-Pittman Archives Press, 1992.

Index